1998

Research Methods in Park, Recreation, and Leisure Services

Ananda Mitra and Sam Lankford

Sagamore Publishing
Champaign, IL
www.sagamorepub.com

Editor: Susan M. McKinney
Book layout: Lisa J. Peretz & Anne E. Kolodziej
Cover design: Joe Buck & Deborah Bellaire

ISBN: 1-57167-030-0
Library of Congress Catalog Card Number: 98-85938

Dedicated to the people who taught me to think–my father, Dr. Kalyan Kumar Mitra, and my mentor, Dr. Joseph Bannon, Sr.

Dedicated to the people who showed me the power of love–my mother, my wife, and my son. —Ananda Mitra

---

For Jill, Jesse, Jordan, and Patch.

Dedicated to Dr. Carl E. Miller, Professor Emeritus, California State University at Bakersfield. A true educator and father in every sense. A person who understood both the value and limitations of research in helping us to understand our world. —Sam Lankford

Table of Contents

Introduction

Purpose of this Book

Research Methods for Leisure Research was written to help beginning researchers and practitioners conduct research in the pursuit of resolving leisure service problems and issues.

What makes this book different from other research methods books? We believe this book is differentiated by the specific application to leisure research. Furthermore, it is our desire to help students and practitioners solve important and complex problems in understanding leisure behavior and in the delivery of services. The book is meant to be used as a guide in the systematic planning and implementation of academic research, planning and policy studies, market research, and evaluation reports. In essence, our intention is to provide a book that illustrates and illuminates the potential contributions of various research methods in the field of leisure services. Similarly, we describe processes that, if followed, lend themselves to the conduct of what is often referred to as basic or scientific research. Therefore, this book emphasizes systematic methods for gathering, analyzing, and reporting information.

The researchers for whom this book is intended may be from a number of subdivisions of leisure services and areas of research interest. Some examples include:

- The researcher concerned with identifying the factors that are promoting the decay of urban parks and with recommending appropriate policy actions;
- A sports management specialist employed by a university athletic department attempting to conduct ad conversion studies to determine the effectiveness of local advertising;
- The marketing director for a local convention and visitor bureau concerned about the image of the community and how it compares with other, competing destinations;

- A program manager attempting to understand what type of recreation and social programs youth-at-risk would be attracted to;
- An open space planner helping a community conduct long-range land use plans that include parks, bike lanes, and river access acquisition and management;
- An academic attempting to study and advance what is known about motivation and leisure participation and subsequent satisfaction levels;
- A parks planner and policy analyst charged with identifying the social, economic, environmental, and personal benefits of recreation in the community;
- A district superintendent concerned with identifying factors that may help to motivate full-time, part-time, and seasonal recreation and park staff;
- A program specialist focused on improving services to seniors, the disabled, and youth-at-risk;
- A community center manager working with the board of directors of the community association to determine the optimal administrative structure;
- A manager working with the board of directors to determine voter attitudes toward a proposed bond issue for an aquatics facility;
- A leisure studies student interested in why some children participate in after-school programs and others do not, and if such participation has some correlation to success in school;
- A program director concerned about the lack of participation by women, seniors, and the disabled.

The field of leisure services is diverse and complicated in terms of the issues and trends impacting the policies, programs, professional needs, and community support for leisure services. In such a diverse field, where do we find answers to our problems? Henderson and O'Neill (1995) note that most of the foundation of our knowledge base comes from allied fields such as psychology, sociology, forestry, and business, as well as criminal justice, urban affairs, and health. Therefore, as a profession, we rely on concepts, models, and theories grounded in the physical (e.g., exercise science and physiology), behavioral (e.g., psychology) and social (e.g., sociology, geography and urban planning) sciences for the provision, management, and evaluation of our services.

Chapter One

An Introduction to Research Concepts and Ideas

WHY DO LEISURE RESEARCH?

Anyone whose job depends on information about what people do or want should know how to obtain that information in a valid and systematic manner (Sommer & Sommer, 1986). This is especially true in leisure services, where professionals deal on a daily basis with "what people do during their leisure time," "what people want to do during their leisure time," and "what people experience during their leisure time." Specifically, leisure professionals must know how to interview, construct questionnaires, observe behavior, evaluate programs, and conduct various kinds of experimental research projects. Kraus and Allen (1987) note a number of specific needs in leisure services that can be met through systematic, carefully designed research and evaluation studies. They identified the need to improve, test, or apply new practices to upgrade leadership and management operations; the need to understand the leisure experience (motivations, structure, and consequences) and needs of clients; and the need to measure outcomes of experiences to provide documentation and support for what we do as a profession.

A review of leisure research literature suggests that the research (1) has been predominantly applied in nature, (2) has not been cumulative, and (3) has relied on survey-related data collection procedures. Discussions of leisure research methodology in turn can be characterized by two dominant streams. The first is concerned with the degree to which research is adding to a verifiable knowledge base that we as a profession can use to improve leisure and recreation as an applied and social science. Second, there exists a concern regarding methodology issues, specifically, whether or not our methodologies can produce usable knowledge. Logically, one must ask, what do science and research methodology have to offer those who take an interest in the leisure phenomenon? The ultimate goal of leisure research is to produce an accumulating body of reliable knowledge that will enable us to explain, predict, and understand leisure phenomena that interest us. Importantly, a reliable body of knowledge could be used to improve the human condition through leisure delivery systems. Therefore, in order to improve the human condition through leisure, we must as a profession become more careful in our approach to studying the leisure phenomenon.

SHORTCOMINGS OF LEISURE RESEARCH

Of particular concern and importance is the number of weaknesses and inadequacies that have been noted with respect to the leisure research being produced. In the area of therapeutic recreation, Bedini and Wu (1994) found in a review of 46 articles published in the *Therapeutic Recreation Journal* that the use of theory, sophistication of designs, strength of measurement, and application continue to be problems in the field. Additionally, in the publication *A Literature Review: The President's Commission on Americans Outdoors* (1986) most of the authors pointed to inadequacies in leisure research. The papers consist of literature reviews of trends and demands, values and benefits, natural resources management, special populations, motivations and barriers, activity participation trends, urban recreation, tourism, financing, and information and communication. What was noted in almost every paper, and certainly in relation to each of the above-mentioned areas, is that the theories, methods, and analysis and statistical treatments are substandard and in need of improvement.

In order to advance the status of leisure research methodologies and findings, certain changes are necessary:

1. *A focus on core leisure services issues*. Specifically, we should study and better understand the characteristics of leisure that distinguish it from other social sciences. Also, communication from the field and between researchers and professionals must identify what is important and what are critical research needs in leisure services. *Parks and Recreation* magazine carries a "Research Update" in every issue, which attempts

to address this issue. As reported in a 1994 Research Update, the papers contained in the 1993 volume of *Leisure Sciences* addressed management decision making in parks and recreation (n=8) working in parks and recreation systems (n=8) fiscal issues (n=3) constraints to participation (n=3) and marketing (n=2). Goodale (1994) notes that *Leisure Sciences* articles could be placed in the following categories: motivation to participate; consumer behavior; constraints to leisure; ethnic, gender, and cultural issues; and equity in service delivery. Perhaps leisure research is beginning to develop a focus on core issues that will distinguish this field from other social services in content.

2. *Specific methodological improvements*. The use of meta-analysis in the synthesis of research findings across fields is timely and important. Leisure services is an interdisciplinary field, and the research generated tends to reflect this diversity. Another area of improvement is in the use of qualitative methods. A number of new research projects in recent years have been based on qualitative methods. Leisure researchers need to become both more proficient practitioners of this craft and contributors to the advancement of these methods. Finally, leisure researchers need to make more substantial use of quantitative techniques, particularly in causal analysis, longitudinal methods, and structural equation modeling. Some attention needs to be given not only to specific techniques for use in leisure research, but to how these techniques can be acquired by students and scholars.

There are signs that leisure research is improving. Goodale (1994) notes that from 1992 to 1994 30% of the articles in *Leisure Sciences* were devoted to improving leisure research. It was also noted that 50% of the articles were devoted to "discovering phenomena related to leisure activities, satisfaction or testing other studies," while another 10% of the articles were aimed at advancing the theory of leisure.

RESEARCH AS DECISION MAKING

Guiding the organization of this book is the recognition that systematic research can lead to improved decisions and problem solving, as well as provide documentation of the worth and value of our services. Leisure services include, but are not limited to, parks planning and design, parks and facilities maintenance, recreation programming, natural resources management, and tourism services. What ties professionals in such diverse fields together at a decision-making and research level? Primarily, there are four main functions that facilitate dialogue and decision making: 1) the recognition that a problem or an opportunity for improvement of services exists, (2) the collection and synthesis of information, (3) generation of alternatives to address the problem or opportunity, and (4) communication of the observations and findings. These functions are merely key tasks in systematically making informed decisions using the research process.

In leisure services, we often work in group decision-making situations. Therefore, it is necessary to develop a range of alternative decisions that will influence leisure service delivery and decision making. Ewert (1990) suggests that collective decision making can produce a research agenda that takes into account a broader spectrum of "customers" and more perspectives than generally is the case for any one individual or a small group of in-house specialists. Leisure professionals need to be aware of and be able to use a range of methods to engage the "public" or "client" in the decision-making process through the research process.

Research that documents the effectiveness of our programs and activities can help increase our visibility and credibility (Bialeschki, 1994). Unfortunately, a rational and scientific sequence of inquiry is often not followed in the documentation of services or in the recognition and resolution of leisure service delivery problems. Why is this so? Often the current political climate is not conducive to the systematic study of service delivery problems. For example, suppose a special interest group is pressuring the Recreation and Park Commission to preserve an open space parcel. Rather than recommend a study to identify whether such a parcel is needed and is financially acceptable, the commission may recommend approval rather than face the angry special interest group. Impending deadlines or budget constraints also may hinder the implementation of appropriate research studies to solve problems. Finally, staff may not have the expertise to conduct the research. One study showed that only 30% of the park and recreation professionals in the Pacific Northwest could conduct a thorough evaluation of programs and services within their department (Lankford, 1990).

Given the above constraints, leisure service professionals, working collectively, can at a minimum address the following questions to make better-informed decisions.

1. What is being studied?
2. Why it is a problem or an opportunity?
3. What concepts or models are available to justify the use of various problem-solving approaches?
4. What accepted theories or assumptions are these concepts or models based on?
5. What are the expected results from the research endeavor?

In leisure services practice, the objective is to improve the quality of life and the human condition. Sylvester (1995) notes that relevant factors in leisure service are where people live their lives, where leisure exists, and how leisure services seek to enhance the quality of people's lives. As Figure 1 shows, the process of leisure services in contemporary society encompasses many political, economic and sociocultural externalities that influence the types of services delivered at the local level.

How is the process of leisure research related to this model of the delivery system? In the provision of services, policy, planning (and design), evaluation (and research), and service implementation are reliant upon each other to address the needs of the community. Furthermore, to design and implement a study successfully, the researcher, policy analyst or evaluator must be able to understand and consider the nature and scope (influence) of all the above components of the system. To facilitate the production of useful and meaningful research, it has been suggested that research training begin early in one's professional career (Bedini & Wu, 1994).

Figure 1
The Political, Economic and Socio-Cultural Environment of the Leisure Service Delivery Systems

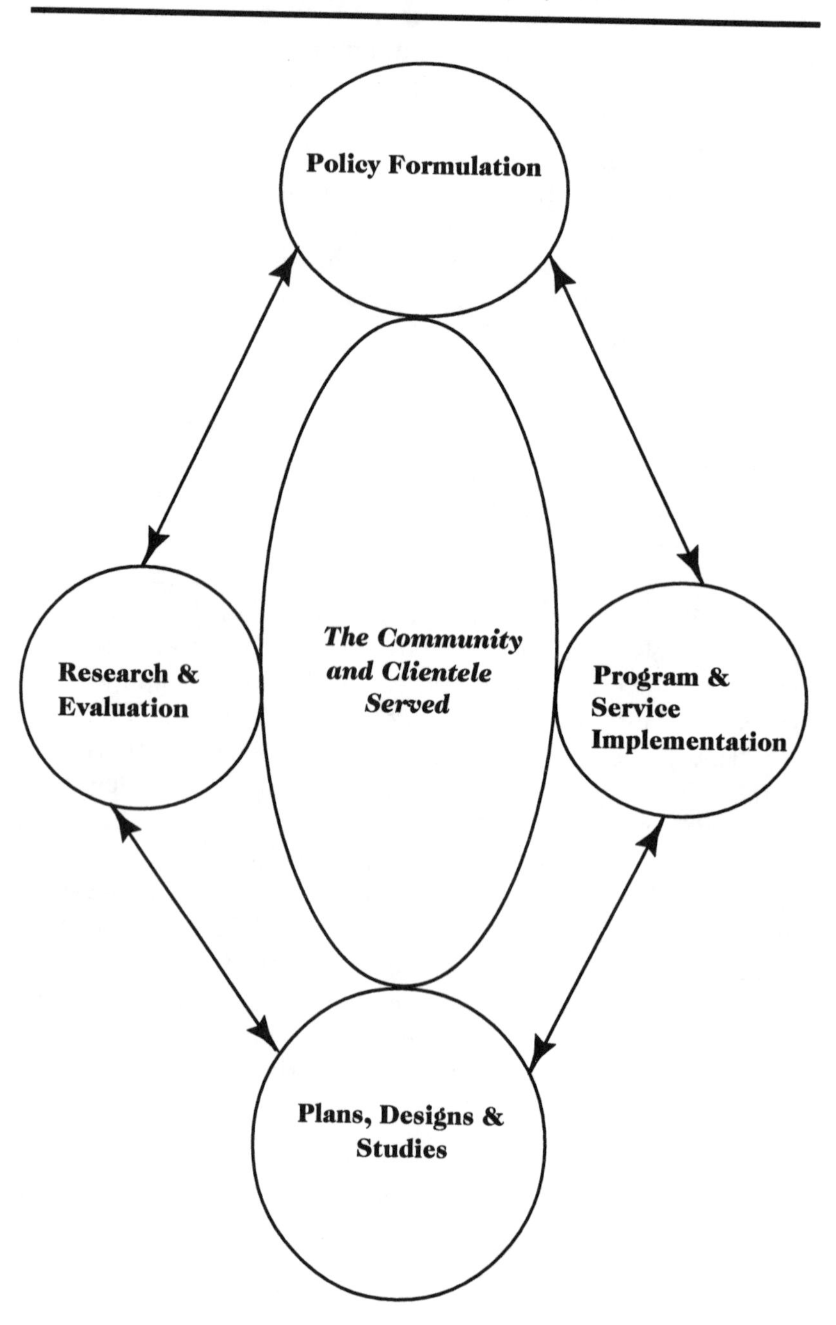

Research is important in the implementation and management of successful and meaningful programs. Research helps professionals understand leisure and recreation behavior better, which may help to justify existing programs and lead to the development of new and better programs (Henderson, 1994). Interestingly, according to Henderson and O'Neill (1995) a recent study suggests that 41% of the respondents regularly read the Research Update, which surpassed the readership of other columns such as "Washington Scene" and "Product Round Up," in NRPA's *Parks and Recreation* magazine. Yet many practitioners criticize the type of research that is conducted in leisure services on the grounds that it is of little use or relevance to practice. Practitioners are usually disinterested in theoretical research studies, tending to view them as "ivory tower" preoccupations that do not get at the concrete issues or the real problems that need to be solved (Kraus & Allen, 1987). Consequently, Henderson and O'Neill (1995) explored the question of whether or not research has contributed to the advancement of professional practice. They note that practitioners and academicians need to participate in the activity of research and communicate what needs to be researched. If the worthy subject of research is agreed upon by both groups, there is a greater chance that the research will help to advance practice. Conversely, if the research and subsequent dialogue is not transmitted through our professional publications, then research may have little impact on practice.

Kraus and Allen (1987) suggest that an emphasis be placed on research studies that occupy the middle ground, that are both academically respectable and clearly relevant to the concerns of recreation agencies and practitioners. This implies an emphasis on applied research (sometimes referred to as action or evaluation research). Furthermore, Henderson and O'Neill (1995) note that theoretical research focuses on the exploration of leisure behavior, not on the management of consumer/client services. Therefore, an effective approach to policy studies and evaluation studies must be grounded in some acceptable theory or have some basis or model to rely upon.

In order to influence practice, improve services, and address the critical issues of today, leisure researchers must become more proactive and action oriented. Many have suggested that unless we as individuals are embedded in the world out there, our understanding of what is relevant can be archaic (Allison, 1995). As Ewert (1990) noted, "Research, whether conducted formally or informally, is an integral part of a park and recreation organization: this is how every agency gleans information regarding how it should use its resources or what problems are being encountered" (p. 1). It is important, then, to develop a closer working relationship between practitioners and researchers. The development of a research agenda and means to contribute to the body of knowledge may include some of the following principles (Henderson & O'Neill, 1995):

1. Researchers and practitioners need to understand the relationship between research and practice and make research a priority in the profession.
2. Research should be presented clearly for application. Academicians should use jargon-free descriptions, and practitioners should learn basic research terminology.
3. Academics should spend some time doing applied research and interpreting research to practitioners.
4. National Recreation and Park Association (NRPA) assistance in ensuring that practitioners receive and have access to research findings of relevance to practice should be expanded.
5. Researchers and practitioners need to work together to determine research needs and agendas, interpret findings, and disseminate the results.

CHARACTERISTICS OF RESEARCH

Research is a careful, patient, and methodical inquiry done according to certain rules (Sommer & Sommer, 1986), guidelines, or accepted practices. Research is the manner in which we attempt to solve problems in a systematic effort to push back the frontiers of human ignorance or to confirm the validity of the solutions to problems others have presumably solved (Leedy, 1985). Research implies a planned systematic approach to solving problems or discovering the answers to complex issues. Tuckman (1978) suggests that there are five characteristics of research:

• *It is systematic.* Problem solving is accomplished through the identification and labeling of variables, followed by the design and implementation of research that tests the relationships of the identified variables through hypothesis testing.

• *It is logical.* The procedures allow other researchers to evaluate the conclusions drawn from your research. Procedures are described in enough detail so that other researchers can review the methods, findings, discussion, and conclusions in order to identify the relevance of the work to their own research agenda, or practical application.

• *It is empirical.* The researcher collects data on the issue or problem on which to base decisions. It should be noted that qualitative methods do produce findings on which to base decisions. These decisions can lead to policy formation, improved understanding of the problem, or further work and research.

• *It is reductive.* Research takes many individual events and/or observations (data) and uses them to establish more general relationships and associations. It is through the use of subject observation or subject response to our methods of collecting data in a carefully controlled study that we can form statements of relationships or begin to understand the underlying dimensions of the issue or problem. Research also allows others to draw generalizations about some issue or phenomenon.

• *It is replicable.* The research process is recorded, enabling others to test the findings by repeating the research or to build future research on previous results. Through careful documentation of our study design, implementation, findings, and conclusions, we allow other researchers or policy analysts to customize their own studies in answering similar research questions within their own context or situation.

These characteristics are based on the more traditional or mechanistic view of research, rather than a conceptual or naturalistic view. However, even qualitative approaches should have some logical and systematic basis within the data collection process. These issues are explored more fully later in this book.

THE SCIENTIFIC APPROACH OF BASIC RESEARCH

The scientific method of research involves the notion of a theory and subsequent development of hypothesis statements. In order to test the theory, the researcher must identify and operationalize variables for study. Then a research design and data collection process are developed, and the process ends with an analysis and reporting of the findings. The scientific method of inquiry, summarized in Table 1.1, includes a sequence of steps to be followed in the course of a research study (Smith & Glass, 1987):

Step 1: A *theory* about the phenomenon exists.
Step 2: The researcher detects a *research problem* within the theory and develops from it a research question to investigate.
Step 3: A *research hypothesis* is deduced from the propositions in the theory. The research hypothesis is a statement about the relationship between constructs.
Step 4: The researcher determines the operations (specific procedures or methods) by which the constructs will be defined and states a hypothesis that can be tested statistically. This hypothesis is called the null hypothesis. A research design is developed as a plan for implementing the operations and testing the null hypothesis. These operations, the null hypothesis, and the design make up the guidelines for the study.
Step 5: The researcher conducts the study according to the guidelines.
Step 6: The null hypothesis is tested based on the data from the study.
Step 7: The original theory is revised or supported based on the results of the hypothesis testing.

Table 1.1
Scientific Method Summarized (Smith & Glass 1987)

Sequence	Example
Step One: Theory, made up of constructs and propositions that link them, already exists.	"Contrived Theory" proposes that deliquency (D) is caused by anomie (An), as socialization (As), deliquent association (DA) and labeling (L).
Step Two: Propositions that are contradictory or lack empirical support are chosen as research problem.	"Is anomie the cause of delinquency?" is chosen as the research problem.
Step Three: Research hypothesis is deduced from theory.	"High anomie is a cause of delinquency" is deduced as research hypothesis.
Step Four: Constructs are operationally defined and assigned functions. Procedures for evaluating evidence are stated.	Anomie is defined as self-reported beliefs about job prospects (independent variable An-op); Delinquency is defined as self-reported acts (dependent variable, D-stated); Sampling, measurement, and analysis procedures specified. The null hypothesis is, "There are no differences in number of delinquent acts reported by groups high and low on An-op" ($p<0.05$).
Step Five Study is conducted according to number of acts committed by the two groups.	Data show an appreciable difference in average specifications in Step Four. Subjects high in anomie reported more acts than those low in anomie.
Step Six: Null hypothesis is tested.	Null hypothesis is rejected based on the difference between the two groups.
Step Seven: Research hypothesis is supported or yields further research hypothesis.	Research hypothesis "anomie causes delinquency"is disconfirmed. The original theory supported. "Contrived Theory" is supported and engenders stronger belief or is revised accordingly.

BASIC AND APPLIED RESEARCH

The two most common reasons for doing leisure research are (1) to obtain answers to pressing questions or problems and (2) to contribute to theories of leisure behavior. Generally, providing answers to pressing questions or problems has been referred to as *applied research*. It is usually conducted to solve some immediate problem or take advantage of opportunities in the market. The objective of applied research is to answer a specific question for a specific group at a given point in time and is less concerned with the discovery of new knowledge (Chadwick, Bahr, & Albrecht, 1984). Examples include conducting a study to determine why some teenagers are not participating in after-school programs or what certain age groups desire in the way of leisure programs.

One type of research that is receiving increasing attention is program evaluation. For the most part, this involves determining the effectiveness of a leisure service or program. Rossman (1995) defines evaluation as "judging the worth of program services on the basis of an analysis of systematically collected evidence." Evaluation is valuable in that it can guide legislative action (Sommer & Sommer, 1986) and it can lead to useful judgments in three ways: program development, organizational management, and establishing accountability (Rossman, 1995). A recent emerging concept, quality assurance, is related to the assessment and evaluation process (Edginton, Hanson, & Edginton, 1992).

Investigations designed to answer general long-range questions about leisure behavior are considered basic research, and are generally motivated by the researcher's curiosity. In practice, the division between applied and basic research studies is far from clear (Sommer & Sommer, 1986). However, basic research is typically directed toward advancing scientific knowledge for its own sake (Rossi, Wright, & Wright, 1978). Thomas and Nelson (1990) note that considerable controversy exists in the literature on psychology, education, and physical education about whether more research should be applied or basic. Some see the distinctions as a reflection of the attitudes and objectives of the researcher rather than the research activity per se

(Rossi, Wright, & Wright, 1978). Others (Leedy, 1985, p. 3) argue that the basic difference between applied research and basic research lies in the depth to which basic research probes the underlying causes and meaning of observed phenomena and in the sophistication with which it demands that the collected data of observation be interpreted. However, Henderson and Bialeschki (1995) note that evaluation (applied) and other forms of research differ only in their objectives or purposes, rather than in their designs or executions. Often the two types of research are indistinguishable (Rossi, Freeman, & Wright, 1979), and most research incorporates some degree of both applied and basic methods (Thomas & Nelson, 1990). In comparing paradigms between research and evaluation, we can generalize and note that research normally utilizes experimental and correlation methods, while evaluation-type research relies on the systems approach (input, processing, and output) and the objectives approach (objectives, means, and measures). For comparative purposes, it is useful to examine the characteristics of basic, applied, and evaluation research as presented in Table 1.2 (McMillan & Schumacher, 1984).

Table 1.2
Characteristics of the Types of Research

	Basic	Applied	Evaluation
Description of Research Type	Physical, behavioral and social sciences	Applied fields such as medicine, social work, engineering, and education	Practice at a given site or sites, specific programs, or policies
Purpose	1. Test theories and discover scientific laws, basic principles 2. Determine empirical relationships among natural and social phenomena 3. Determine analytical relationships among events	1. Test the usefulness of scientific theories within a given field 2. Determine empirical relationships within a given field. 3. Determine analytical relationships among events within a field	1. Assess the merit, or worthiness of a specific practice or program 2. Assess the worth of a specific practice
Typical Role of Investigator	Scientist	Researcher within a given field	Researcher/and or practitioner at a site(s)
Level of discourse	Abstract, general within science	Abstract, general within a given field	Concrete, specific to a particular practice

Table 1.2 Cont.

Generalizability of explanations	Relate to physical, behavioral, and social sciences	Apply to a given field	Apply to a specific practice at a given site(s)
Functions	1. Add to scientific knowledge of basic laws and principles 2. Advance further inquiry and methodology	1. Add to research-based knowledge in a given field 2. Advance research and methodology in a given field	1. Add to research-based knowledge and method of a specific practice or program 2. Aid in decision-making at a given site(s)
Intended ultimate	Accepted body of scientific knowledge in physical, behavioral, and social sciences	Accepted body of research-based knowledge in a given field	1. Change of practice at outcomes site(s) and knowledge in field of application

Source: Adapted from McMillan, J. H., & Schumacher, S. 1984. *Research In Education.* Little, Brown & Co. Boston.

In our estimation, the distinctions between basic or pure research and applied or action research are vague and rather meaningless in the resolution of problems or confirmation of knowledge. In fact, all research types are a form of inquiry. Inquiry can take any form as long as it is systematic and consistent (Short, 1991). The following guidelines can be used to determine what constitutes a quality research effort (modified from Nachmias & Nachmias, 1987; Thomas & Nelson, 1990; Stoddard, 1982). It should be noted that this refers to the deductive (quantitative) mode of research, as opposed to the qualitative approach.

1. Identification and delimitation of the problem and the subproblems, stating the relationships;
2. A thorough review and analysis of relevant literature;
3. Specifying and defining testable hypothesis or developing research questions;
4. Designing a research study and method to test the hypothesis or address the research questions, developing a research plan;
5. Choosing the subjects, administering the tests and questionnaires, or conducting observations;
6. Analyzing and reporting the results; and
7. Discussing the implications of the findings and making any necessary adjustments in programs or recommending further research.

Quality research, whether basic or applied, involves much more than designing and implementing an appropriate methodological plan or analysis of data. Some of the most important activities or tasks occur prior to designing the technical methodology or analysis (Majchrzak, 1984). The researcher must focus on selecting and defining the problem. The following section delineates the steps in defining the problem, collecting data, and reporting data.

THE RESEARCH PROCESS

The conduct of research is a process consisting of generic steps. In general, seven distinct steps or tasks can be identified relative to a quality, comprehensive research project. Frequently, the resolution of one research problem gives rise to new questions and further research problems that require a repeat of the research cycle. This cyclic approach continues indefinitely, reflecting the progress of a scientific discipline (Nachmias & Nachmias, 1987). The seven steps are graphically depicted in Figure 1.2 and are elaborated upon below. The arrows in Figure 1.2 note the direction or sequence of steps, and the connecting lines suggest the interrelatedness of the tasks or steps within the research process.

1. Identify the Problem or Issue, and State the Possible Relationships of Variables

Kerlinger (1986) suggests that a research problem begins as a question, and that the question usually asks something about the relations among the variables under consideration. Primarily, the researcher attempts to brainstorm the possible variables related to the research question. The investigation of a research topic can start from a variety of questions or problems that have one common characteristic: they are such that observation or experimentation can provide the needed information for some answers (Dandekar, 1988). Topics can be generated by personal or theoretical interest, gaps in the literature, or by practical concerns and issues in the field and society.

At this stage, the researcher starts with the identification of a problem or opportunity, stated in clear, unambiguous terms. The primary research problem is worded as a simple statement that expresses the core of the research (Stoddard, 1982). Many research efforts are limited in scope or quality due to the fact that the researcher did not adequately consider the complexity of the problem or opportunity. A concise statement guides the research project through the many steps and complicated procedures to be utilized. Without this statement, we may deviate from the original purpose and get lost in side issues, or be distracted from answering and validating what we wanted to originally address. This statement is integral to the overall research process.

Problems must be made concrete and specific. The topic chosen must be narrowed so that the task is manageable in size and can be completed within a single study, within budget, and within the given time and staffing constraints. It is difficult for many researchers to choose the right level of focus in defining what elements of a system (problem) they will study and to what detail. The key is the ability to home in on what is significant and avoid the peripheral but potentially interesting questions about the problem.

The problem or research statement invariably mentions the phenomenon being studied, which may be termed the problem variable. The problem variable therefore is one of the phenomena that must be measured by an appropriate field technique. In other words, is the problem measurable or does it have characteristics that can be observed and described in components? Once the researcher defines the topic or research problem, criteria are required for making the decision to conduct the research (adapted from Creswell, 1994; Isaac & Michael, 1985):

a. Is the topic researchable, given the allotted time, resources, and availability of data?
b. Is there sufficient personal interest in the topic to sustain attention over the long haul?
c. Will the results of the study be of interest or of use to others in the field?
d. Is the topic publishable, adequate for a terminal degree or course, or of use in making change in policy and programs?
e. Does the study (1) fill a void in the literature, (2) replicate other work, (3) extend other work, or (4) develop new ideas and concepts in the scholarly literature?
f. Will the project contribute to career goals? Is it in line with personal goals and expectations?
g. Is there administrative, financial or other support for the work?
h. Do I possess the technical skills, or do I need help?

Figure 1.2
Research Process

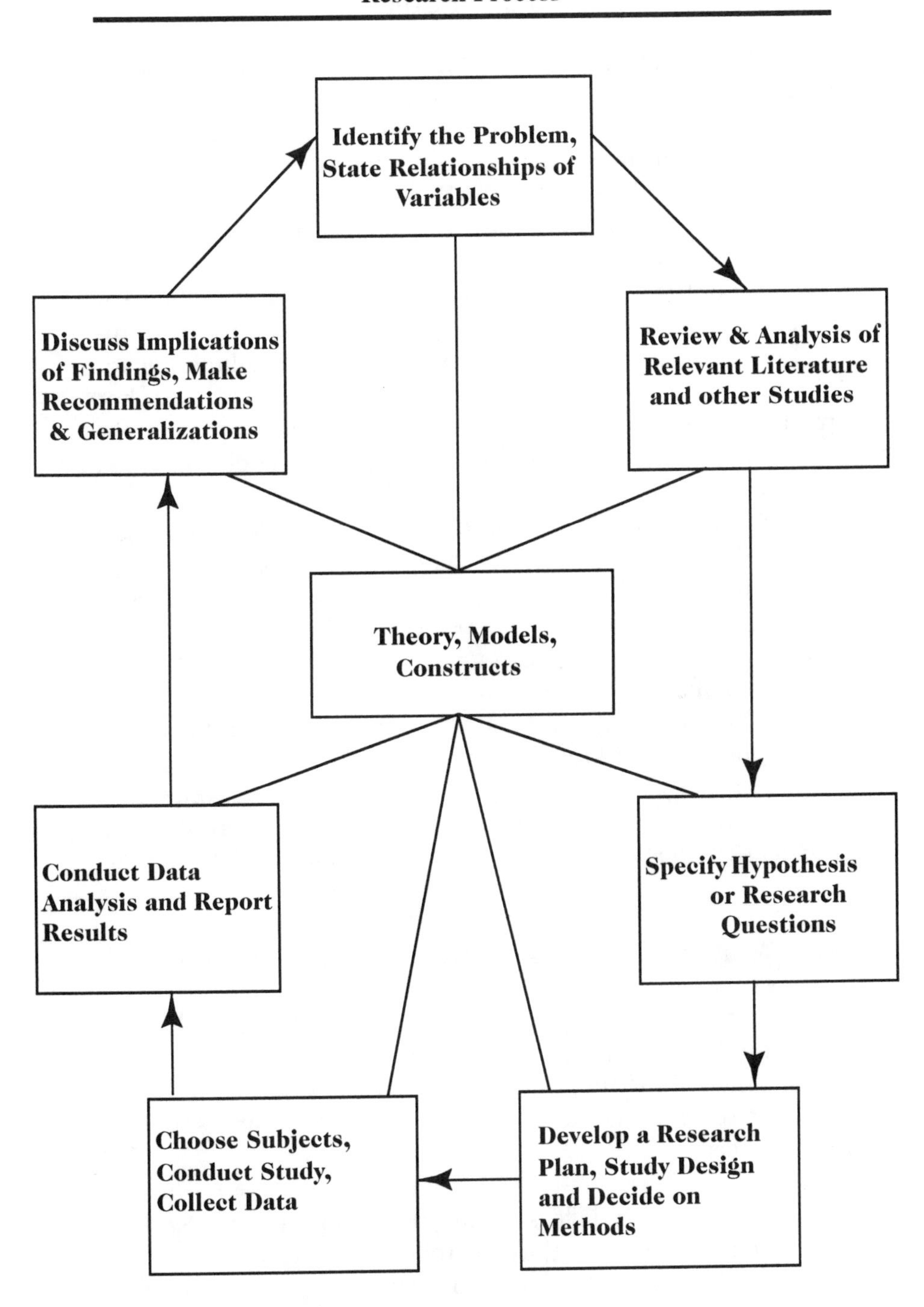

2. Review and Analysis of Relevant Literature and other Studies

The goal of the literature review is to develop knowledge and understanding of previous work or activity in regard to the topic being researched. The researcher should carefully read and evaluate the literature reviews contained in journal articles. Attention should be paid to the dates of material cited, type of publication (journal vs. trade), and analysis of literature cited by the writer being reviewed.

Use of the literature in the identification of possible variables having relationships to the problem or opportunity is crucial at this stage. Examining previous studies or obtaining advice and opinions from local experts provides the researcher with some level of assurance that the project is on the right track. The task of the literature review is intricately entwined with the research problem and formulation task. The goal is to work toward specifying the problem so that it become manageable in the course of the research project. As a word of caution, Isaac and Michael (1985) note some common errors in conducting literature reviews. These include hurriedly conducting the review and proceeding before understanding the problem; relying too heavily on secondary sources; concentrating on research findings, and overlooking methods and measures; and faulty copying of citations and notes.

A first step in specifying a problem is to immerse oneself in the literature on the subject. Some questions the researcher might ask of the literature include (Williamson, Karp, & Dalphin, 1977):

a. What are the various theories or concepts offered to explain the topic under investigation?
b. Do the theories or concepts seem to contradict one another, and if so, in what ways?
c. Which of the theories or concepts seems most plausible?
d. Do the authors themselves call attention to unresolved issues?

As problems and ideas for the project begin to emerge while reviewing the literature, the researcher must consider the kinds of data and what methodological techniques are called for to adequately address the potential problems generated or identified out of the literature.

A number of specific steps can be used to successfully complete a literature review.

Step One. Have the topic clearly focused and reviewed by other pertinent individuals.

Step Two. Become familiar with the library. Proceed with a general word search of the topic.

Step Three. Read sources collected and begin note taking. Summarize each article or source by citing the topic, research questions or hypothesis tested and used; the sample size and method of selecting subjects (e.g., convenience vs. random); research design and methods; and findings and conclusions. A word of advice: Make a *complete* citation of the source and library call number. This saves time in the final writing of the bibliography or reference section. The following outline can be used for all sources (it is advisable to use a standard format such as American Psychological Association [APA] style to save time): Author. (date). *Title*. Source, volume (no.), pp.

Step Four. Arrange the sources and summaries of work by the most important sources or by date of publication. Citing the most important sources first allows the reader to quickly move through a research paper. The date format allows the researcher to insert another source should one surface. In order to propose hypotheses or research questions, use the following guidelines (adapted from Adams & Schvaneveldt, 1991) during the literature search: (1) identify specific statements related to the project; (2) group statements by theme, method, findings, etc.; (3) integrate statements in terms of agreement in findings and direction of hypothesis and research questions; (4) develop hypotheses statements from previous studies; and (5) arrange findings of previous studies on the topic that range broadly (multiple studies) and those that are emergent or isolated (single studies).

This step concludes with writing a first draft of the introduction of the study and literature sources.

3. Specify the Hypothesis or Researchable Questions

The researcher at this stage of the process should consider the use of theory within the context of the question. Simply put, a theory is an effort to explain a phenomenon, an effort to understand why something occurs or not (Goodale, 1994). The researcher searches the literature to identify an existing theory about the phenomenon.

The theoretical basis for the work will provide the researcher with an ability to define the subproblems or components of the larger issue in question, and allow a reasonable guess as to the direction of subsequent efforts (hypothesis). This effort should conclude in a clear diagram of the variables and their relationships and should provide precise direction for solving the problem or exploring the opportunity.

Creswell (1994) offers a model of the quantitative (deductive) mode of research and how theory is related and addressed (Figure 1.3). It should be noted that this model is top-down, starting with the realization of a theory or conceptualization and testing that theory. The researcher then proceeds to test the hypothesis, operationalize variables, and use a data collection method.

Figure 1.3
The Deductive Mode of Research in a Quantitative Study

Researcher Tests a Theory

Researcher Tests Hypotheses or Research Questions Derived from the Theory

Researcher Operationalizes Concepts or Variables Derived for the Theory

Researcher Uses an Instrument to Measure Variables in the Theory

The inductive mode of research begins in quite another manner (Creswell, 1994). This model suggests a bottom-up approach, where the researcher is searching for relevance and information upon which to build a theory or suggest a theory (Figure 1.4). This method is sometimes referred to as the interpretive method. More detail regarding this mode of research is offered in Chapter 2. This model is shown here to allow the reader to see the relationships between theory, data collection, and instrumentation.

Figure 1.4
The Inductive Mode of Research in a Qualitative Study

Researcher Develops a Theory or
Compares Pattern with Other Theories

Researcher Looks for Patterns (Theories)

Researcher Forms Categories

Researcher Asks Questions

Researcher Gathers Information

Research Questions and Subproblems

Sometimes it is difficult to identify or separate the problem from the subproblems. Use of experts and literature often helps to define the issue under question and lead the proper identification of the components of what one is examining. An example of problems and subproblems may be viewed as follows. Recreation and leisure professionals cite problems with youth-at-risk for use as a justification for additional taxpayer support. Recreation and leisure professionals profess that providing recreation programs will positively impact the youth and reduce crime and gang activity. A number of variables may have some influence on the findings and outcomes. The problem, then, is to justify the influence of recreation programs on youth-at-risk. Subproblems or related variables that need to be defined, measured, and controlled for could include the facilities used (adequacy, equipment, lighting, location etc.); leadership presence (style, personality, knowledge, etc.); type of program (sports, social); number, age, and gender of participants; self-concept of participants; local police support, attitude, or presence; parental involvement and awareness; gang activity or influence; drug and alcohol use and abuse; and school-related programs and support. Table 1.3 provides examples of research questions and subordinate questions to illustrate the considerations that the researcher must be attentive to and be prepared to address (adapted from Hedrick, Bickman, & Rog, 1993).

Table 1.3
Examples of Primary and Subordinate Questions

Primary:	How prevalent is drug use among high school students?
Subordinate:	What percentage use cocaine at least weekly?
	What percentage use marijuana daily?
	What percentage sell drugs to other students?
Primary:	How many homeless children are there in town?
Secondary:	How many are below age 12?
	What percentage are black, white, Hispanic, and Asian?
	What percentage are living in parks?
Primary:	Is the park district making optimum use of its staffing?
Secondary:	What are the qualifications of staff and their expertise?
	How much time is consumed by maintenance and administrative tasks?
Primary:	Did the after school study hall and play program increase graduation rates for 7th and 8th graders?
Secondary:	Were there different rates for male and female students?
Secondary:	What kinds of subsequent after school opportunities did the students pursue?
Secondary:	What was the cost per student?

Assume that we conducted research on a particular community and concluded that recreation programs had a positive impact on youth and lowered crime rates. However, given the nature of the variables listed above, we must question whether the increased police activity and involvement had anything to do with lowering the crime rates in the area. Did the school institute drug, alcohol, and gang awareness programs? How did this influence perceptions and rates of leisure involvement? Did the new program make parents more aware of their children's activities? Did the parents make more of an effort to become directly involved with their children's leisure time involvement? As you can see, the issue becomes quite complex; consequently, we must identify the components (subproblems) of the topic in question in order to better understand the issue, design appropriate methods, and interpret the findings.

Hypothesis Statements

As already noted, research looks for facts and meanings guided by the problem and research question, or hypothesis. Hypothesis statements are educated guesses (or proposed generalizations) about the relationships thought to exist between the research phenomenon and other pertinent phenomena, which are frequently termed explanatory variables (also predictor or independent variables) (Stoddard, 1982; Dandekar, 1988). Having stated the problem and attendant subproblems, each of the subproblems is then viewed through a logical construct called a hypothesis (Leedy, 1985). Sometimes researchers do not present hypotheses (or research questions) at the beginning of the research. By postponing an identification of potential relationships, data needs and issues are put in question. If no hypotheses are stated or relationships are only vaguely implied, important decisions about explanatory variables are, in effect, delayed until the stage of data collection (Stoddard, 1982).

The role of the hypothesis in research is to suggest explanations for certain facts and to guide in the investigation of others, essentially providing direction for solving the problem. A hypothesis may be based on a hunch or intuition that may ultimately make an important contribution to leisure research. If a hypothesis has been tested in only one study, there are two limitations to its usefulness (Dandekar, 1988): (a) there is no assurance that the relationship between two variables found in the given study will be found in other studies, and (b) there is no clear connection with the body of knowledge. Fortunately, if a hypothesis arises from other studies and recommendations, the first limitation is lessened. If the hypothesis was derived from other studies and also from a theory, then the hypothesis is freed from both limitations. The key point is that one-case or one-shot studies are suspect and need replication and proof or discussion of generalizability to a larger sample. This problem is important and points to the necessity of conducting thorough literature reviews (step 2) and problem identification and clarification (step 1).

The following are some examples of research hypotheses. Note that hypotheses state the expectations of the researcher in positive terms. The null hypothesis statement of "no relationship or difference" is the one actually statistically tested. It usually states that the relation or difference in the findings is due to chance or sampling error and puts this supposition to a probability test (Isaac & Michael, 1985).

a. Positive reinforcement of acceptable behaviors increases the incidence of such behaviors among youth at risk. (Null: Behaviors of youth are not influenced by positive reinforcement.)
b. Urban density causes alienation and lack of recreation participation. (Null: Lack of recreation participation and alienation are not related to urban density.)
c. Satisfaction with a leisure activity is enhanced by the ability of the participant and concept of perfectionism. (Null: Satisfaction is not related to ability and/or perfectionism.)
d. Frequency of television viewing is positively related to passivity among adolescents. (Null: Any differences in passivity and television viewing occur by chance.)
e. Anxiety decreases performance on complex psychomotor tasks, thereby decreasing satisfaction in leisure. (Null: Anxiety is not correlated with satisfaction.)
f. A child's involvement in recreation programs decreases as the number of siblings in the family increases. (Null: The number of siblings does not have an effect on involvement.)
g. Delinquency and gender are related; males are more likely than females to become delinquent. (Null: The means in the two populations from which the samples were respectively drawn at random are equal.)

Dandekar (1988) suggests that much exploratory research and learning through trial and error must take place before hypotheses can be formulated. Hypotheses are not quickly deduced from preliminary work. However, exploratory work is necessary to develop theories and models, and to help practitioners utilize theories in problem solving. The development of clear hypotheses and research questions facilitates the design of a quality study.

4. Develop a Research Plan and Study Design, and Decide on Data Collection Method(s)

A decision about which phenomena are meaningful is only one of several decisions that must be made prior to collecting data. Because the decisions are interdependent, it is wise to organize these decisions into a research plan (Stoddard, 1982) or map. It is often said that "you have to plan to plan." The same is true for research: we have to plan to conduct research. The research plan provides a guide as to the procedures, definitions, and direction of the project. Since research efforts need to be concise, defined, and purposeful, the research plan can improve the quality and efficiency of our efforts. It allows us another opportunity to view the project as a whole, ask relevant questions, and seek expert advice from statisticians, methodologists, and supervisors in order to address various limitations such as samples, methods, analysis, and reporting. In other words, we must not go in an aimless, undirected manner hoping to discover some "interesting facts." We have set out to address the problem statement and examine the variables in question as set forth above. Figure 1.5 shows an example research plan for a quantitative study.

Specifically, the research plan or map identifies the necessary steps and methods to be used. This allows the researcher an opportunity to think through the design of the study as well as analyze the types of variables and their relationships to the study issue. In the case of Figure 10.5, the study was designed to measure resident attitudes toward tourism. The researcher hypothesized from the literature that the three groups would have different attitudes toward tourism, and that various independent variables would be correlated with the dependent variable (attitude toward tourism).

In terms of choosing methods, the problem must come first. The problem should drive the data collection and analysis procedures. Specifically, the researcher must ask, "what questions must be answered?" and "how will they be approached?" The next issue involves the time and resources available. Considerations include the researcher's time and budget, the subject's time limitations, and setting or ethical questions.

The researcher constructs a research design to maximize internal and external validity (see Chapter 3). Attention should

Figure 1.5
Research Plan/Map

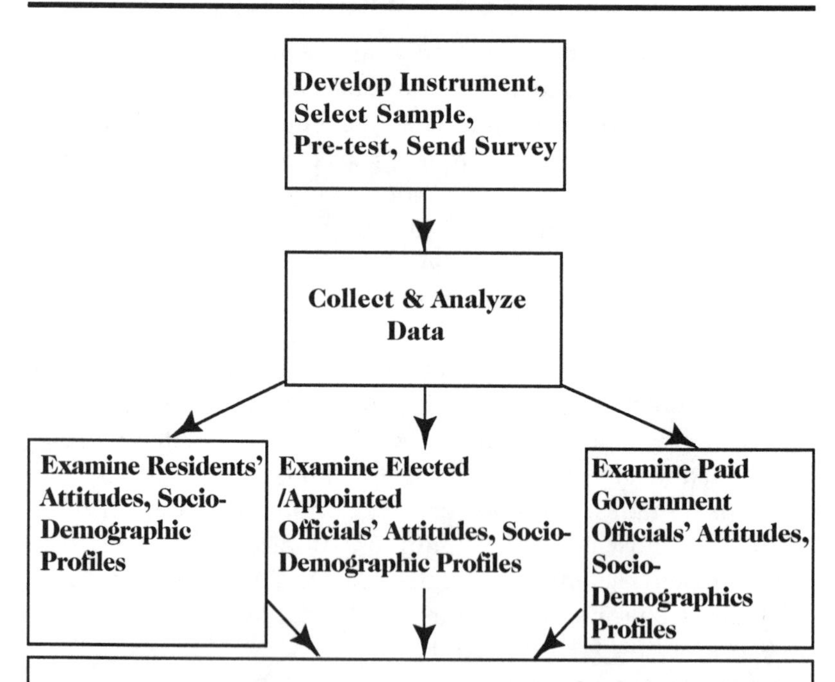

Measure Attitudes Using a One–Way Analysis of Covariance with Two Covariates: Analysis of Covariance of Tourism Attitudes (3 Groups) Scores, Using Length of Residency (RES) and Whether or Not Individual Works in a Tourist Related Business (WRK) As Covariates

Conduct Duncan's Multiple Range Test to Determine Which Group(s) if Any Differed in Regard to Attitude

Conduct Multiple Correlational Study to Determine Which of the Following Independent Variables Helps to Explain Attitudes Toward Tourism. Independent Variables: Age; Income; Sex; Length of Residence; Work in Tourism Industry; and Place of Birth

Make Conclusions and Recommendations About Tourism Development Issues in the Columbia River Gorge

be paid to the control and manipulation of variables, establishment of criteria to evaluate the data, and instrumentation (i.e., develop an instrument or adapt an existing instrument). As can be seen in the research plan in Figure 1.5, the researcher paid particular attention to variables of interest and influence, controlled them through statistical methods, and indicated the development of an instrument. Figure 1.6 illustrates the transition from the conceptual level (hypothesis or research question) phase to the operational level (adapted from Nachmias & Nachmias, 1987). We illustrate this point using the conceptual understanding that people seek benefits from leisure and that the provision of leisure services provides a number of benefits to people and communities (social, personal, economic, and environmental). The conceptual level, conceptual components, and conceptual definitions are at the theory level. Again, this points to the importance of theory and literature in study design. Operational definitions and the operational level are at the research level. This component points to the importance of understanding methods and analysis procedures.

To implement the study, the researcher has a number of data collection methods available. Table 1.4 provides a listing of examples of the various methods available to the leisure services researcher (adapted from Sommer & Sommer, 1986). Additional clarification of these techniques is provided in Chapters 2 and 3.

Table 1.4
Choosing A Data Collection Technique

Issue/Problem	Approach	Data Collection Technique
To obtain reliable information under controlled conditions about attitudes toward leisure due to exposure to virtual reality.	Conduct experimental design in controlled setting (room or area)	Laboratory experiment, simulation
To find out how people behave and interact in public open spaces.	Observe them	Systematic observation
To find out how people behave in private recreation settings.	Ask them to keep diaries	Personal documents

Table 1.4 Cont.

Issue/Problem	Approach	Data Collection Technique
To learn what people think about leisure motivation.	Ask them	Interview, questionnaire, attitude scale
To find out where people go for their leisure pursuits.	Chart their movements	Behavioral mapping, trace measures
To identify relationships between motivation and satisfaction levels of the experience.	Administer a standardized scale	Attitudinal Scale with known Psychometric properties
To identify trends in leisure research	Systematic tabulation and literature review	Content analysis
To understand an event in leisure services or an experience.	Detailed investigation of secondary sources and interviews	Case study

Source: Adapted from Sommer & Sommer, 1986.

There are disadvantages and advantages to all the methods listed in Table 1.4. When researchers choose a methodology to study a problem, they must weigh the advantages and disadvantages of their options in the context of the overall goals of the research (Cozby, 1993) or project. Issues of consideration include artificiality of experiments, ethical considerations, subject variables, and predictions of the future. Artificiality of experiments refers to problems associated with replication of the findings (in laboratory settings) in the field. Specifically, did subjects respond differently in the laboratory or other controlled setting due to testing or tester presence and bias? In terms of ethical considerations, the researcher should make certain that any experimental methods employed are suitable for a group or problem. Subject variables are of concern in that information such as age, sex, education, and marital status, may be important to a study. Care should be taken not to offend respondents.

Figure 1.6
From Conceptual to Operational in a Study

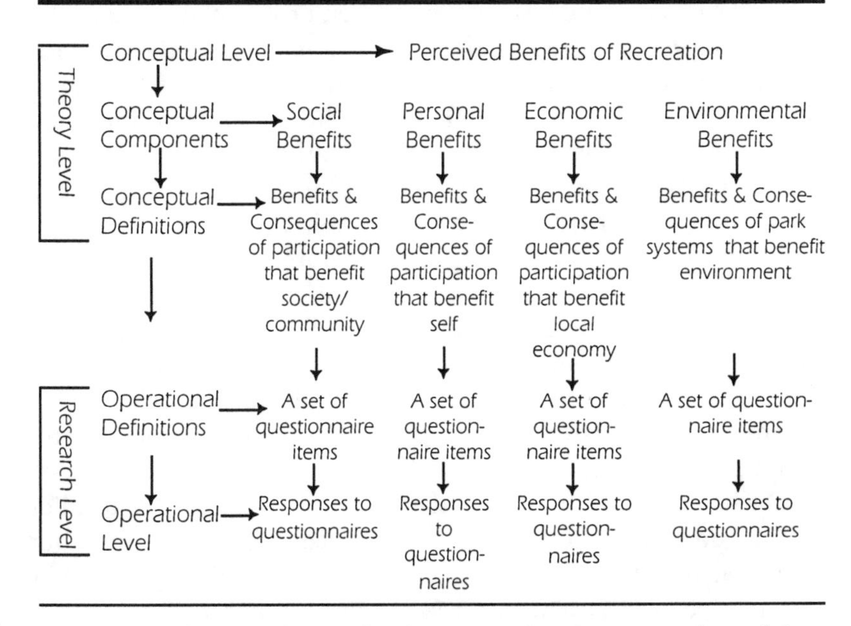

To implement the study, the researcher has a number of data collection methods available. Table 1.4 provides a listing of examples of the various methods available to the leisure services researcher (adapted from Sommer & Sommer 1986). Additional clarification of these techniques is provided in Chapter 2 and 3.

Additionally, the researcher should determine which subject variables are most important in the final analysis and description of the findings. Finally, predictions are of both interest and concern. In order for other researchers to assess the reliability of the predictions or inferences derived from the data, the measurements used and the validity and reliability of measurement systems must be both understood and reported by the researcher. This issue is central to the concept of generalizability.

5. Choose Subjects, Conduct the Study, and Collect the Data

The primary focus of this book concerns the various methods used to collect data in leisure services. Specific details and concerns are discussed in Chapters 2 and 3. The researcher should note that the data collected are meaningful only as a means to answering a specific research problem and are useful to the degree that they can be analyzed and reported to provide a solution to a problem or address a hypothesis. Of particular importance is that the data produced by various techniques are valuable only insofar as they satisfy overall research goals.

Pitfalls the researcher must avoid in the gathering of data include (adapted from Isaac & Michael, 1985) paying insufficient attention to establishing and maintaining a rapport with subjects, which may lead to refusals to cooperate or errors in measurement; failure to evaluate available measures in terms of appropriateness to the study purpose and subjects and validity of the instrument; use of methods that the researcher is not trained to administer, analyze, or interpret; and failure to pretest the instrument.

Generalizability is related to the problem of external validity and data collection (sample size). Essentially, the researcher attempts to determine in what situations the results apply, other than the sample on which the results are based. The results obtained in a study are limited to the population from which the sample was drawn, if simple random sampling methods are employed (sampling is described in greater detail later in the book). Researchers can enlarge the study to include subjects from other areas in order to generalize. If studies repeatedly turn up the same differences or similarities, then the results can be considered generalizable and not simply characteristic of a single situation.

While some sample designs such as nonprobability and simple random designs are limited in generalizability, steps can be taken to increase the validity of a study. Specifically, purposive or quota samples should employ random selection of subjects. Observational studies should employ random selection of days, times, events, sites, etc. to reduce bias. Interviews conducted as intercept surveys should include every nth person entering the interview site. The point is to try to approximate randomness in the technical sense (to provide as equal an opportunity for selection as is possible) and to devise ways of reducing or eliminating sources of error (Sommer & Sommer, 1986).

Beyond the sampling technique, the next obvious issue concerns the sample size requirements. Larger samples generally provide more reliable and representative data than small samples. Specifically, larger samples have lower sampling errors and greater reliability, and increase the power of statistical tests applied to the data. However, the reduction in sampling error may not be worth the additional time, money, and resources. There are arguments in favor of small sample sizes. For example, small samples of subjects cost less to administer tests and conduct the analysis of the findings and small samples are sometimes more manageable and convenient, especially in exploratory work. The following should be considered when deciding on the sample size:

1. *Statistical probability level desired.* This is explained later in this book.
2. *Available resources and time constraints.* Small samples take less time to manage.
3. *Number of subsets to compare or differentiate.* The sample must contain large enough subsamples, such as age and gender, in order to make meaningful comparisons.
4. *Refusals and bad addresses.* Samples sometimes must be increased to allow for unusable data or rejections. For example, for a survey given to employees, we can generally expect higher return rates than would occur with the general population. The researcher must consider the topic, its potential interest to the sample, the length of the survey, and the convenience of the instrument when determining sample sizes.

Finally, a clear description of the sampling method and return rate should be developed for the written report. This allows readers an opportunity to evaluate the generalizability of the data. Perfectly representative samples are difficult to obtain due to out-of-date or incomplete listings of potential respondents. Many researchers often settle for a less-than-perfect sampling procedure in order to obtain samples which are accessible and cooperative (Sommer & Sommer, 1986). However, the researcher should strive for a comprehensive sample method and report the procedures fully.

6. Conduct Data Analysis, and Report Findings and Results

As a guide for analysis and writing, the researcher should consider three questions (Schmerl, 1988): (1) How much? (2) how many? (3) compared to what? Questions 1 and 2 are easily communicated and analyzed in most studies. However, the "compared to what" question is at the heart of what we are trying to do in research; it guides us in the collection, analysis, and compilation of data. Schmerl (1988) notes that it is an organizing principle beginning with the tentative idea of how the data might be usefully compiled (displayed) for comparisons. Specifically, the researcher needs to focus on the hypothesis and raw data and then determine the most efficient and comprehensive means of designing tables and graphs to present the important pieces of data.

Data analysis refers to the process by which the researcher organizes and summarizes the accumulated data into a form that addresses the issue or problem at hand. The analytical process usually involves calculating and summarizing statistics and notes taken during observations or reducing the observations into a small, manageable format. The researcher should have been aware of the type of data and their characteristics prior to data collection. Data analysis opportunities may be limited by the data characteristics. For example, if the data consist of numbers, certain statistical treatments can be applied. If data are written comments or classified phenomena without numerical associations, then fewer kinds of statistical summaries (or no statistical summaries) are available. This issue is explained in greater detail in the following chapters.

A number of common errors occur in the analysis of data (Isaac & Michael, 1985) due to:

1. The researcher selecting statistical tools that are not appropriate for the proposed analysis. Sometimes the data fail to meet the assumptions of the tests used,

2. The researcher collecting data and then trying to find a statistical technique that can be applied in the analysis. The researcher must have a clear understanding of the measurement characteristics and options for analysis prior to data collection.

Through the literature review, the researcher can discover the measurements and statistical tools applied in similar work. A researcher who lacks the training and expertise can proceed to acquire assistance or the necessary training. Specifically, the researcher should be aware of which statistical techniques require which type of data (nominal, ordinal, interval, or ratio) and which type of test is appropriate based on statistical assumptions and sample size (nonparametric or parametric).

7. Discuss Implications of the Findings, Make Recommendations, and Generalize Results

Finally, the researcher is in a position to present the findings and make recommendations regarding the issue or problem. The parts of the research report are relatively simple and straightforward. The written document should achieve three objectives (based on Leedy, 1985): (1) It should acquaint the reader with the problem researched and explain the implications sufficiently so that readers can understand the problem or issue being researched. (2) It should present the data fully and adequately. (3) It should interpret the data for the reader and demonstrate how the data address the problem or issue being researched.

Displaying the data is the beginning of the interpretation of the findings, which is the purpose of research. At this point, the researcher interprets the meaning of the facts (data), which hopefully will lead to a resolution of the problem, or confirmation or rejection of the hypothesis. In fact, without an inquiry into the intrinsic meaning of the data, no resolution of the research problem or its attendant subproblems is possible (Leedy, 1985).

In standard scientific methodology, the formal testing of a hypothesis leads directly to a conclusion about its acceptability. Even a less formalized procedure (evaluation research or some forms of qualitative research, for example) should produce evidence about the correctness of the hypothesis or one's initial intuition about the relationships. The statement of the acceptance or nonacceptance of the hypothesis is the goal of the entire undertaking. All who acknowledge and accept the conclusion recognize that its validity is highly contingent upon the quality of the data (Stoddard, 1982). The research process or cycle must be carefully and successfully implemented at each stage in order to produce valid and reliable data.

To address the implications of the study, the researcher can begin discussing findings by asking simple questions of the data set. First, address the research questions or hypotheses that were framed before any data were collected. Remember, the hypothesis is a proposition linking two concepts (or variables). The link may be simply one of association, where X is related to Y. But potentially more useful hypotheses are those that suggest a causal relationship, that X causes Y (or possibly contributes to Y, as there may be other factors involved as well).

Other questions the researcher should consider are as follows. How do these data relate to the other studies? Was the experimental service program effective? Have we learned which tactics work well with which population? What did this study accomplish or contribute to the body of knowledge? Did the study address the problem or issue? What implications to practice are suggested by this study?

If the researcher is thoroughly familiar with the literature, this task becomes easier to address. Thomas and Nelson (1990) suggest some simple rules for organizing the discussion of the findings:

1. Discuss your actual results, not what you wish they were.
2. Relate your results back to the introduction, literature review, and hypotheses or research questions.
3. Explain how your results fit within the theory presented.
4. Interpret the findings and recommend applications of your findings.
5. Summarize and state conclusions with supporting evidence.

A note of caution is prudent at this point. Never believe one piece of data until other data dealing with the same topic are considered for consistency of results, and never assume that there is only one way to perceive the truth on a question or problem (Bloom, 1986). Additionally, never be lulled into believing that there is only one way to conduct research. As Chapter 2 points out, there are many methods available to the leisure researcher.

CONCLUSION

Information in this chapter introduced concepts and models of research in the social sciences and leisure research. The purpose of this section was to help the reader gain an understanding of the characteristics of research in both its applied and basic form. Where possible, references were made to leisure research strengths, weaknesses, and purposes. Changes were recommended to advance leisure research, such as a "focus on core issues," and "specific methodological improvements."

This chapter addressed the research process and its relationship to decision making in leisure service delivery. Importantly, the research process facilitates the recognition and definition of problems or opportunities; collection and synthesis of information; generation of alternatives; and communication of the findings. These tasks are inherently part of any sequential and systematic problem-solving model. It was noted that many practitioners do not read the findings of leisure research. Yet, these very same practitioners do in fact solve problems in the field. One aim of this section of the book was to introduce to the reader the symbiotic relationship between leisure service delivery and leisure research.

In order for the student and practitioner to understand the value of research fully and judge its adequacy and quality, characteristics of research were introduced. Finally, a generic research process was introduced in order to inform the reader of the basic steps of any research project. Many details were included in the discussion of this research process, such as the use of a research plan or map. This information was provided early in the book to provide a solid framework for understanding later chapters. The intention here is to have the reader understand early on what we believe to be a systematic and thorough research process. Additionally, later chapters come back to these very same concepts and process in the areas of research design, reliability and validity, analysis, and reporting.

Chapter Two

Methods of Data Collection in Leisure Research

INTRODUCTION

Researchers must understand methodological issues in data collection in order to be effective in the provision of quality research. Clearly, one must be knowledgeable about the methods of acquisition (Adams & Schvaneveldt, 1991) in order to produce research findings that impact the provision of leisure services. Of particular importance here is the realization that data or information can be partially defined by the methods used to gather it; consequently, understanding methods of data collection will make the information more meaningful. The meaningfulness of data is usually determined via concepts such as validity, reliability, utility, and generalizability. Once data have been accumulated, we generally can refer to or infer a theory. To illustrate the intricate interrelationships between theory, research methods, and data, the diagram (adapted from Adams & Schvaneveldt, 1991) in Table 2.1 is provided.

The model in Table 2.1 suggests that theories or concepts are used to provide some level of understanding about leisure services. Various research methods are utilized to collect information, thereby providing a data source or observation about the leisure phenomenon being explored. Finally, the effort leads to a level of understanding that provides conclusions, and then new or confirmed models and theories are established. Of particular importance are the interrelationships between the methods, theory, and data. Researchers must have a grounding and understanding in all these areas in order to impact the field through the conduct of leisure research.

This chapter discusses the various methods of collecting data and the issues and concepts surrounding qualitative and quantitative methodologies

LEISURE RESEARCH METHODS

Once the researcher has formulated a research plan or map as discussed in Chapter 1, the next step is to construct the research design. The researcher must begin to identify the approach to the problem, what methods will be used, and why the methods chosen are the most effective or appropriate. Obviously, these decisions will be based on the purpose of the study, the nature or type of problem being addressed, and what alternatives exist for addressing the requirements of the study. The alternatives for data collection can be organized into functional categories as shown in Table 2.1.

It should be pointed out that the scheme is overlapping as presented. There are many similarities and many differences, and the categories are not always mutually exclusive. For example, an interview could be highly structured, which would place it in the survey method section. However, another interview could be unstructured and free-form, placing it within the category of observations. The characteristics of each methodology are described in the following section.

Table 2.1
Various Techniques of Data Collection in Leisure Services

Data Collection Methods	Examples
Documents Historical Literature review Meta-analysis Diaries Content Analysis Secondary Data	To find out how people behave in private and public spaces. To identify trends in leisure research and practice. Participants keep diaries and journals researcher conducts content analysis of studies, reports and diaries.
Observations Interpretive Ethnographic Participant observer Case study	How people behave and interact in public open spaces. Observe systematically, become a participant observer.

Table 2.1 Cont.

Survey	
Questionnaire Interview Standardized Scales/ Instruments	To learn what people think about leisure motivation. To identify relationships between motivation and satisfaction. Use interviews, surveys and standardized scales.
Experiments	
True designs Quasi designs	Obtain information under controlled conditions about leisure attitudes and experience with virtual reality. Subjects may be randomly assigned to various tests and experiences then assessed via observation or standardized scales.
Other Field Methods	
Nominal Group Technique Delphi	To identify trends and issues about leisure services, management and delivery systems. Focus Group systems. Various group, question and pencil paper exercises are used by facilitators.
Multimethods Approach	
Various Means as above	How senior citizens view leisure in the context of living alone. Interviews, journals and quantitative measures are combined to provide a more accurate definition and operationalization of the concept is confirmed.

Modified from Isaac & Michael, 1985; Leedy, 1985; Dandekar, 1988, Thomas & Nelson, 1990.

QUALITATIVE AND QUANTITATIVE METHODOLOGIES

There are two broad types of quantitative data collection methods: experiments and surveys. Experiments include true experiments (which are virtually nonexistent in leisure services research) using random assignments to treatments, and quasi-experiments using nonrandomized designs. Surveys include cross-sectional and longitudinal studies using questionnaires or interviews that may or may not contain attitudinal scales. This is probably the dominant data collection form within leisure research and allied fields.

There are four broad areas of qualitative data collection methods. These include ethnographies (observations of groups over a period of time), grounded theory (using multistaged data collection over time to develop a theory), case studies (using a variety of data collection procedures to explore the case over time and by activity), and phenomenological studies (involving the study of subjects over a period of time through the development of relationships, and reporting findings based on researcher "experiences"), These are referred to as participant observer methods. Further breakdown of these methods includes field methods, documents, and observations. As noted in Table 2.2, Creswell (1994) suggests a number of methods of data collection in qualitative research studies. These include observational methods, interviews (unstructured), analysis of secondary data sources (journals, case studies, historical documents, etc.), and use of electronic devices (photographs, recordings, and videos).

Table 2.2
Data Collection Approaches in Qualitative Research

- Gather observational notes by conducting an observation as a participant, or being an observer.
- Conducting an unstructured, open-minded interview and take interview notes, or using audio tapes and transcribing the interview later.
- Keep a journal during the research study, or have the informant keep a journal during the research study.
- Collect personal letters from informants.
- Analyze public documents (e.g., official memos, minutes, archival material).
- Examine autobiographies and biographies
- Examine physical trace evidence (e.g., footprints in the snow).
- Videotape a social situation or an individual/group.
- Examine photographs or videotapes.
- Have informants take photographs or videotapes.
- Collect sounds (e.g., musical sounds, a child's laughter, car horns honking).

At this point, it is obvious there are a number of options in the use of qualitative methods and variations of these options. Each option, as with any research method, has specific advantages and limitations. Table 2.3 provides a partial listing of the issues that the leisure service researcher should be aware of when utilizing any of these methods. Care should be taken to reduce the possible impacts of the limitations upon one's own research study. At a minimum, the researcher should be fully aware of the limitations of the methods employed.

As with any study design and process, the researcher should ask some specific questions during the design and completion of the qualitative study procedure. Creswell (1994) offers a list of possible questions the researcher might want to respond to before embarking on the study, during the conduct of the study, and in the writing and presentation of the study. Many of the considerations address the eventual write-up of the results and possible sources of error or concern relative to the data. The checklist in Table 2.4 is designed to help the research convey the validity and reliability of the qualitative process used.

Table 2.3
A Checklist of Questions for Designing a Qualitative Procedure

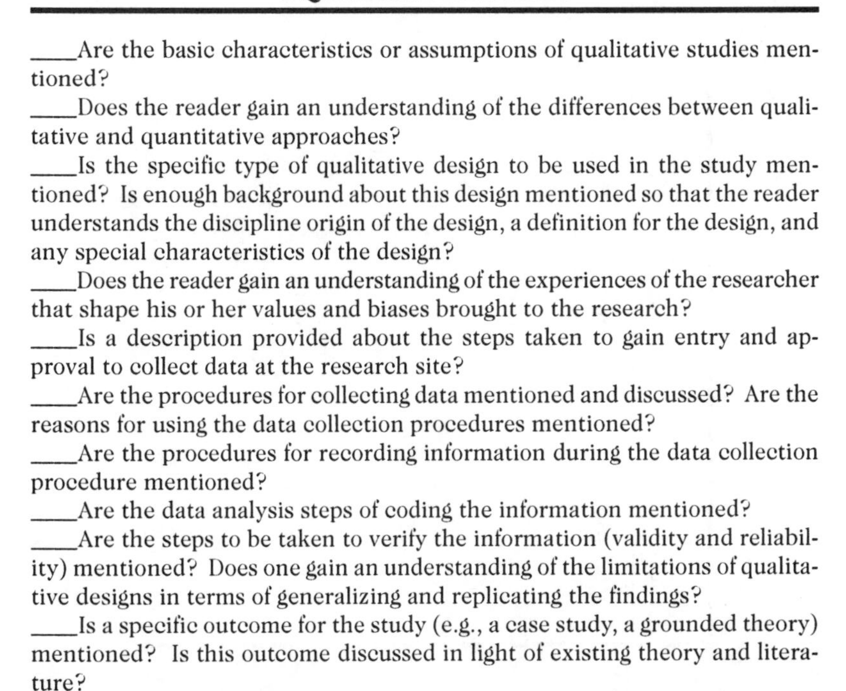

____Are the basic characteristics or assumptions of qualitative studies mentioned?

____Does the reader gain an understanding of the differences between qualitative and quantitative approaches?

____Is the specific type of qualitative design to be used in the study mentioned? Is enough background about this design mentioned so that the reader understands the discipline origin of the design, a definition for the design, and any special characteristics of the design?

____Does the reader gain an understanding of the experiences of the researcher that shape his or her values and biases brought to the research?

____Is a description provided about the steps taken to gain entry and approval to collect data at the research site?

____Are the procedures for collecting data mentioned and discussed? Are the reasons for using the data collection procedures mentioned?

____Are the procedures for recording information during the data collection procedure mentioned?

____Are the data analysis steps of coding the information mentioned?

____Are the steps to be taken to verify the information (validity and reliability) mentioned? Does one gain an understanding of the limitations of qualitative designs in terms of generalizing and replicating the findings?

____Is a specific outcome for the study (e.g., a case study, a grounded theory) mentioned? Is this outcome discussed in light of existing theory and literature?

Table 2.4
Qualitative Data Collection Types, Options, Advantages, and Limitations

Data Collection Types	Options	Advantages	Limitations
Observations	Complete participant researcher conceals role Observer as participant –role of researcher is known.	Researcher has firsthand experience with informant. Researcher can record information as it occurs.	Researcher may be seen as intrusive. "Private" information may be observed that cannot be reported.
	Participant as observer –observation role secondary to participant role Complete observer –researcher observes without participating	Unusual aspects can be noticed during observation. Useful in exploring topics that may be uncomfortable for informants to discuss.	Researcher may not have good attending and observing skills. Certain informants (e.g., children) may present special problems in gaining rapport.
Interviews	Face-to-face–one on one, in person interview Telephone–researcher interviews by phone Group–researcher interviews informants in a group	Useful when informants cannot be directly observed. Informants can provide historical information. Allow researcher "control" over the line of questioning.	Provides "indirect" information filtered through the views of interviewees. Provides information in a designated "place," rather than the natural field setting.

Table 2.4 Cont.

Interviews			Researcher's presence may bias responses. Not all people are equally articulate.
Documents	Public documents such as minutes of meetings, newspapers Private documents such as journal or diary, letter. –an unobtrusive source of information.	Enables a researcher to obtain the language and words of informants. Can be accessed at a time convenient to researcher in hard-to-find places.	May be protected information unavailable to public or private access. Requires the researcher to search out the information
	Represents data that are thoughtful in that informants have given attention to compiling.		Requires transcribing or optically scanning for computer entry.
	As written evidence, it saves a researcher the time and expense of transcribing.	The documents may not be authentic or accurate.	Materials may be incomplete.
Audiovisual Materials	Photographs Videotapes Art objects Computer software Film	May be an unobtrusive method of collecting data. Provides an opportunity for informant to share directly his or her "reality." Creative in that it captures attention visually.	Maybe difficult to interpret. May not be accessible publicly or privately. The presence of an observer (e.g., photographer) may be disruptive and affect responses.

NOTE: This table includes material taken from Creswell, 1994; Merriam, 1988; Bodgan & Biklen, 1992; Leedy, 1985; Isaac, 1985.

There is much debate within the leisure services field regarding the use, or overuse, of quantitative methodologies. A number of leisure researchers (Mannel, 1980; Ellis & Williams, 1987; Sylvester, 1995; Henderson, 1991) suggest that we are overly reliant on quantitative data and analysis and that we are missing rich sources of information by not utilizing suitable qualitative methods when the research question warrants the application. Allison (1995) notes that it is problematic when we, as a profession, reject new approaches and new techniques in favor of the way things have always been done in science.

Rather than take sides on this recurring issue, we suggest that multimethod approaches can provide a more accurate and detailed research project than the traditional unidimensional (qualitative or quantitative) approaches provide. Techniques and considerations will be more fully discussed later in the book. In the meantime, it is important to point out the various differences between qualitative and quantitative methods. Framing the discussion in terms of these epistemological poles is important in alerting us to the fact that there are competing claims regarding what constitutes warrantable knowledge (Henwood & Pidgeon, 1993).

The notion of quantitative versus qualitative research methods has its roots in 20th-century philosophical thinking (Creswell, 1994). During the 19th century, qualitative methods of investigation began as a countermovement to the traditional use of quantitative methods through the works of Weber, Dilthey, and Kant (Smith, 1983). The qualitative approach to research has since taken on a number of descriptive terms for the purpose of defining its characteristics. Qualitative methods have been referred to as the naturalistic approach (Lincoln & Guba, 1985), the postmodern approach (Quantz, 1992), or the interpretive approach (Smith, 1983) to research.

Quantitative approaches have been referred to as the traditional, the positivist, the experimental, or the empiricist paradigm. Quantitative methodological emphasis in research originated from an empiricist tradition established by Comte, Durkheim, and Locke (Smith, 1983).

Assumptions of Differences and Similarities between Qualitative and Quantitative Methods

Firestone (1987), Guba and Lincoln (1988), and McCracken (1988) (as cited in Creswell (1994)) define the differences between the two research choices regarding assumptions used to define the differences between the two research choices. Essentially, the opposing paradigms differ with regard to how reality is defined, the relationship of the researcher to the subjects, influences of researcher-to-subject bias, acceptable research language and terminology, and the process itself. Reliance on the summarization by Creswell (1994) in describing these differences is acknowledged here. A number of comparisons between qualitative and quantitative methods can be made, as shown in Table 2.5.

Quantitative researchers generally view reality as objective, as something that can be measured and is separate from the researcher. These researchers assume they are independent of the study population so as to not allow their values to bias the study and influence the outcomes. Great efforts are taken to minimize instances of study bias and maintain some distance from the study population. There are acceptable methods, definitions, and language used to describe the research, process, analysis, and discussion of findings. Cause-and-effect relationships are sometimes established, normally based on a deductive process. Variables of study are identified and used to frame the study, leading to descriptions of the problem, prediction, and explanation. Finally, relevance, accuracy, and reliability of findings are established through reliability and validity procedures.

Table 2.5
Characteristics of Qualitative and Quantitative Research

Point of comparison	Qualitative research	Quantitative research
Focus of research	Quality (nature, essence)	Quality (how much, how many)
Philosophical roots	Phenomenology, symbolic interaction	Positivism, logical empiricism
Associated phrases	Fieldwork, ethnographic, words, naturalistic, grounded, subjective	Experimental, empirical, statistical, numbers
Goals of investigation	Understanding, description, discovery, hypothesis generating	Prediction, control, description, confirmation, hypothesis testing
Design characteristics	Flexible, evolving, emerging	Predetermined, structured
Setting	Natural, familiar, real life	Unfamiliar, artificial, controlled, laboratory
Sample	Small, nonrandom, theoretical	Large, random, representative
Data collection	Researcher as primary instrument, interviews	Inanimate instruments (scales, tests, surveys, questionnaires, observations computers)
Mode of analysis	Inductive (perspectives by researcher)	Deductive (by statistical methods)
Findings	Comprehensive, holistic, expansive, perspectives	Precise, narrow, reductionist, prediction

Qualitative researchers, on the other hand, view reality as subjective, as seen by the study participants through interaction with the sample. Values and interpretations of the researcher are introduced, and biases may or may not occur. As the researcher progresses with the study, decisions about the findings, data, and methods evolve and an inductive process is used to shape definitions and factors that emerge. Context-bound findings are described, which may or may not lead to patterns, theories, or understanding of the factors and variables (categories). Accuracy and reliability are established through verification of data with the study population. Table 2.6 describes some of the assumptions surrounding the qualitative and quantitative paradigms.

In terms of similarities, each method must begin with a well-established research question, list of potential subproblems/issues, and a sense of the direction of outcomes (hypothesis testing). It is our belief that any research effort, regardless of whether it is quantitative or qualitative, must begin with defining and framing the study. Methodological concerns and choices naturally follow the definition and framing of the study.

Some (Creswell, 1994) suggest that researchers are seldom trained to conduct studies using more than one paradigm (qualitative or quantitative). Consequently, individuals learn one method, and this becomes the dominant research approach. In fact, Sylvester (1995) observes that leisure studies students who receive instruction in rational inquiry get their primary and often their only preparation in empirical methods, and are offered little or nothing in the way of historical, interpretive, or critical methods. Table 2.6 characterizes why some researchers select one paradigm of research methodology over another (Creswell, 1994).

Table 2.6
Reasons for Selecting a Paradigm

Criteria	Quantitative Paradigm	Qualitative Paradigm
Researcher's Worldview	A researcher's comfort with the assumptions and methods	A researcher's comfort with assumptions and methods
Training and Experience of the Researcher	Writing skills, computer statistical skills, library skills	Writing skills, computer text-analysis skills, library skills
Researcher's Psychological Attributes	Comfort with rules and guidelines for conducting research, low tolerance for ambiguity, time for a study of short duration	Comfort with lack of specific rules and procedures for conducting research, high tolerance for ambiguity, time for lengthy study
Nature of the Problem	Previously studied by other researchers so that body of literature exists, known variables, existing theories	Exploratory research, variables unknown, context important, may lack theory base for study.
Audience for the Study (e.g., journal editors and readers, graduate committees)	Individuals supportive of of quantitative studies	Individuals supportive of qualitative studies

Source: Creswell, J. W. (1994)

It is debatable whether certain research problems are better suited for qualitative to quantitative methods (Creswell, 1994). The nature of the problem should drive the research design and data collection methods, emphasizing (a) operational definitions of constructs and variables, (b) controlled observations and empirical data, and (c) generalized and repeated observations (Iso-Ahola, 1980).

In broad terms, quantitative methods rely heavily upon literature, which can be used to build upon, test theories or ideas, or establish a new knowledge base. Using the literature, leisure researchers can replicate studies to confirm various positions (hypotheses) within leisure services. This is not to say that qualitative methodologists do not rely on previous literature; however, qualitative studies generally start out by exploring the research problem with study participants. Many times the variables are not known prior to the study, but are identified in the exploration and interview process. The literature review is then further refined, and explanations of the findings are then supported. Based on the work of Patton (1980), Henderson (1991) provides a checklist (Table 2.7) for those leisure service researchers who may not know which research paradigm to utilize in the conduct of a particular study. According to Henderson (1991), if the answer is yes to any of the questions in Table 2.7, the researcher should at least consider qualitative methods as possible ways to approach the research question being addressed.

Table 2.7
Checklist for Considering Qualitative or Quantitative Approach

- Is the researcher interested in individualized outcomes?
- Is the researcher interested in examining the process of research and the context in which it occurs?
- Is detailed, in-depth information needed in order to understand the phenomena now under study?
- Is the focus on quality and the meaning of the experiences being studied?
- Does the researcher desire to get close to the data providers and immersed in their experiences?
- Do no measuring devices exist that will provide reliable and valid data for the topic being studied?
- Is the research question likely to change depending upon how the data emerge?

Table 2.7 Cont.

- Is it possible that the answer to the research question may yield unexpected results?
- Does it make more sense to use grounded theory than existing *a priori* theory in studying the particular phenomena?
- Does the researcher wish to get personally involved in the research?
- Does the researcher have a philosophical and methodological bias toward the interpretive paradigm and qualitative methods?

The following sections detail the characteristics of specific data collection methods available to the leisure service researcher within the qualitative and quantitative paradigms. Occasional reference to qualitative or quantitative methods is made; otherwise we leave it to the reader to determine which method is best suited to his or her own research and paradigm.

DATA COLLECTION TECHNIQUES

There are many different ways to collect data about leisure and recreation. In general, there are two fundamental methods. First, when it is necessary to collect data about people, it is possible to use surveys, experiments, and observation studies to investigate the different recreation-related attributes of people. Sometimes such studies can be supplemented by analyzing secondary data about people's behaviors and opinions. On the other hand, if the interest is in recreation-related documents, then techniques such as content analysis, document analysis, program analysis, and meta-analysis can be used to identify the different ways in which leisure is conceptualized. This section provides a detailed examination of some of the key data collection techniques used in survey research.

Surveys

Survey research is the systematic gathering of information from respondents for the purpose of understanding and/or predicting some aspect of behavior of the population of interest (Tull & Hawkins, 1987). The term "survey" implies that data have been gathered using some form of questionnaire. Four data gathering methods are common in survey research: mail out questionnaires; face-to-face interviews, telephone interviews, and self-administered surveys. Surveys can provide data on feelings, perceptions, attitudes, needs, knowledge, past and intended behaviors, and other descriptive items. Leedy (1985) provides a list of salient characteristics of surveys:

1. The survey method deals with a situation that demands the technique of observation of phenomena as the principal means of collecting data.
2. The population for the study must be carefully chosen, clearly defined, and specifically delimited in order to set precise parameters for ensuring generalizability and representation.
3. Data can be susceptible to distortion through the introduction of bias in the design (interviewer bias or poor sampling).

Questionnaires

A person may be hesitant to answer questions verbally but willing to write out answers. Self-administered (mail-out or intercept surveys) questionnaires also permit the use of graphics, detailed and more complex response scales, checklists and other forms of measurement. Respondents can respond at their leisure and at their own pace. However, mail-out surveys generally require more than one mailing in order to generate an appropriate response rate. Multiple mailings require additional time and money. Use of the telephone in survey research has reduced the costs and time required to gather data. Dillman (1978) recommends the combination of mail and telephone surveys to increase response rates.

Since the questionnaire is often mailed, the following considerations must be accounted for in the execution of the survey method. First, the language must be clear in soliciting exactly what the researcher is trying to understand. The researcher should determine if the question or assumptions of the question fit the scope and purpose of the study. A pretest of the instrument will indicate problematic questions. Secondly, the instrument as a whole should fit the specific research objective, be simple and brief, and be consistent in format and response information. Providing a cover letter and postage for return is essential with mail-out questionnaires. For intercept methods, a badge of identification, a letter explaining the purpose and other particulars, and a clipboard are essential.

Procedures for the implementation and use of surveys must be carefully planned, and provisions must be made to guard against bias. The general steps taken in a survey study are:

1. Formulating the objectives of the study.
2. Designing data collection methods with the notion of reducing bias and increasing reliability and validity.
3. Selecting the sample.
4. Collecting data, checking the data set for errors, and coding the questionnaire.
5. Analysis of data. Prior to conducting the study, the researcher will have determined the steps and techniques to be used in the analysis.

In terms of survey design, two basic methods are utilized (Nishikawa, 1988): cross-sectional surveys and longitudinal surveys. Unweighted cross-sectional survey design consists of a one-time "snapshot" for measuring some characteristic of the population. Weighted cross-sectional surveys deliberately oversample a minority within the total population to allow enough cases for analysis. When the researcher knows that groups vary on certain topics of interest, samples are drawn from the respective groups for comparison purposes (contrasting samples design).

The two basic types of longitudinal surveys are before-and-after studies and trend analysis. Before-and-after studies measure change or stimulus on a target population. Trend analysis is the act of collecting data over a specified period of time, normally much longer than for other methods.

Panel Questionnaire Designs

Another extension of the survey is the panel design. Essentially, this technique allows the researcher to interview and collect data over a period of time with the same subjects. The obvious benefits are that the study can be longitudinal and that recall bias is reduced.

An example of a panel design is a series of studies (Howard, Lankford, & Havitz, 1991; Howard, Havitz, Lankford, & Dimanche, 1992) on authenticating the expenditures of pleasure travelers. The researchers obtained permission from traveling couples to conduct the study over a period of a few months. First, one member of the traveling party was asked to keep notes of expenditures each day. A special diary method was developed for recording the expenditures. Second, the traveling partner was asked to estimate the trip expenditures in a survey during an interview prior to departing the area. The recording partner was also interviewed, and data were collected on the recorded expenses. Third, the cooperating couples were sent surveys three months later to test the hypothesis that recall accuracy is not a problem. Thus, initial contact was made, data collection was performed, and exit interviews and surveys were used over a period of months to conduct the study.

There are both advantages and disadvantages to panel studies. Obviously, the ability to interview subjects over a period of time is an advantage. When cross-sectional (one-shot) studies are conducted, for example, we have to compare two samples. Any differences could be due to sampling error or to real changes in the population. Sampling error can be ruled out when we use a panel design (Williamson, Karp, & Dalphin, 1977). Other benefits of the panel design include the ability to collect more data and the ability to customize the questions for each successive survey.

As for the disadvantages, there will be a loss of panel members over time (e.g., due to lack of interest, lack of cooperation, movement, and death). Additionally, the process takes some time due to the need for multiple mailings of questionnaires, interviews, etc. Finally, attitudes and behaviors may change as a result of the mere act of continual interviewing. Williamson, Karp, and Dalphin (1977) note that respondents might start reading about and becoming familiar with the issue and start answering from an "informed" point of view, one not representative of the sample.

Details concerning the construction of questionnaires and the utilization of survey methods are presented later in the book. Isaac and Michael (1985) have identified a number of errors in questionnaire-type studies that should be addressed by the leisure service researcher. Specifically, they note that researchers utilize questionnaires too often when the problem can be better addressed through other methods; give insufficient attention to pretesting; ask too many questions, some of which are not relevant; overlook details of format, grammar, and printing; and fail to check nonrespondents for possible bias.

Interviews

An interview is a purposeful conversation conducted in a disciplined manner. The interview is more than a conversation, because one participant is recording or guiding the discussion and one is considered the informant. Classification of interview type is based on the amount of control exercised by the researcher. Some researchers may choose a passive role, along the lines of the participant observer. Others may desire a more controlled and structured situation.

Interviews are usually characterized as one of three types:

1. *Structured* or standardized interview questionnaires. All questions are asked in exactly the same way and in the same order for all respondents. Precisely worded questions are used, and sometimes are lengthy and intensive.
2. *Nonscheduled standardized.* All questions are asked of each respondent, but they may be asked in different ways and in different sequences. Some questions may be changed due to the circumstances.
3. *Unstructured* or nonstandardized. No standardized schedule of questions is used, and the interview is free form. The researcher is free to change topics and carry on a more relaxed and in-depth discussion on any topic or issue that surfaces.

These differences address the degree of structure of the interview.

Structured interviews include face-to-face interviews as well as telephone interviews using questionnaires. The researcher sets out with specific questions in a certain order or sequence. Since the researcher has developed specific questions and determined the order in which they are asked, the structured interview is considered a quantitative method. However, there is a fine line by which this distinction is made. For example, if the questions contain predetermined response categories, the method is leaning toward being quantitative or structured. However, if the questions are open-ended, then the method may be categorized as qualitative or unstructured.

The degree of structure refers to the extent to which the interviewer is restricted to the question wording and instructions in a questionnaire. An interviewer in an unstructured setting can omit, alter, add, or probe for responses, thereby changing the design. Structured interviews tend to minimize biases of the interviewer more than unstructured interviews. They also allow the hiring of unskilled interviewers because they basically just read the questions and record answers. Unstructured interviews offer rich data that is most useful in exploratory stages of research. However, this technique requires more highly trained and skilled interviewers.

There are advantages to interviewing over surveying. The interviewer can better arouse the respondent's interest in the study or problem and thereby increase the likelihood of participation. Additionally, complete and accurate responses can be obtained, and the interviewer can complete all the questions. Other positive aspects are that the interviewer can obtain information on the condition of the site or respondent, and interviewing can provide data on subjects who would be missed in a survey effort. However, the high costs of travel and the amount of time required for interviewing can be drawbacks. Potential bias problems also exist in that the respondent may not provide accurate or "true" answers due to the interviewer's presence. Therefore, the interviewer should consider the nature of the questions and the potential for embarrassment on the part of the respondent.

If possible, and within the scope of the study, researchers should attempt to randomize the interview time, day, place, and respondent in order to generalize results and provide a reasonable degree of accuracy. To gain even greater control of responses, an interviewee may be asked to refer to maps, pictures, and models as part of the response system. For example, in a study of tourists along the Oregon coast, interviewers intercepted travelers at random sites, days, and times and asked predetermined questions related to economic impact regarding their travel. In addition, the travelers were shown a series of pictures depicting various landscapes and asked to indicate their preferences. In actuality, these pictures were images with differing vegetation types and densities. Surveys and pictures were also randomly mailed to residents of the region and placed in the local newspapers for mail-back to the university research team. This provided a multimethod approach (discussed in further detail at the end of this chapter) to studying the issue prior to recommending action. The study group was commissioned by the Oregon Department of Transportation to identify the appropriate level of tree and vegetation removal for this important scenic corridor (Knowles-Lankford, 1990).

Some guidelines for consideration of the interview method include preparing the interview, approaching the interview, questioning, closing, and recording. To prepare for the interview, the researcher should consider the time of day of the interview, be knowledgeable about the scope and purpose of the study, develop a letter of introduction, and carry an identification badge for the interview. When approaching the interview, the researcher should provide his or her name in the introduction to reduce suspicion as well as for common courtesy. Additionally, the researcher should avoid the word "investigation," as this sets a negative tone. The ingredients of a successful introduction include (1) a statement about the purpose of the study, (2) identification of the sponsoring agency, (3) affirmation regarding confidentiality, (4) a description of how the respondent was selected, and (5) an explanation of how the results will be utilized.

Experimental Treatments

Chapter 4 presents actual designs and procedures for conducting experimental and quasi-experimental studies. This section presents the characteristics of experimental designs. Experimental designs are the basis of statistical significance. An experimental or research design has two purposes (Huck, Cormier, & Bounds, 1974): to help a researcher answer a research question and to control for possible rival hypotheses or extraneous variables that might compete with the independent variable as an explanation for the cause-effect relationship.

For example, the leisure service researcher might be interested in the effect of recreation programs (the independent variable, experimental treatment, or intervention variable) on behaviors (dependent or outcome variables) of youth-at-risk. In this example, the independent variable (recreation program) is presumed to effect change in the dependent variable. The primary question remains, how can the researcher be confident that the changes in behavior were caused or influenced by the recreation programs, and not some other, intervening variable? An experimental design does not eliminate intervening variables; however, it can account for their effects.

While the experimental approach is powerful due to the control over variables and tests, it is the most restrictive and artificial method of data collection. When humans are manipulated or controlled during any systematic observation or evaluation, some question remains as to the effects of a laboratory setting versus a natural setting. Therefore, some researchers prefer to conduct field-based experiments. Field experiments tend to have higher external validity (Sommer & Sommer, 1986), but it is difficult to control extraneous conditions and variables in the field.

Experimental control is associated with the following factors (Huck, Cormier, & Bounds, 1974): (1) the random assignment of individual subjects to comparison groups, (2) the extent to which the independent variable can be manipulated by the researcher, (3) the time when the observations or measurements of the dependent variable occur, and (4) which groups are measured and how. The portion of the sample or population that is exposed to a manipulation of the independent variable is known as the treatment group. For example, youth who enroll and participate in recreation programs are the treatment group, and the group to which no recreation services are provided constitutes the control group.

There are two primary criteria for evaluating the validity of an experimental design. The first is internal validity. Did the independent variable make a difference in the study? Can a cause-and-effect relationship be observed? To achieve internal validity, the researcher must design and conduct the study so that only the independent variable can be the cause of the results (Cozby, 1993). The second criterion is external validity, which refers to the extent to which findings can be generalized or be considered representative of the population.

Chapter 3 provides detailed information regarding the validity and reliability of tests and measures. However, at this point it is useful to review several types of errors that can confound experimental results (i.e., confuse the effect of the independent variable with that of some other variable or variables) (based on Cozby, 1993; Thomas & Nelson, 1990; Tull & Hawkins, 1987; Huck, Cormier, & Bounds, 1974; Campbell & Stanley, 1966):

1. Premeasurement and interaction error occurs when the effects of taking a preliminary measurement impact subsequent measures by changing the respondent's sensitivity or re-

sponsiveness to the independent variable(s). That is, the independent variable is more likely to be noticed and reacted to than it would without the initial measurement. For example, residents of one community were given questionnaires regarding the impact of tourism in their community, causing them to be more aware of local tourism development issues. Thus, any activity related to tourism would cause the respondents to be more sensitive in their follow-up measurements.

2. Maturation error represents the biological or psychological processes that systematically vary with the passage of time, independent of specific external events. Respondents grow older, tired, etc. between the pre- and postmeasures. Maturation is a plausible rival hypothesis in many studies because people change naturally.

3. History refers to any variables or events, other than the ones being tested and manipulated that occur between pre– and postmeasurement and affect the dependent variable. For example, for a study of the effects of organized city recreation programs that is conducted on youth-at-risk, the fact that 40-50% of the youth also participate in the police activities league would constitute a serious threat to internal validity.

4. Instrumentation refers to changes in the instrument over time. This is especially problematic in observational work, where the observer gains skill yet becomes fatigued over time.

5. Selection bias errors occur when the subjects are not randomly assigned or groups are unequal. When treatments are administered, the question remains if selection bias has influenced the outcomes. Statistical regression bias is a related concern, in that individuals are assigned to groups because of scores on some measure, not based on random selection.

6. Mortality refers to the loss (from refusal or inability to continue) of subjects from the groups being studied.

A research design that is similar to experimentation, but with the critical difference that the treatment and control groups are selected after the introduction of the potential causal variable, is the ex post facto design. True designs use random assignment of subjects to the control groups and treatment groups, identification and manipulation of the independent and dependent variables, and pre- and post-testing. Quasi-experimental designs are distinguished from true experimental designs primarily by the lack of random assignment of subjects to treatment and control groups. In leisure service evaluation, it is sometimes impossible to conduct a true experimental design. Following are descriptions of these three designs.

True Designs

In a true design, three principles apply: (1) at least two groups or conditions are compared, (2) the researcher has control or can predict and evaluate the experimental treatment, and (3) subjects are randomly assigned to treatment groups. True experiments may be conducted in the laboratory or the field (classrooms, streets, parks, etc.).

For example, suppose two groups of subjects are randomly selected and assigned, and each is administered a questionnaire designed to measure support for park and recreation tax levies. One of the groups—the experimental group—is shown a film on the benefits of parks and recreation. Later the researcher administers the post-test of support measures to both groups. Use of the control group allows the researcher to determine if the park and recreation film actually has an influence on taxpayers' attitudes toward financial support of parks and recreation systems.

There are seven basic steps to experimental research.

1. Survey the literature.
2. Define the problem, formulate a hypothesis, define basic terms and variables, and operationalize variables.
3. Develop a research plan:
   a. Identify confounding or mediating variables that might contaminate the experiment, and determine how to control them.
   b. Select a research design (see Chapter 3).
   c. Randomly select subjects and randomly assign them to groups.
   d. Validate the instruments and measures used.
   e. Develop data collection procedures, conduct a pilot study, and refine the instrument.
   f. State the null and alternative hypotheses and set the statistical significance level of the study.
4. Conduct the experiments.
5. Analyze the data, apply appropriate statistical tests, and report results.

Quasi Designs

Random assignment is not a characteristic of quasi designs (also known as the natural experiment) because it is impossible to randomize subjects into treatment or control groups in the field. Consequently, internal validity is at question because subjects are self-selected or some other bias may be present. Quasi designs attempt to approximate the features of true designs to infer that a treatment did have an effect. Essentially, groups are formed (nonrandomly) and given pretests, one group receives treatment and then both are given a post-test.

Steps in the conduct of quasi experiments are generally the same as those in true designs, with the exception of randomization. Internal and external validity remains a concern and a limitation.

Ex Post Facto Designs

Essentially, an ex post facto design is used to determine which variables can discriminate between groups. For the most part, the research question asks "Did these variables influence the way these groups responded?" An example involves youth who are having personal and social problems and youth who seem well adjusted. An examination of the factors and characteristics of the two groups would provide an indication of predictors of behaviors and tendencies. The first step in ex post facto research is formulation of the research problem with the identification of what may influence the dependent variable(s). Second, the researcher identifies plausible rival hypotheses that might explain the relationships. Third, the researcher identifies and selects groups to be studied. Fourth, the researcher collects and analyzes the data. Rival hypotheses and factors affecting the dependent variable are identified. It should be noted that these studies cannot prove causation and are vulnerable to the errors described above. However, like quasi experiments, they provide valuable data lead to an understanding of phenomena if the researcher is careful in the design of the instruments and measures.

Other Field Methods/Group Techniques

Nominal Group Technique

The nominal group technique (NGT) is a group discussion structuring technique that has been used for a number of purposes. It is useful for providing a focused effort on topics of importance to the agency or researcher. The NGT provides a means to identify issues and opportunities and ways to reach customers. Ewert (1990) noted that the NGT is a collective decision-making technique for use in park and recreation planning and management. A few published leisure services studies have utilized the NGT as either the primary data collection method (Lankford & DeGraaf, 1992; Little, Lankford, DeGraaf, & Tashiro, 1995) or as a basis for further data exploration (Williams, Lankford, DeGraaf, & Chen, 1995). The technique is very useful in gaining insight into group issues and behaviors.

Backoff and Nutt (1988) refer to the NGT as a silent reflective technique. Silent reflective techniques enable each member of the management group to identify strengths, weaknesses, opportunities, threats, and issues before group discussion takes place. Disadvantages of typical interacting groups is that members often make premature commitments, have inhibitions, or deliver hasty evaluations, thus shutting off valuable lines of inquiry (Bouchard & Hare, 1970). The NGT (Delbecq & Van de Ven, 1971) is a widely used silent reflective technique.

The NGT is an effective tool for decision making, strategic planning, policy development, and goal formulation. NGT is a more structured approach compared with techniques such as brainstorming for generating a list of options and narrowing it down. The power of this technique is that it is structured, yet it allows each participant a chance to express his or her opinion in a nonthreatening environment. Consequently, consensus is obtained on high-quality, realistic ideas and strategies.

According to Scholtes (1988), due to the relatively low level of interaction, NGT is an effective tool when all or some group members are new, when issues are highly controversial, or when a team is stuck in disagreement. Delbecq and Van de Ven (1971, 1975) noted the NGT can be used for (a) identifying strategic problems and (b) developing appropriate and innovative programs to solve them.

Delbecq and Van de Ven (1971, 1975) outlined a six-step process for implementation of the NGT. Step 1 consists of introducing the technique and explaining the questions. During step 2, participants are asked to write their responses to the questions on five-by-seven-inch cards. Step 3 consists of listing the responses on flip charts. Once subjects have completed the task of responding to the question(s), a facilitator records their ideas on a flip chart in round-robin fashion. The fourth step consists of having the group discuss each item for clarification, elaboration, and/or defense. After the discussion, step 5 involves voting on the top five items listed on the flip chart. Finally, during step 6, the facilitator tabulates the votes for the items.

Scholtes (1988) describes a two-part process for implementation of the NGT. Part 1, entitled "a formalized brainstorm," consists of six steps: (1) the facilitator and client define the task(s) in the form of a question(s); (2) the facilitator describes the purpose of the process and meeting; (3) the facilitator introduces and clarifies the question(s); (4) participants individually write down responses to the questions; (5) the facilitator asks each participant to read one idea off his or her list and records ideas on a flip chart; (6) if necessary, ideas are clarified and defined by the originator of the idea.

Part 2 is entitled "making the selection" and consists of an additional six steps. Step 1 is implemented only if the group wants to reduce the list; however, the originator must agree to drop or consolidate the original idea. For step 2, participants are given cards or paper on which to record their ideas. The number of cards is a rough fraction of the number of items on the list. Generally, it is recommended that four cards be used for up to 20 items, six cards for 35 items, and eight cards for 35 to 50 items. Step 3 consists of having participants write down one item per card (one card per item). During step 4, the participant assigns the highest point value to the most important item (in an eight-card system, eight points is given to the most preferred item, seven points is given to the second most important item, etc.). For step 5, the facilitator collects the cards and tallies the votes for each item. The totals are marked on the flip chart so that the participants can view the results. Finally, step 6 consists of discussion and reaction to the results.

In summary, a systematic five-step procedure characterizes the NGT: (1) members of the group identify ideas in written/silent form; (2) each member lists his or her own ideas and then rank-orders the ideas (silently); (3) a facilitator gives each participant an opportunity to state his or her ideas (one item per person at a time, in round-robin fashion) until all ideas are exhausted; (4) as a group, participants discuss and consolidate ideas into a list; and (5) finally, members vote to select priority ideas. The final list of ideas becomes the focus of further research and discussion. These ideas can also be used to generate a work plan for a formal strategic planning process, a basis for a survey or interview, or the development of a scale.

Delphi Method

The delphi method was originally developed to structure discussions and summarize options from a group to avoid meetings, collect expertise from afar, and save time through the elimination of direct contact. Although the data may prove to be valuable, the collection process is generally too time consuming for most researchers and agencies to utilize. When time is available and respondents are willing to be queried over a period of time, the technique can be very powerful in identifying trends and predicting future events.

The technique requires waves of questionnaires and feedback reports to a group of individuals. Each wave is analyzed and the instrument/statements are revised to reflect the responses of the group. A new questionnaire is prepared that includes the new material, and the process is repeated. An example of such a study follows.

The researcher chooses a panel of experts or respondents and provides the necessary background material and questionnaire. Participants are asked what project or policy options or issues (depending on the research topic) there are, and asked to rank-order the importance of the items or issues on the questionnaire. This ranking and discussion of items is fairly open-ended. The resulting list represents a list of the initial issues. The lists of the respondents are synthesized and returned to the panel group, with the request that additional rankings of importance be given to the consolidated list. The researcher might add a question asking the respondent to indicate the likelihood of an event happening. Consequently, the researcher is able to identify issues and trends as well as possible future outcomes. Additional rounds may be utilized until it is felt that a consensus exists on the panel. These additional rounds may also include questions regarding groups who may be affected by the change, for example, or what the policy implications will be if the event occurs.

The primary disadvantage, obviously, is the time needed for the researcher to compile and analyze the data, and the possibility that the respondent group may not remain interested or intact (due to transfers, new jobs, etc.). The important features are that the technique allows the researcher to start with open-ended questions, narrow a topic or issue, and conclude with some potentially useful information. Compared with single-survey designs, this technique may provide more detailed information.

Focus Group Interviews

A focus group interview generally involves 8-12 people chosen because they are from a market segment or other group of interest to the researcher. The group is interviewed for 1-3 hours by a moderator who guides discussion about a product, concept, or service. In contrast to interviewing one individual in an in-depth interview, the researcher can obtain findings from 8-12 people, provided the moderator is trained and sensitive to the group.

Focus groups are generally used for (a) basic exploration of an idea for a new or existing service or product (policies, facility proposals, and management procedures could also be explored); (b) service or product positioning studies; (c) advertising and marketing research; (d) establishment of clientele understanding of a leisure service and vocabulary as a preliminary function in developing a questionnaire (Tull & Hawkins, 1987); (e) identification and exploration of attitudes and behaviors regarding leisure issues; and (f) interpreting previously obtained survey results (Rossman, 1989). The value of the group interviews (focus groups) lies in their ability to stimulate new ideas among participants by allowing spontaneity and candor (Henderson & Bialeschki, 1995).

Respondents are selected according to some sampling plan or design and are asked to meet at a certain time and place. It has been suggested that a number of focus groups should be used until one stops receiving new ideas or information

(O'Sullivan, 1991). The moderator attempts to establish rapport with the group and sets the stage for interaction. During the process, the moderator provokes discussion relative to the topic and then proceeds to summarize the responses to determine the extent of agreement on the issue. Following the interview, the moderator (or a second person) should organize the notes and review the tape recordings as soon as possible (O'Sullivan, 1991).

The following procedure is typical of most focus groups situations.

1. Utilize an office with a large table, equipped with a tape-recording device (video recorder, audiotape machine, or both).
2. Provide a short warm-up and introduction. The moderator provides ground rules and other pertinent information.
3. Provide a discussion regarding the context in which the service, product, or issue is bought, used, or thought about. This will include general reactions to the topic. Next, panelists are asked to write (privately) about any physical form of the topic (product, drawings, registration forms, advertisements, etc.). A discussion follows. This pattern continues (write and then discuss) for each physical piece of evidence or proposal.
4. The discussion ends with a wrap-up of summary statements by the moderator. Before concluding, survey data (demographics) are collected from the respondents.

O'Sullivan (1991) notes that the moderator should encourage all to participate, should not allow domination by one person, and should not demand a consensus. Some questions the researcher should consider are, how do you judge one person's comments against another's, and what effect did the setting have on the statements made?

Among the advantages of focus groups is that the process allows individuals to express themselves and refine ideas using the group interaction process. The group interview is generally more exciting and stimulating than the standard interview (Tull & Hawkins, 1987). The process allows people to explore ideas, similarities, and differences. This technique has also proven useful with children (McDonald, 1982) and with adults in developing countries or in cultures with low literacy rates (Goodyear, 1982). However, a number of disadvantages exist. Since the process is lengthy, securing the random sample is difficult. Those who attend these sessions are not likely to be similar to those who do not agree to the process, thereby limiting the generalization of the results. Second, the loud, controlling type of respondent can sway the group outcomes if the moderator is not skilled at working with groups and the public. In any case, focus groups are useful for providing feedback from users and nonusers on a variety of topics when the recreator requires additional insights (O'Sullivan, 1991).

Behavioral/Cognitive Mapping

One way of identifying heavy use areas or the perceived importance of various natural resources and tourist destinations would be to intercept users at the beginning of their vacation/recreation visit using cognitive and spatial mapping techniques to allow for identification of recreation resources. Specifically, the information provides a spatial map of the current recreation use, the most significant recreation resources, and the approximate number of visitations to these areas.

Perception of the environment has received extensive research attention within the fields of environmental psychology (Ittelson, 1973) and geography (Tuan, 1975). The application of cognitive mapping procedures to the study of recreation and tourism activities has been tested on a limited basis (Walmsley & Jenkins, 1992; Fridgen, 1987; Pearce, 1981; Britton, 1979). Yet, as noted by Downs and Stea (1977) and Fridgen (1987), recreation and cognitive maps are inseparable. All forms of recreation and travel involve some form of environmental cognition because people must orient, traverse, and locate recreation destinations and attractions.

Specifically, cognitive mapping allows recreation resource managers the opportunity to identify where users and visitors perceive the best recreation areas of the state, island, etc. to be located. It is important to understand these perceptions in order to manage intensive use areas appropriately in terms of maintenance, supervision, budgeting, and planning. In addition, public policies and land use planning adjustments may be required for authorized land uses, resource protection laws, off-road use, liability, and law enforcement. Analysis of important recreation areas will also allow for better interagency coordination. Local government can organize task forces made up of local, state, and federal representatives to address use levels and policy questions as needed. Finally, once high-impact areas are identified, economic analysis of recreation sites and uses can be conducted by pertinent state and local organizations for policymaking decisions. Lankford (1994, 1996) prepared a series of studies for the Hawaii State Department of Forestry to track tourists' use of the hiking and trail system in order to better understand the eco-tourism market. An integral part of the research was the use of cognitive maps, as well as basic survey research data.

Cognitive maps are prepared in order to grid the research site into zones. These zones take into consideration existing geographic, climatic, landscape, marine resources, and recreation sites. The grids allow respondents to indicate primary recreation sites, and the composite will allow the researcher to identify high impact areas. After discussion with park and recreation managers, researchers collect data at beach and camping sites by interviewing visitors and recreationists. Random sites, days, times, and respondents (every nth) should be chosen for data collection in order to increase the reliability and generalizability of the data.

Respondents identify, rank-order, and rate (Likert-type scale) the top three zones on the map. In addition, some sociodemographic information and questions related to the management of the areas may be collected. Following the methods of Fridgen (1987), respondents are asked to circle the three most important recreation areas and then place an X in the circle they thought best for their particular recreation activity. In this way, a recreation location score (RLS) was derived as follows for each area of the island of Oahu:

a: A tally of circles for each part of the island was made.

b: A tally of partial circles for each part of the island was made.

c: A tally of X's for each part of the island was made.

As a result, the calculation of the RLS would look like: RLS = (.4A + .4C +2B). This score allows the researchers to determine which areas of the island had the most relative use and to monitor the site for the satisfaction of the user.

Observations

Observations are not only useful data collection methods but are important as an prelude to other procedures. Many types of observational methods exist, such as casual, systematic, participant observer, and ethnographic observation. Use of any of the variations requires an understanding of the situation and problem at hand. Primarily, the leisure studies researcher heeds to know where to find subjects, the length and intensity of site usage, physical and geographic layouts, and possible distractions at the site that might limit the use of observational methods.

Observational research is ideal for studying commonplace nonverbal behaviors, such as gestures, pastimes, or public open space use, in which people may not be conscious of how they are acting. One fear of most researchers is that the process or method employed will meet with resistance from the respondent group. Observational methods provide an option to the interview or questionnaire. The researcher can observe people using an area, their times of arrivals and other factors.

Like the survey method, the observation schedule should be carefully designed to minimize inaccuracy and bias. A list of observable items should be developed prior to the field work. This allows the observer to concentrate on the important aspects of the research design. Creswell (1994) offers a comparison of the observation methods available (complete participant observer, observer as participant, participant as observer, and complete observer) in Table 2.8.

Table 2.8
Observation Data Collection Types, Options, Advantages, and Limitations (Creswell 1994)

Observation Options	Advantages of the Type	Limitations of the Type
Complete participant -researcher conceals role	Researcher has firsthand experience with informant.	Researcher may be seen as intrusive.
Observer as participant -role of researcher is known	Researcher can record information as it occurs.	"Private" information may be observed that researcher cannot report.
Participant as observer -observation role secondary to participant role	Unusual aspects can be noted during observation.	Researcher may not have good observation skills.
Complete observer -researcher observes without participating	Can explore topics that may be uncomfortable for informants to discuss.	Subjects (e.g., children) may present special problems in gaining rapport.

In the preparation of a research design that employs observation, a number of procedural steps for systematic observation research are necessary (Sommer & Sommer, 1986) to assist the leisure services researcher. These are as follows:

1. Specify the question(s) of interest (reason for doing the study).
2. Are the observational categories clearly described? What is being observed and why?
3. Design the measurement instruments (checklists, categories, coding systems, etc.).
4. Is the study designed so that it will be *valid* (i.e., does it measure what it is supposed to measure, and does it have some generalizability)?
5. Train observers in the use of the instruments and how to conduct observational research.
6. Do a pilot test to (a) test the actual observation procedure and (b) check the reliability of the categories of observation using at least two independent observers.
7. Revise the procedure and instruments in light of the pilot test results. If substantial changes are made to the instrument, run another pilot test to make sure changes will work under the field conditions.
8. Collect, compile, and analyze the data and interpret results.

Casual observation is normally done without prearranged categories, much like unstructured interviews. At early stages of the research process, casual observation allows one to observe subjects prior to designing questionnaires and interview formats. Sommer and Sommer (1986) suggest that the observer record first impressions immediately and daily. Sometimes recorders become desensitized to what is occurring.

Participant Observer

In the participant observation study, the researcher becomes a member of the group under study to collect data about the participants. There is a fundamental dilemma in the method: how secretive or open should the researcher be in recording activities of the participants (Dandekar, 1988)? These are methodological and ethical questions. It is the researcher's ethical responsibility to keep information confidential on the subjects, not exploit subjects, and be open with them regarding the study and the intended uses of the data. However, the researcher may bias the outcomes by possible actions, words, and presence within the study group.

The participant observer needs to find a good vantage point from which to observe the group. There should be a regular routine of visits for observation. Observations must not be classified in terms of one's own cultural experience, but within the framework of the group under study. The observer should also try to be inconspicuous in the note taking. Field notes should include maps, descriptions, comments, and analytic themes as necessary to better understand the data.

Windshield Surveys

Windshield surveys are quick site surveys of large areas (by car, on foot, or on a bicycle) to record initial impressions about an area or group. Park planners and maintenance personnel often employ such a technique, which allows for the recording of the general ambiance of the area. The survey is repeated at different times of the day, during various days of the week, in different seasons, and during special occasions (Dandekar, 1988), such as a concert in the park, a party, or other gathering.

Often, a researcher will inventory the facilities, and map and record observations using photographs and sketches of current site conditions. Later this information will be overlaid on base maps and validated for accuracy. Obviously, awareness of available source material is necessary to create the maps and other inventory information. Ideally, the windshield survey is made by two or more people—one to drive, one to comment, and one to record. Recordings can be done on maps and comments added during the survey or later.

Case Study

Case studies tend to be used in policy research because they are usually quick, cost efficient, and allow some room for impressionistic analyses of a situation (Majchrzak, 1984). However, Henderson (1991) notes that case studies often take a long time to complete and may result in massive, difficult-to-read documents.

Case studies supplement statistical analyses and allow us a better understanding of behavioral aspects of the issue. Case studies allow the researcher to examine the extent to which a policy or plan has been implemented and has changed a situation. Basically, case studies are in-depth investigations of a single instance. They provide a real opportunity to apply a multimethod approach to research and problem solving. Case studies are likely to use observations, secondary data sources, testing procedures, and other techniques (Kraus & Allen, 1987).

The researcher searches for themes in the data to use in developing a "story." Analysis consists of selecting data from the sources available that best describe and represent the researcher's understanding and interpretation of the event (Smith & Glass, 1987). The analysis for a case study consists of examining, categorizing, tabulating, and recombing evidence, just as for other forms of qualitative data interpretation (Henderson, 1991). The write-up includes a narrative account of the event with images, photos, and maps, if pertinent.

Specific steps in the conduct of case study research are as follows: (1) state the objectives of the research and determine the unit of study, characteristics, relationships, and processes that will provide direction for the study; (2) design the approach, state how will units be selected, and identify what sources of data exist; (3) collect the data; (4) organize the data to form a coherent reconstruction of the event; and (5) report and discuss findings.

Generalization from a case study is necessarily limited (Sommer & Sommer, 1986). The study was conducted in a single area; consequently, the findings may not apply to other areas or situations. However, the lack of generalizability does not make this type of study less important in leisure research. Case studies merely reflect the immediate purpose of the research: to discover and clarify the complexities of a single phenomenon (McMillan & Schumacher, 1984). Additionally, the case study occurs after the fact, thus requiring secondary data which may or may not be accurate. One difficulty is that the measurement of change in a situation normally requires analysis of the situation before, during, and after the events have taken place. Often it is difficult to locate reliable baseline data for comparisons and analysis.

As with any data collection method, there are a number of problems and issues the leisure service researcher should be aware of with regard to using any type of observational research (adapted from Isaac & Michael, 1985; Sommer & Sommer, 1986):

1. Reactive effect from being observed— a guinea pig effect in which awareness of being watched changes behavior.
    a. People become self-conscious and do not behave as they normally would.
    b. People attempt to accommodate the observer, doing what they believe the observer wants them to do.
    c. The observer's specific appearance or manner influences peoples' actions.
    d. Subjects change in accommodation to the observer during the course of the study.
2. Investigator error
    a. Unclear and unreliable observational categories.
    b. Bias on the part of the observer.
    c. Changes in the observational procedures in the middle of the study.
3. Sampling error
    a. People being observed are not representative of the groups to which the results will be generalized. This may be due to weather, day, location, etc.
    b. Inadequate time periods may have been selected for observation, causing a misrepresentation of the population using the area.

Documents

Using the sources of secondary data mentioned earlier in this chapter, the researcher has a number of options for the collection of important data relative to a problem. Among the types of methods that utilize documents are content analysis of studies, diaries, letters, case studies, and historical studies.

Secondary Data

The data sources for leisure research come from a variety of sources and agencies. Table 2.9 illustrates the depth and variety of these sources for leisure researchers. Primary sources consist of data that the researcher generates through a systematic process of data collection. Secondary sources consist of data that the researcher gathers from existing studies, libraries, and agencies. O'Sullivan (1991) notes that organizations such as the U.S. Census Bureau, chambers of commerce, public libraries, trade and professional organizations, and government agencies are sources for these types of information. Secondary information offers relatively quick and inexpensive answers to many questions and is almost always the point of departure for primary research (Stewart & Kamins, 1993).

Use of secondary data is common in both qualitative and quantitative research. However, all researchers should utilize secondary data in order to provide a framework for the study, develop the research question(s), and validate study findings. Findings from primary data studies should be compared to data such as U.S. Census figures in order to validate the study.

Table 2.9
Sources of Data In Leisure Research

Method and Data Source	Types of Information Available
EXISTING SOURCES (Secondary Data Collection)	
U.S. Census	Extensive demographic data including age, sex, distribution, education, ethnicity, migration patterns, service industry, etc.
Bureau of Labor Statistics	Extensive information on such things as employment, unemployment, types of employment, income, etc.
National Center for Health & State Department of Health	Information on vital rates such as births, deaths, health, etc. marriage and divorce rates, etc.
State Employment Departments	Number employed by industry, projected levels of employment growth, available jobs skills and skill shortages
Federal Land Management	National Parks, historic sites, scenic ar eas, forests by acres, budget and visitation rates.
State Highway Departments	Miles and condition of highways, bike lanes, and streets, capital and maintenance costs of highways
Law Enforcement Agency	Number and types of motor vehicles, types of crimes and violations, number of police officers by county and city, law enforcement

State Outdoor Recreation	Number and type of parks, number and type of Agency/Dept. campgrounds, location, and use rates for parks, lakes, rivers, etc.
Welfare/Human Services Department	Number of families on various types of assistance such as Aid to families with Dependent Children, Social Security, and SSI. Number of alcohol and drug abuse counselors, number of family counselors. Number and cases of child abuse, spouse abuse, desertions, child adoptions
State Fire Marshal's Office	Number of fires, location of the departments, fire personnel by type (volunteer or professional) and location, fire equipment by location
Secretary of State's Office	Political precincts and jurisdictions, elected officials by area, voting patterns
Environmental Impact	Environmental statements will have data for other park and recreation projects in the area.
Local Histories	Local authors frequently have written local histories that can be helpful in developing a broader understanding of the area and its people
Local Newspapers	Scanning local newspapers is an excellent means to become better acquainted with a community and its principal actors as well as the issues tha thave been of greatest local concern.
MULTIPLE DATA SOURCES (Primary data collection)	
Multiple methods Observation, interviews Official Documents: Project proposals, Surveys and planning studies	Use statistics, behaviors, needs, desires and concerns, and attitudes
Single Methods Experimental and Non-experimental studies to include qualitative and quantitative methodologies	Use statistics, behaviors, needs, desires and concerns, and attitudes
Adapted and Modified from Chadwick (1984), McMillan & Schumacher (1985), and Dandekar (1988).	

There is little excuse for not utilizing secondary data. In fact, many primary data collection efforts duplicate existing sources of data, and often are inferior in terms of reliability and validity. Secondary information is a vital resource for planning and decision making in leisure services.

The following steps are presented as a guide for exploring secondary data sources (adapted from Stewart & Kamins, 1993).

Step 1: Identify what needs to be answered or addressed.

Step 2: Develop a list of key terms and names of organizations and individuals that may provide access to the information.

Step 3: Conduct library or organization searches. Utilize general directories (e.g., *American Statistics Index* (ASI), *Business Index, Business Information Sources, Encyclopedia of Geographic Information Sources*, and *Marketing Information: A Professional Reference Guide*) and guides to academic literature (e.g., *Dissertation Abstracts International; Education Index; Management Contents; Leisure, Recreation & Tourism Abstracts; Psychological Abstracts; Social Science Citation Index* (SSCI); and *Sociological Abstracts*) to initiate the search. Key words should be utilized. It is advisable to limit the search within the last few years, as new sources would address previous work.

Step 4: Compile relevant sources, and evaluate the findings of the material. At this point the researcher would determine the need for more specialized sources and data needs. Consulting the reference librarian for more specific needs and utilization of the CD-ROM materials may be appropriate at this time. If further data needs are required, consult local authorities for additional information.

In analyzing each of the secondary sources, the researcher should be able to answer the following questions (Stewart & Kamins, 1993):

1. What was the purpose of the study, and why were the data collected?
2. Who collected the information? What qualifications and potential biases are represented in the conduct and reporting of the study?

3. What type of information was actually collected? How were the units and concepts operationalized and defined? How were direct measures utilized?
4. When was the information collected, and is it still current? Were there specific events that might have influenced the findings or outcomes?
5. How was the information collected? What was the methodology employed?
6. How consistent is the information obtained from one source with other sources or the researcher's own experience?

U.S. Census Data: Some Special Sources for the Leisure Services Professional

The U.S. government conducts 11 censuses on a regularly scheduled basis. This information is particularly helpful for the leisure service programmer, manager, planner, and researcher. Census information is available on households, businesses, government units, transportation, and natural resources. Some of the publications available that provide information and introductions to these data sources are: *American Statistics Index: A Comprehensive Guide and Index to the Statistical Publications of the U.S. Government; Census Catalog and Guide; Historical Statistics of the United States: Colonial Times to 1970; Statistical Abstracts of the United States;* and *Statistics Sources.* In addition, much of the census of housing and basic demographic information that is useful in leisure services is available on CD-ROM in most public libraries. Every major metropolitan area has at least one regional depository of federal documents.

In addition to the CD-ROM format, another exciting and useful development in the presentation of census data is the Topologically Integrated Geographic Coding and Referencing (TIGER) system. The TIGER system gives the user the ability to generate a digitized street map of the entire United States. A researcher can chart literally every block in every county and city within the United States by integrating economic, topographic, and demographic information. Businesses, planning departments, and other organizations utilize TIGER to define boundaries of customers for the optimal allocation of resources. TIGER can give the leisure services professional the tools necessary to pinpoint customers for the purposes of segmentation.

The U.S. Census Bureau provides a list of software vendors for utilization of this data set.

Content Analysis

The technique of content analysis systematically describes the form or content of written and spoken material. It is frequently used for quantitatively studying mass media (print, audio, etc). This technique allows one to conduct research without coming into contact with other people (Sommer & Sommer, 1986). The technique uses secondary data and is considered unobtrusive research. An additional aspect is that the researcher has no effect on the material; the data are already collected. The technique is a quantification of events or observations within the media being investigated.

The first step is to select the media to be studied and the particular issue. Then some sort of classification scheme to record the information is developed. The analysis can emphasize the content of the material (specific topics or themes), its structure (location, format, illustrations, etc.), or both. To increase the reliability of the process, Sommer and Sommer (1986) suggest that two or more judges be trained in the scoring system. The judges should come up with similar results in the scoring of data sources, provided that categories are clearly stated and don't overlap. Reliability coefficients can be computed to make sure that there is high agreement among the raters (Cozby, 1993).

The process is tedious due to the requirement that each data source be analyzed along a number of dimensions. If one is studying open-ended survey responses, the researcher must list all responses, and then collapse the items into similar categories and quantify the number of occurrences of each.

Lankford (1990) conducted a content analysis of open-ended questions with regard to tourism impacts in the Pacific Northwest. A total of 1400 surveys were reviewed, representing a random sample of six counties and 14 cities. All responses were read, key words listed, and categories determined. Differences were noted between residents of the various cities and counties. The research indicated that people are concerned with the following issues: economic impacts, traffic, governmental involvement, rate of development and growth, the environment, and level of tourism development.

Establishing categories is difficult and necessary in order to code and score the data. It is best to skim the data to identify major or reoccurring themes. Decisions about the unit of analysis must be made as well. Do the researchers examine every article, every nth article, or every paragraph of each article? Once categories are defined, the process is one of locating words, phrases, ideas, or meanings that fit into the codes (Adams & Schvaneveldt, 1991).

Henderson (1991) notes that the process can be inductive or deductive—deductive in that a quantification of frequencies occurs in the tabulation of codes, and inductive in that themes and patterns emerge and are noted during the process. Altheide (1987) promotes the idea of using both approaches, which are referred to as ethnographic content analysis and quantitative content analysis. It involves utilizing the quantitative approach and enriching the data with the reflective and highly interactive nature of the investigator, concepts, data collection, and analysis. Primarily, the purpose is to provide information that can still be counted and put in emergent categories, and that provide good descriptive meaning as well.

The results of the content analysis are descriptive yet can provide an indication of trends and issues in society. For example, Naisbitt (1982) produced the high-impact publication *Megatrends* using this technique. The availability of information is limited only by the topic. If a researcher wanted to study the application of a certain type of chemical used on golf courses, it is unlikely that many sources would be available; however, the researcher who wanted to examine maintenance practices for parks in general would find more sources available.

Meta-Analysis

The conclusions in a literature review are based on the impressions of the researcher. In recent years, the technique of meta-analysis (Rosenthal, 1984) has emerged for combining the actual results of the studies being reviewed. The idea is to utilize statistical techniques to estimate the strength of a given set of findings across many different studies. This allows the creation of a context from which future research can emerge (Smith & Glass, 1987). The main point is to determine the reliability of a finding by examining the results from many different studies (Cozby, 1993).

Researchers analyze the methods used in previous studies and then quantify the findings of the studies. Thomas and Nelson (1990) detail the steps to meta-analysis:

1. Identification of the research problem.
2. Conduct of a literature review of identified studies to determine inclusion or exclusion.
3. A careful reading and evaluation to identify and code important study characteristics.
4. Calculation of effect size. Effect size is the mean of the experimental group minus the mean of the control group, divided by the standard deviation of the control group. The notion is to calculate the effect size across a number of studies to determine the relevance of the test, treatment, or method. For more details, refer to Thomas and French (1986) and Hedges and Olkin (1985).
5. Reporting of the findings and conclusions.

Meta-analysis allows the researcher to identify the underlying principles and impacts of a large number of studies. These findings can become the basis for establishing theories, models, and concepts. The difficulty lies in the lack of adequate reporting of means and standard deviations in many journal articles. Consequently, the researcher must locate the author or obtain the data file from the researcher.

Historical Research

Historical research in leisure studies may focus on biographies of park and recreation pioneers (Joseph Lee, Jane Adams), institutions (public parks and recreation, federal land management agencies), movements (playgrounds, leisure education), and concepts (professionalism, certification and licensure, play). Historical research is sometimes referred to as analytical research, along with policy studies and legal research (McMillan & Schumacher, 1984). Underlying the varieties of analytical research are common methodological characteristics including a research topic that addresses past events, primary and secondary data, techniques of criticism for historical searches and evaluation of the information, and synthesis and explanation of findings. Historical studies provide knowledge and understanding of past historical, legal, and policy events.

Wesner (1994) notes that although historical research is seemingly rare in leisure studies, it is important for both practitioners and academics. Specifically, historical research allows us to better understand our profession, reminds us where we have been, and provides a glimpse of where we might be headed relative to services, trends, and needs. Interestingly, in the last decade 32 different journals have published articles about leisure, mostly by people outside of the leisure profession (Wesner, 1994). Historical studies fall into one of six categories (Wesner, 1994): (1) the history of movements, (2) the history of individual people, (3) the history of groups of people, (4) the history of a single subject, (5) the history of a geographical area, and (6) the history of an idea. Historical research is much more than a literature review; it is more exhaustive in that sources are diverse and often include older, unpublished sources and accounts.

The purpose of historical research is to interpret facts by systematically and objectively collecting, evaluating, and verifying evidence. The historical researcher attempts to verify facts through the use of triangulation methods, in which other data sources are checked and cross-checked to confirm the events being reported. Two data sources are utilized in this verification process: primary and secondary data. Primary data sources include the author witnessing the event, while secondary sources are others who witnessed the event from whom the author obtains verbal or written verification.

Historical researchers must weigh the value of the data collected by way of external and internal criticism (Isaac & Michael, 1985). Internal criticism asks if the sources are authentic, if the data supplied are accurate and relevant to one's particular study or problem. Specifically, the researcher is making a judgment of the source to determine if there were biases, motives, or limitations of the author which might have influenced the findings. The external criticism of historical information addresses whether or not the document or other material is authentic. Typical considerations are, who wrote the document, when and where, and what was the intention? In qualitative analysis, the simple agreement of statements from independent sources can be misleading since the research is dependent upon preserved sources (McMillan & Schumacher, 1984). Therefore, identification of agreement with other known facts

Figure 2.2
Example of A Leisure Service Policy Framework of Issues/Trends, Policy Questions and Proposals Which Lead to Specific Research Designs (Adapted from ICMA 1988)

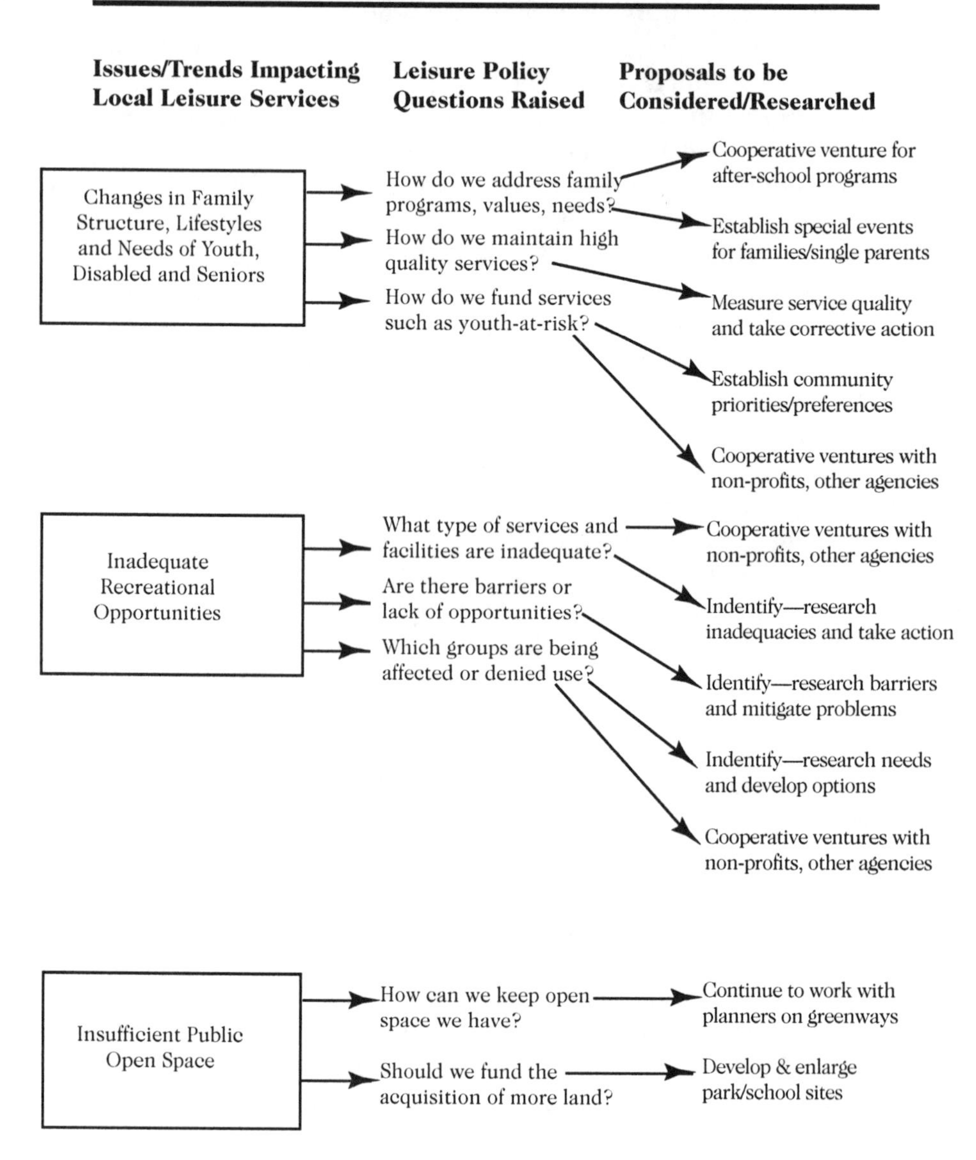

or circumstances surrounding the event lends credibility to the source and information. Consequently, validity of historical research lies in the procedures inherent in the methods utilized, specification of the search process and sources, criticisms of sources, and the final interpretation of sources and materials (McMillan & Schumacher, 1984).

There are five basic procedures common to the conduct of historical research. Essentially, these steps are common to all research projects and methods in that they provide a systematic approach to the conduct of the research.

Step 1: Define the problem, asking pertinent questions such as: Is the historical method appropriate? Are pertinent data available? Will the findings be significant in the leisure services field?

Step 2: Develop the research hypothesis (if necessary) and research objectives to provide a framework for the conduct of the research. Research questions focus on events (who, what, when, where), how an event occurred (descriptive), and why the event happened (interpretive). This contrasts with quantitative studies, in which the researcher is testing hypotheses and trying to determine the significance between scores for experimental and control groups or the relationships between variable x and variable y.

Step 3: Collect the data, which consists of taking copious notes and organizing the data. The researcher should code topics and subtopics in order to arrange and file the data. The kinds of data analysis employed in historical research include (based on McMillan & Schumacher, 1984):

a. *Analysis of concepts.* Concepts are clarified by describing the essential and core concepts beginning from the early developmental stages. Clarification allows other researchers to explore the topic in other fashions.

b. *Editing or compilation* of documents, to preserve documents in chronological order to explain events. For example, an edition of Butler's park standards, the National Recreation and Park Association's first minutes, or letters from early pioneers in the field preserves the documents for future researchers.

c. *Descriptive narration* tells the story from beginning to end in chronological order, utilizing limited generalizations and synthesized facts.

d. *Interpretive analysis* relates one event to another event. The event is studied and described within a broader context to add meaning and credibility to the data. For example, an examination of the development of a local jurisdiction's ability to dedicate land for parks may be related to the urbanization and loss of open space in our communities.

e. *Comparative analysis* examines similarities and differences in events during different time periods—for example, the budget-cutting priorities and procedures of the Proposition 13 era of the early 1980s in parks and recreation as compared to the budget-cutting priorities and procedures of today.

f. *Theoretical and philosophical analysis* utilizes historical parallels, past trends, and sequences of events to suggest the past, present, and future of the topic being researched. Findings would be used to develop a theory or philosophy of leisure. For example, an analysis of public recreation agency goals and objectives of previous eras can be used to describe the future in the context of social, political, economic, technological, and cultural changes in society.

Step 4: Utilizing external and internal criticism, the research should evaluate the data. Sources of data include documents (letters, diaries, bills, receipts, newspapers, journals/magazines, films, pictures, recordings, personal and institutional records, and budgets), oral testimonies of participants in the events, and relics (textbooks, buildings, maps, equipment, furniture, and other objects).

Step 5: Reporting of the findings, which includes a statement of the problem, review of source material, assumptions, research questions and methods used to obtain findings, the interpretations and conclusions, and a thorough bibliographic referencing system.

To assist the historical researcher, a number of issues and common errors in historical research have been noted (Isaac & Michael, 1985). First, for some topics or problems addressed through research, there may be insufficient data available to utilize historical methods. Therefore, redefinition of the problem or use of another method should be considered. Second, the topic must be narrowly defined yet broad enough to identify patterns for interpretation. Third, some researchers allow their bias to show when reviewing and reporting on historical events. Careful editing and cross-checking (triangulation) of references is necessary. Finally, some researchers can accurately recite the facts of events in chronological order but fail to integrate these facts into meaningful generalizations. It is essential that the researcher be fully knowledgeable about the era and key issues being addressed.

A MULTIMETHOD APPROACH TO LEISURE RESEARCH

To illustrate the complexity and range of issues facing the leisure professional, Figure 2.2 provides a policy framework that addresses proposals and research questions. It is important to note the range and types of research methods we can utilize in the resolution of a problem. In fact, it is prudent for the researcher to utilize both qualitative and quantitative methods for each study, as well as a number of methods within each paradigm. In other words, a multimethod approach leads to better data for improved decision making. In studying the issues and trends presented below, it is apparent that a researcher could utilize personal interviews, telephone and mail questionnaires, quasi, and ex post facto research, in addition to case studies and historical methods, in the resolution of these issues.

Yoder, McKinney, Wicks, and Espeseth (1995) note the need for new ways of gathering information, both "hard" and "soft," from different places, groups, and individuals. They define the process as triangulation—the theory and process of collecting, analyzing, and integrating data from multiple sources with multiple research methods. For the purposes of this discussion, the term *multimethod approach* will be used.

Glancy and Little (1995) utilized observations, interviews, and primary and secondary records to suggest how time and proximity to the interactive context/incident can be operationalized to examine the social factors of personal leisure. Williams and Neal (1993) studied motivational issues in leisure services using importance-performance analysis. Techniques used included content analysis, panel of experts and interviews and survey research. Robertson (1993) studied delinquent behavior of adolescents using initial and exit interviews, personal workbooks and journals, a leisure awareness workshop, and quantitative questionnaires. Lankford (1995) utilized focus groups, intercept survey interviews, nominal group methods, and quantitative surveys in the exploration of leisure needs, issues, attitudes, and opinions of U.S. Army personnel and their dependents. Hines (1993) linked qualitative and quantitative methods to show how a multimethod approach can be used to study diverse cultural and ethnic minority groups. Dennis, Fetterman, and Sechrest (1994) utilized participant observation, interviews, and surveys to show how both qualitative and quantitative research methods can be used in substance abuse research. In the development of recreation and tourism plans for a community (Lankford, 1988; Povey, Lankford, & Knowles-Lankford, 1989), a series of nominal group methods, interviews, open-ended and closed-ended surveys, and design charrettes were utilized over a three-year period to research proposals and develop recommendations for the community.

It should be obvious at this point that multimethod research is being used successfully in the field of leisure services. The arguments regarding quantitative versus qualitative research become moot in light of the current efforts of leisure researchers. The important point is that the researchers are moving beyond a two-dimensional argument and are utilizing all of the methods available in the conduct of research.

Each technique has shortcomings: experimentation is artificial, observation is unreliable, interviews are biased, and so forth. There is no ideal method in leisure research. The advantages of some relate to economy of time and money, while disadvantages may concern objectivity. For most leisure research problems, several methods are applicable and should be used to fully address the project. Brewer and Hunter (1989) address a number of advantages of multimethod research. First, theories do not respect conventional methodological boundaries. We know in leisure research that our strongest theories come from multiple studies using multiple methods that arrive at similar conclusions. Second, any research problem of importance is the subject of repeated investigations. Repeated investigations can utilize other methods in the exploration and definition of the problem, once the original methods have established the significance of the problem. Finally, overreliance on one method fails to guard against specific sources of error. No matter what method(s) the leisure services researcher chooses, adherence to a carefully designed study design will provide meaningful results.

CONCLUSION

Following the research process guidelines set forth in the previous chapter, we can help to ensure that the research results will produce meaningful and useful results. Additionally, this chapter pointed out the strengths and weaknesses of various data collection methods used in leisure research. Some discussion of qualitative and quantitative methodology was included to assist the researcher in determining the best method for the research problem. The aim here is to avoid the ongoing debate about qualitative vs. quantitative and theory-then-research or research-then-theory. Importantly, the message delivered here is that the research problem or issue will drive the methods used in the research process.

Chapter Three

Measurement in Leisure Research

THE NATURE OF MEASUREMENT

Measurement is perhaps the most fundamental feature of the social scientific investigation process (Wagenaar, 1981). Measurement contributes objectivity, reliability, and validity to research. Measurement and research design are closely intertwined, and are both essential to the research process. To complete useful research, one must implement the best design for a given problem (Adams & Schvaneveldt, 1991). Without the ability to apply measurement concepts, many questions regarding the study of leisure could not be answered through the research process.

Adams and Schvaneveldt (1991) have pointed out some of the important functions of measurement in research:

1. Measurement produces data to be used in a variety of ways and helps promote the world of discovery.
2. Measurement helps the researcher better understand the properties of objects or events.
3. Measurement is the mechanism for helping the researcher view the relationship of one property to another in testing hypotheses, propositions, and theories.
4. Measurement helps establish the presence or absence of a factor and its degree of influence.
5. Measurement allows us to make meaningful observations about reality.
6. Measurement is a detailed way of looking at or assessing certain aspects of the data collection process.

In order to measure, one must first apply the meanings and values to the concept in question. For example, research into youth-at-risk would involve a significant amount of thought and reading in order to clarify what exactly is meant by this concept. A conceptual definition of youth-at-risk might include relationships with peers, parents, and other adults; association with drugs and alcohol; sexual behaviors; and involvement in school and after-school activities.

Once a conceptual definition has been developed, the researcher begins to operationalize the concept by specifying the measurement procedures. A set of specific indicators that reflect aspects of the concept are identified to produce a valid operational definition of the concept. For example, to operationalize the concept of youth-at-risk, the researcher may choose to measure the frequency, number, and closeness of contacts with adults, parents, and peers. Obviously, another measurement issue is raised in terms of what constitutes "closeness." It is possible that a scale has been utilized in other studies that may be adaptable for use in a youth-at-risk study.

VARIABLES AND UNITS OF ANALYSIS

In order to move from the conceptual to the operational level, we convert concepts into variables by assigning values to them. A variable is an empirical property that takes two or more values (Nachmias & Nachmias, 1987). As an example, leisure participation is a variable in that it can be differentiated by frequency of participation (daily, weekly, monthly, etc.). Wright and Goodale (1995) operationalized participation as frequent, moderate, infrequent, former, and nonparticipant. Similarly, leisure satisfaction can be assigned values such as highly satisfied, satisfied, dissatisfied, and highly dissatisfied. Assume we wish to measure a relatively straightforward variable such as income. Does this mean household income, individual income, or family income? Obviously, one must define family, individual and household income for the purposes of the study. Is the income gross, net, or after in-kind transfers from social programs (food stamps, housing programs, etc.)?

The obvious point is that the researcher must define each variable in order to measure accurately the concept in question. Therefore, a variable is not fixed in reality but is tied to the purposes of the research project. The assumption that reality has been captured in a data set can lead the researcher to ignore the steps used to operationalize the variable by converting a property of reality into a set of numbers. The researcher must constantly remain aware during the analysis phase of the project that many decisions were used in operationalizing the variables.

Classification of Variables

Variables can generally be classified into three categories: independent, dependent, and control (also known as intervention, mediating, and extraneous).

Independent Variables

Independent variables are also referred to as predictor, input, manipulated, treatment, stimulus, intervention, experimental, or moderating variables. This type of variable is presumed to cause, affect, or influence the outcome measures of a study or test. The researcher designs a situation where subjects are exposed to a condition or problem, which is called the independent measure because the subject has no control over it. The subject's response to the condition or problem becomes the dependent variable. For example, if two methods of leisure counseling are being tested, the counseling methods are the independent measures, and the measurement of attitudes toward leisure upon termination of the counseling session constitutes the dependent variable.

Another example is a study to determine whether age, sex, and occupation (independent variables) positively or negatively affect attitudes toward leisure time (dependent variable). The independent variable is what the researcher is manipulating, that is, the condition (age, sex, occupation, income, etc.) that might influence an attitude or response.

Dependent Variables

Dependent variables represent the effect or influence of the independent variable. They are sometimes referred to as outcome, output, or response variables. They are "dependent" in that the outcome depends on the effects of the variables being managed. For example, if two leisure counseling methods are compared, the resulting change in attitude toward leisure time is the dependent measure.

Control Variables

Control variables, also known as background or classification variables, are so called because they need to be controlled, held constant, or randomized so that their effects are neutralized or accounted for during the study. Examples are gender, age, IQ, income, and educational level. Obviously, any of these measures could also be classified as independent or dependent based on the purpose of the study. By applying the previous example to the analysis of the possible effect of a control variable, can the researcher be sure which, if any, of the two leisure counseling methods (independent variables) produced changed attitudes toward leisure time (dependent variables)? Could it be that another causal agent or independent variable has influenced these attitudes?

The quality of the research design determines the degree to which rival hypotheses or extraneous variables can be controlled or ruled out. This, in turn, is determined by the researcher in the following ways: (1) the random assignment of subjects, (2) the ability to manipulate the instrument or test (in this example, the leisure counseling method), (3) the time when the measurements of the dependent variable occur (randomized data collection times are necessary), and (4) which groups are measured. These issues are obviously related to quasi and experimental designs, which are described in Chapter 4.

In Chapter 9, more detail and other examples are explained relative to classification of variables. The intention here is to provide a framework for the reader in order to further understand measurement concepts and experimental designs which follow this section.

LEVELS OF MEASUREMENT

In order to measure, the researcher assigns numerals or other symbols to variables according to some established rules. Nachmias and Nachmias (1987) define a numeral as a symbol (I, II, III, ... or 1, 2, 3, ...) that has no meaning until the researcher assigns it meaning. Once numerals have been assigned meaning, they become quantitative values for use in statistical analysis to describe, explain, and predict. In measurement, the term *assignment* means mapping numerals to objects or events according to certain rules in order to clarify or arrange the data. For example, a mapping rule for classification of respondents may be that a value of 1 indicates a female respondent and a value of 2 a male respondent. Another mapping rule might involve having respondents enter a value of 3 if they are satisfied with a recreation program, 2 if they are neutral or not sure, or 1 if they are dissatisfied. Therefore, measurement can be viewed as an assignment of numbers to objects or events according to some predetermined rules established by the researcher, in a consistent manner.

There are various levels of measurement (sometimes referred to as scales of measurement). These are the nominal, ordinal, interval, and ratio levels, which are related to one another in a nested hierarchy: nominal data are only nominal; ordinal data are also nominal; interval data are also ordinal and nominal; and ratio data are also interval, ordinal, and nominal. These distinctions are very important to the researcher, in that the ability to apply various statistical techniques for analysis is based on the level of measurement used. In some instances, statistical treatments designed for interval data cannot be used for nominal data. In some cases, the analysis can proceed, but with a compromise in the strength of the findings due to violation of the assumptions.

Nominal Level

Nominal scales of measurement have no numerical or quantitative properties. There is no quantitative difference between the groupings. For example, classifying people by gender merely allows the researcher to distinguish male and female respondents; it does not imply that one is greater or less than the other. The two groupings are different, but one group does not possess more of the variable "sex" than the other. The nominal scale is used for naming, labeling or classifying people, objects, or events. Examples include yes-or-no questions, male or female status, occupational category, day of week, and leisure program type. The only rules are that all members of a category or class have the same number and that no two classes or categories have the same number.

An example of the use of the nominal scale is a recreation center programmer who wants to determine whether adults enroll in aerobics on weekends because of the hours of the program, instructor reputation, or price. The programmer randomly samples 100 customers and finds that 45 come because of the instructor, 30 because of price, and only 25 because of the hours of operation. The programmer has formed a three-category nominal scale, counted the number of cases (in terms of both frequency and percent), and identified the modal category (instructor reputation). Suppose the programmer also identified the sex of the respondents, allowing further analysis as follows:

Gender	Instructor	Issue Hours	Price	Total
Male	20	7	11	38
Female	25	18	19	62
Total	45	25	30	100

The data above can be analyzed using the modes (female and instructor) and the percentage values, and such data are often analyzed statistically using the chi-square test to determine if there is a significant association between females and males and the issue that is attracting them to the aerobics course. To summarize, nominal scales of measurement are for classification, no ordering of the categories is possible, and categories are exhaustive and mutually inclusive.

Ordinal Level

Ordinal scales of measurement allow the researcher to rank-order data (people, objects, events, etc.) as first, second, third, and so on using numbers, letters, or other symbols. Measurement at this level involves the same principle as nominal measurement—classification of objects—and an additional rank-ordering of the objects. However, no particular value is attached to the intervals between the numbers used in the scale. The ordinal scale of measurement allows the researcher to determine what is more or less only, not how much more or how much less.

A significant amount of research in leisure centers relies on ordinal measures. One of the most common applications involves preference measurements of competition between service providers. For example, a customer may be asked to rank preferences for several aerobics classes, instructors, times, and prices from a number of recreation centers. The following question would produce ordinal data:

How would you rate the quality of aerobics classes offered at the YMCA compared with the selection offered at the City Parks and Recreation Community Center?

___Better___The Same___Worse

The recreation programmer could arrange the data as follows:

Quality Rating	Number of Responses
Better	65
Same	35
Worse	50

The programmer examining the data would be faced with resolving the issue of why so many are saying that the YMCA has better a program (the mode), yet nearly as many say it is worse. Obviously, further research would be needed to determine the characteristics of respondents in each category and why there is such a division.

In terms of analysis, researchers using the ordinal scale can establish the mode, median, percentage and frequency of occurrence, and percentile rank of a variable. Additionally, the range and maximum and minimum values can be specified, and chi-square can be utilized to analyze the statistical significance of the data. Also, inferential statistics such as Mann-Whitney U, Friedman two-way ANOVA, and rank order correlation can be applied. The branch of statistics that deals with nominal and ordinal measures is referred to as nonparametric statistics.

Interval Level

Interval scales measure the magnitude of differences between cases in uniform increments or degrees of difference. There is an arbitrary zero point, and the unit of measurement established is arbitrary. The scale is subject to direct arithmetic manipulation, and the zero in an interval scale indicates absence of the variable.

The most common form of interval measurement in leisure services is attitudinal measures. A Likert scale, for example, requires respondents to state their level of agreement or disagreement with a statement by selecting a response such as:

1. Strongly Disagree;
2. Disagree;
3. Neutral;
4. Agree;
5. Strongly Agree.

It is doubtful that the intervals between items are all exactly equal (Tull & Hawkins, 1987). However, researchers treat the data as if the intervals were equal since most statistical techniques are not affected by minor deviations (Albaum, Best, & Hawkins, 1977).

In a study of selected recreation activities, Havitz, Dimanche, and Howard (1993) compared two samples using the Personal Involvement Profile (PII) and Involvement Profile (PI) scales. A five-point Likert scale like the one described above was used. They analyzed the data using factor analysis, Cronbach's alpha coefficient (explained later in this chapter), MANOVA, and Pearson's correlation coefficient.

Scores can also be compared across groups using T-tests and ANOVA. Data can be described and analyzed using the mode, mean, standard deviation, factor analysis, regression, and the product moment correlation. Virtually the entire range of statistical analyses can be applied to interval scales (Tull & Hawkins, 1987).

By now, the reader should start to realize the important relationship between the levels of measurement and use of statistical techniques for analysis later in the research process. The mention of these statistical techniques is meant to indicate how many more are available when the level of measurement increases in complexity and detail. Having a variety of ways to analyze a particular level of measurement allows the researcher to report the data in more meaningful ways in the hopes of resolving problems in the field. For more examples and detail with regard to measurement and analysis, refer to Chapters 9 and 10 in this book, and refer to any multivariate statistical methods textbook.

Ratio Level

Ratio scales measure data using equal intervals and an absolute zero point (meaning a zero amount of the variable). Variables such as weight, time, length, geographic distance, and area have natural zero points and are measured at the ratio level (Nachmias & Nachmias, 1987). It has also been demonstrated that ratio-level scales of measurement can be developed to measure attitudes, opinions and preferences (Tillinghast, 1980). The ratio scale is most common in physical sciences where all four of the following conditions exist: equivalence (nominal), greater than (ordinal), known distance of two intervals (interval), and a true zero (ratio) (Nachmias & Nachmias, 1987). An important distinction between the ratio and interval scales is that numbers applied in ratio scales are measured from absolute zero, whereas interval measures apply numbers to indicate differences from an arbitrary zero. The mean, median, and mode can be used to describe the results in the ratio scale. Virtually all statistical treatments are available to the researcher using the ratio scale.

VALIDITY AND RELIABILITY

A major feature of good research is validity. There are two types of validity: internal and external. Internal validity refers to whether the instrument measures what it is suppose to measure. It represents the freedom from bias in forming conclusions in view of the data. It guarantees that the changes in the dependent variable are the result of the influence of the independent variable rather than the manner in which the research was designed. Therefore, it is important to carefully operationalize variables and conducts studies that control for possible violations of internal validity.

External validity refers to whether or not we can "generalize" the findings beyond our immediate situation. This type of validity is concerned with the ability to extend the conclusions reached through observation of a sample to the universe. More simply stated, can the conclusions drawn from a sample be generalized to other cases?

Scales and measurement instruments can be evaluated according to four elements: validity, accuracy, precision and reliability. A scale is valid if it in fact measures the variable for which it was designed and measures it consistently. There is no intrinsic statistical test to ascertain the validity of a scale.

Accuracy refers to the extent to which a variable is classified correctly. If the best measure was utilized in a study, then we can estimate the amount of error by comparison to other, alternative measures.

A scale is accurate if it is free from systematic and variable errors. A systematic error (a bias) is one that occurs each time we measure something. A variable error is one that occurs randomly when we measure something. For example, the mood of respondents is a variable error. Variable error also relates to reliability.

A scale cannot be accurate beyond its precision. A precise scale is one which measures a phenomenon in fine detail. For example, it is impossible to measure the U.S. dollar more precisely than to the nearest penny. Measurement in more detailed intervals (e.g., hundredths vs. 10ths vs. whole numbers) is more precise.

Validity

Researchers rely upon various types of validity to verify the effectiveness of measurement procedures. The following discussion summarizes the principal types of validity (based on Adams & Schvaneveldt, 1991; Babbie, 1986; Leedy, 1985; McMillan & Schumacher, 1984; Campbell & Fisk, 1959).

Content Validity

Content validity is sometimes equated with face validity. Content validity estimates are essentially systematic but subjective evaluations of the appropriateness of the instrument being used. Content validity concerns the accuracy with which an instrument measures the factors or situations under study. For example, if the "content" being elicited is familiarity with a certain area of knowledge, then content validity is an estimate of how accurately the questions asked tend to elicit the information sought. For example, a scale designed to measure attitude toward a recreation program would not be considered to have content validity if it omitted items such as instructor, cost, and reputation. This is the most common form of validation used in leisure research.

Face Validity

Face validity relies basically upon the subjective judgment of the researcher or a panel of experts. It involves two questions the researcher must answer: (1) Is the instrument measuring what it is supposed to measure? (2) Is the sample adequately representative of the behavior or trait being measured?

Construct Validity

A construct is any concept, such as honesty, that cannot be directly observed or isolated. Construct validation pertains to the degree to which the construct itself is actually designed to be measured. A procedure has been developed by Campbell and Fisk (1959) known as the Multitrait-Multimethod Matrix Method. It makes use of the traits of convergence and discriminability. Convergence examines the effect of various methods of measuring a construct. Different methods of measurement of the same construct should "converge" in their results. Discriminability means that the measuring instrument should be able to discriminate, or differentiate, the construct being studied from other, similar constructs. The researcher is concerned with the interpretation and proper use of a set of scores in order to provide a meaningful explanation of the unobservable construct. This is accomplished by using different methods to assess the same construct.

Criterion Validity

Criterion validity usually employs two measures of validity; the second is a check against the accuracy of the first measure. The essential component in criterion validity is a reliable and valid criterion— a standard against which to gauge the results of the instrument that is doing the measuring. The data of the measuring instrument (e.g., test scores) should correlate highly with equivalent data of the criterion scores. Specifically, does the individual test score predict the probable behavior on a second variable (criterion-related measure)?

Two types of criterion validity checks exist. The first is concurrent validity, which is the extent to which one measure of a variable can be used to estimate an individual's current score on a different measure of the same or a closely related variable. The second is predictive ability, which is the extent to which an individual's future level or attitude relative to one variable can be predicted by his or her score on a similar variable.

Reliability

In addition to being valid, research should also be reliable. Reliability refers to the repeatability or replicability of findings. Instruments and procedures should produce the same results when applied to similar people in similar settings, as well as to the same people as a posttest or follow-up.

It is essential in research that evidence be presented on the reliability and validity of the measurement(s). This allows the reader to determine the applicability and generalizability of the findings to other situations. It also allows others to test and replicate various scales and instruments. To assess whether a researcher has used reliable and valid measurements, the reader should look for evidence that (Adams & Schvaneveldt, 1991):

1. The assessment predicts theoretically appropriate behaviors.
2. The measure can differentiate between groups of individuals known to behave differently within the situation.
3. The assessment includes appropriate conceptual or theoretically based content.
4. Individuals behave (respond) similarly when measured two or more times over a short period of time.

If the assessment meets these four requirements, the consumer can assume that the measure has reasonable validity and reliability. The following discussion reviews the various types of reliability checks for use in leisure research (adapted from McMillan & Schumacher, 1984; Adams & Schvaneveldt, 1991).

Test-Retest Reliability

Does an individual respond to an assessment device in the same general way when the test is administered twice? Essentially, the researcher attempts to determine if the findings are consistent and stable over time by administering the same test. The greater the differences, the lower the reliability. Some common examples are aptitude and IQ tests. Some problems exist with this method: (1) Some items can be measured only once because initial measures may alter the respondent's awareness of the issue. (2) The reuse of the instrument may lead to anger, boredom, and attempts to remember answers from the previous test. (3) Outside factors may cause shifts in attitude over time.

Alternative or Equivalent Form Reliability

When two measurement instruments, which are equivalent in their degree of validity, are given to the same individual, is there strong convergence in how that person responds? The researcher is interested in comparing two measures given at about the same time to determine if items are similar or dissimilar between the two test versions. The researcher may also compare the two measures over a given period of time to the same individuals. Two problems are associated with this method: (1) the extra time, expense, and trouble of obtaining two equivalent methods; and (2) the problem of constructing two truly valid equivalent forms of the instrument.

Internal Comparison or Consistency Reliability

Reliability can be estimated by the correlation among the scores on a multiple-item scale or index in which all items are designed to measure the same thing. The split-half method is the simplest form of internal comparison. The scores on half of the test are compared to the scores on the remaining half. The researcher is interested in whether or not the halves of a measure assess a single trait or dimension through a correlation (measure of similarity). SPSSX and other statistical programs allow the researcher to split the sample for this purpose.

A better approach is to calculate the coefficient alpha (Cronbach, 1951). This method produces a mean of all the possible split-half coefficients resulting from different splittings of the measurement instrument (Tull & Hawkins, 1987). The coefficient alpha can range from 0 to 1. A value of less than .60 is viewed as unsatisfactory (Churchill & Peter, 1984).

CONCLUSION

Measurement is the assignment of numbers to objects or variables that need to be measured. The way in which we measure in research contributes objectivity, reliability, and validity to our findings. There are four levels of measurement: nominal, ordinal, interval, and ratio. For the most part, quantitative analysis on a given set of numbers is dependent on the level of measurement applied.

Validity and reliability are inseparable from measurement. Traditionally, four types of validity have been distinguished: content, face, construct, and criterion. Validity refers to whether a test or scale measures what it is supposed to measure, reliability refers to the stability of this measurement over time. Reliability indicates the extent to which a measure contains variable errors. This refers to the consistency of measurement. For example, a person's score on two scale forms should be similar. This measurement can be estimated by the test-retest method. Understanding concepts in this chapter will facilitate the use of the concepts and methods described in the remaining section of this book.

Chapter Four

Research Design in Leisure Research

RESEARCH DESIGNS

There are two types of research design methods (McMillan & Schumacher, 1984), experimental and non-experimental. Campbell and Stanley (1966) divided experimental studies into four general areas: pre-experimental designs, true experimental designs, quasi-experimental designs, and correctional and ex post facto designs.

Six characteristics distinguish experimental research from other methods: (1) statistical equivalence of subjects in different groups, which is achieved by random assignment of study subjects; (2) comparison of two or more groups or sets of conditions; (3) direct manipulation of at least one independent variable; (4) measurement of each dependent variable; (5) use of inferential statistics; and (6) a design that provides maximum control.

The experimental method deals with the phenomenon of cause and effect. The method is simple. First we assess each situation to establish comparability. Then we attempt to alter one of these situations by introducing an extraneous variable and conducting an evaluation of the effects of the variable on the situation. Whatever change is identified is presumed to have been caused by the extraneous variable.

Experimental research needs to be planned; this is often referred to as the design of the experiment. Design has an important meaning in reference to research. It encompasses the total structure of the research framework, beyond the mere selection of statistical tools to process data, test hypotheses, or effect prediction.

Creswell (1994) provides the following checklist for designing an experiment.

- Who are the subjects in the study? To what populations do these subjects belong?

- How were the subjects selected? Was a random selection method used?

- How will the subjects be randomly assigned? Will they be matched? How?

- What is the dependent variable(s) in the study? How will it be measured? How many times will it be measured?

- What is the treatment condition(s)? How was it operationalized?

- Will covariation of variables be used in the experiment? How will they be measured?

- What experimental research design will be used? What would a visual model of this design look like?

- What instrument(s) will be used to measure the outcome in the study? Why was it chosen? Who developed it? Does it have established validity and reliability? Has permission been sought to use it? Has the author requested a fee for use of the instrument?

- What are the steps in the procedure (e.g., random assignment of subjects to groups, collection of demographic information, administration of pretest, administration of treatment(s), administration of post test)?

- What are potential threats to internal and external validity for the experimental design and procedure? How will they be addressed?

- Will a pilot test of the experiment be conducted?

- What statistics will be used to analyze the data (e.g., descriptive and multivariate)?

Additionally, Sommer and Sommer (1986) have identified important considerations relative to design issues in an experiment. Many are similar to the ideas expressed by Creswell (1994). Of particular importance in both lists are questions related to the rationale and development of the research problem.

A. Design considerations, preliminary to performing the experiment
   1. Is the rationale of the research question spelled out and are the hypothesis clearly stated?
   2. Are the independent and dependent variables specified and operationally defined in a logically justifiable manner?
   3. Does the research design control for:
      a. Subject error?
      b. Experimenter error?
      c. Environmental error, including apparatus, setting, time of the day, and so on?
   4. Is the subject sample representative of the population of concern?
   5. Have you met local requirements concerning the use of human (or animal) subjects?

B. Pilot test (trial experiment)
   1. Are directions clearly understood?
   2. Does the apparatus work correctly?
   3. Is the experimenter performing correctly?

C. Correct any anticipated problems. If they are extensive, do a second pilot test and, upon satisfactory completion, proceed with the experiment.

D. On completion, debrief participants and thank them for their cooperation. Answer any questions and explain where and when the results will be available.

INTERNAL AND EXTERNAL VALIDITY IN EXPERIMENTAL DESIGNS

The test of internal validity asks the question, did the experimental treatments in fact make a difference *in this specific instance?* The test of external validity asks the question, to what populations, settings, treatment variables, and measurement variables can this effect be generalized? The selection of designs that stand up to both validity tests is obviously the ideal. Internal validity issues will be highlighted in relation to each of the following research designs.

The following classes of extraneous variables, if not controlled for in the experimental design, may produce effects that confound the effect of the experimental variable(s) (i.e., compromise internal validity):

1. *History*— Specific events occurring during the research that affect the results.
2. *Maturation*— An effect is due to natural changes in the subjects (older, wiser, weaker, more tired, etc.).
3. *Testing*— Testing may have effects upon the scores of subsequent testing.
4. *Instrumentation*— Changes in obtained measurement result from changes in the instrument or changes in the observers.
5. *Statistical Regression*— This phenomenon occurs when groups have been selected on the basis of extreme scores (high or low).
6. *Selection*— Biases resulting from the difference in subjects between groups may result in outcomes that are different.
7. *Mortality*— This involves the differential loss of subjects from the comparison groups.
8. *Diffusion of Treatment*— Subjects in one group learn about conditions in another group.
9. *Statistical Conclusion*— Assumptions are violated or statistics are misused.
10. *Experimental Bias*— The researcher is responsible for deliberate or unintended effects on subject responses.

External validity (representativeness) is jeopardized by the following four factors:

1. *Interaction* effects between *Selection* biases and the experimental variable.
2. *Reaction* or *Interaction* effects of *Pretesting*— The pretesting modifies the subject in such a way that he or she responds to the experimental treatment differently than will persons in the same population who are not pretested.

3. *Reactive* effects of experimental procedures— Effects arise from the experimental setting that will not occur in non-experimental settings.
4. *Multiple-Treatment Interference*— Effects are due to multiple treatments applied to the same subjects, where prior treatments influence subsequent treatments in the series because their effects are not erasable.

EXAMPLES OF EXPERIMENTAL RESEARCH DESIGNS

Most research methods books utilize a notation system to signify randomization of subjects, pretests, treatments (experiments), and the post-test. The following notation applies to the designs discussed below.

T^1 = Pretest
T^2 = Post-test
R = Randomly selected/assigned
X = Treatment of subjects (independent variable)

Pre-Experimental Designs

The following designs are referred to as pre-experimental designs because they lack control of internal validity which characterizes true experimental research designs. However, given appropriate circumstances, when acceptable theories form the basis for the work, or when other data exist, the threat to internal validity may not be of significance.

Research Design with No Control: One-Group Post-test Only Design

A typical example of this study design would be as follows: Expose youth-at-risk subjects to a series of after-school basketball programs to determine whether or not leisure activities deter delinquent behaviors. A post-test is administered to measure attitudes and behaviors after exposure to the leisure programs. This design may be of use in the exploration of problems and issues or the development of ideas in action or evaluation research. A major disadvantage, obviously, is that there is no control and no internal validity in this design. By not having a control group, we are not able to make meaningful comparisons except through intuition. Basic to research is the process of securing scientific evidence for comparative purposes. The design is as follows:

Treatment	Post-test
X	T_2

Research Design with Minimal Control: The One-Group Pretest/Post-test Study

The one-group pre- and post-test design is a type of experiment where a single group has (1) a pre-experimental evaluation, (2) exposure to the influence of the variable, and (3) a postexperimental evaluation. This method differs from the one-group post-test method in one way: the addition of a pretest. An advantage of this test is that the pretest provides a comparison of the performance by the same group of subjects before and after exposure to X (the experimental treatment). It also provides a control for selection and mortality variables if the same subjects take T^1 and T^2.

Unfortunately, there are many threats to the validity of the study. Primarily, there is no assurance that the difference between T^1 and T^2 is due to X and not some other factor. There are five other possible sources of error in this test. Selection bias and mortality are of concern in that if the subjects did not take both T^1 and T^2, the differences may be due to other factors. Maturation (growing older, tired, less attentive, etc.) of subjects may also be a problem if there is a considerable amount of time between pre- and post-tests. Testing effects may increase or decrease motivation, or change attitudes toward the issue. Any changes in the test or instrument will also change the T^1 and T^2 results.

Finally, statistical regression may be a problem if an extreme group is selected. For example, suppose a leisure researcher selected a group of youth who are labeled at-risk by the local authorities. These children, many of whom have little or no access to leisure resources at home or the local parks, are given a pretest of their concept of free time using the Caldwell, Smith, and Weissinger (1992) leisure experience battery. A leisure counseling process is used on the group. Finally, a post test evaluation suggests that there were positive changes in their personal concept of free time. It is possible that the counseling did have an effect; however, it is also possible that the nature of the sample (no leisure resources available) created a simple regression of low pretest and higher post-test scores.

The one-group pretest-post-test study design is as follows:

Pretest	Treatment	Post Test
T_1	X	T_2

Threats to Internal Validity of Pre-Experimental Designs

ITEMS	One-group post test only	One-group post test only with pretest-post test groups	Nonequivalent
History	-	-	?
Selection	-	NA	-
Statistical Regression	-	-	+
Testing	NA	-	NA
Instrumentation	NA	-	-
Mortality	-	-	-

Threats to Internal Validity of Pre-Experimental Designs Cont.

ITEMS	One-group post test only	One-group post test only with pretest-post test groups	Nonequivalent
Maturation	-	-	?
Diffusion of Treatment	NA	NA	?
Experimenter Bias	?	?	?
Statistical Conclusion	NA	?	?

In the table a minus sign means a definite weakness, a plus sign means that the factor is controlled, a question mark means a possible source of invalidity, and NA indicates that the threat is not applicable to this design (and is also, then, not a factor). (Based on Leedy, 1985; McMillan & Schumacher, 1984; Isaac & Michael, 1985).

Quasi-Experimental Designs

True experimental designs provide the strongest arguments for causal effects of the independent variable because of the incoherent control and ability to explain or account for extraneous factors. However, in leisure research there are many instances when experimental research is not possible, yet causal inference is desired. The purpose of the quasi-experimental design is to approximate the conditions of the true experiment. However, the researcher must be familiar with the compromises that exist in terms of the internal and external validity of the design and proceed within these limitations in mind. The research is characterized by methods of partial control of the study. The steps used in quasi-experimental methods are essentially the same as in true experimental methods.

McMillan and Schumacher (1984) provide guidelines in the assessment of the quality of quasi-experimental designs.

1. Was the research design described in detail sufficient to allow for replication of the study?

2. Was a true experiment possible?
3. Was it clear how extraneous variables were controlled or ruled out as plausible rival hypotheses?
4. Were all potential threats to internal validity addressed?
5. Were the explanations ruling out plausible rival hypotheses reasonable?
6. Would a different quasi-design have been better?
7. Did the design approach a true experiment as closely as possible?
8. Was there an appropriate balance between control for internal validity and for external validity?
9. Was every effort made to use groups that were as equivalent as possible?
10. If a time series design was used, was there an adequate number of observations to suggest a pattern of results? Was the treatment intervention introduced distinctly at one point in time? Was the measurement of the dependent variable consistent? Was it clear, if a comparison group was used, how equivalent the groups were?

The following are examples of quasi-experimental methods.

Nonequivalent Pretest-Post Test Control Group Design

This design is very useful in leisure services settings. The researcher administers a pretest to an already organized group, administers the treatment, and then gives a post test. Only one group receives the treatment; the other group is the control. The issue of selection bias as an internal validity problem is very real. There are a number of variations of this design. Suppose, for example, that a researcher has two or more groups of children with different camp leaders. The researcher is interested in testing various leadership models on students' perception of leisure satisfaction while at camp. Obviously, it is impossible to randomize the entire group, so the researcher gives a different treatment (group leadership model) to each of the groups. A pretest is given, followed by the treatment and then a post test. Interpretation of the results is difficult in that it depends on whether the groups differed on some characteristic related to the independent variable. Therefore, comparisons of age, sex, size of group, etc.are necessary. Maturation and statistical regression variables are also potential validity problems. The design is illustrated below.

Group	Pretest	Treatment	Post test
A	T_1	X	T_2
B	T_1		T_2

Single Group Interrupted Time Series Design

Time series experiments consist of taking a series of evaluations and then introducing a variable or a new treatment or condition into the system, after which a new series of evaluations are made. If a substantial change occurs in the second series of evaluations, we may assume with reasonable confidence that the changes observed were due to the treatment. The design is as follows:

Pretest	Treatment	Post test
$T_1T_2T_3$	X	$T_4T_5T_6$

The weakness of this design is that an extraneous event may be introduced along with the pretest evaluations, test, or post test evaluations. Obviously, history is the most serious threat to validity due to changes in circumstances and subjects.

Control Group Time Series Design

Version 1 of this design is essentially the same as the uninterrupted design above; however, to control for the effects of maturation, pretesting, and statistical regression, a number of groups are pretested simultaneously but post tested at different times (of equal increments). In version 2, a control group is added, to control for history.

Version 1

Version 2

Group	Pretest	Treatment	Post test
Experimental	T_1	X	T
Control	T_1		T_2

Single-Subject Designs

Studies involving one person or group are referred to as single-subject designs, and have a sample size of one. The approach is to study an individual in a non-treatment condition, and then in a treatment condition, with performance on the dependent variable measured continually in both conditions. Single-subject designs differ from case studies in that procedures are used to control extraneous variables to allow for reasonable causal inferences.

Many observations of behavior are used for collecting data in a standardized fashion (time and location, use of trained observers, etc.) in order to ensure reliability of data. Single aspects of behavior are measured many times in the same way (repeated measurement). Precise, detailed descriptions of the conditions before, during, and after the study are recorded. Baseline data are recorded for comparison, and only one variable is manipulated to be able to assess any changes due to the treatment. If more than one factor were manipulated, the researcher would not be sure which factor caused the change.

Two types of this design are presented. Version 1 has weak validity in that factors such as testing and history are not well accounted for. However, version 2 allows strong causal inference if the pattern of behavior changes during the treatment and returns to about the same as it was prior to treatment. The following additional notation is used: A= baseline condition; B= treatment condition.

Version 1: AB Design

Baseline Data A									Treatment Data B			
				Intervention								
									X	X	X	X
T1	T2	T3	T4	T5	T6	T7	T8	T9	T10			

Version 2: ABA Design

Baseline Data A					Treatment Data B					Baseline Data A				
						X	X	X	X					
T1	T2	T3	T4	T5	T6	T7	T8	T9	T10	T11	T12	T13	T14	T15

Threats to Internal Validity of Quasi-Experimental Design

ITEMS	Nonequivalent pretest-post test control group design	single group interrupted time series	Control group interrupted time series
History	?	-	+
Selection	-	?	?
Statistical Regression	?	+	+
Testing	+	?	+
Instrumentation	?	?	?
Mortality	?	?	?
Diffusion of Treatment	?	NA	?
Experimental Bias	?	+	?
Statistical Conclusion	?	?	?

In this table a minus sign means a definite weakness, a plus sign means that the factor is controlled, a question mark means a possible source of invalidity, and NA indicates that the threat is not applicable to this design (and is also, then, not a factor). (Based on Leedy, 1985; McMillan & Schumacher, 1984; Isaac & Michael, 1985).

True Experimental Designs

Most definitions of true experimental designs specify that procedures are taken that rule out inter-subject differences through randomization of the selection of subjects and assignment to groups, and manipulation of the treatment variable is included. The purpose of true experimental design methods is to investigate cause-and-effect relationships by exposing one or more experimental groups to one or more treatment conditions and comparing the results to one or more control groups not receiving the treatment (Isaac & Michael, 1985). The procedures for research using experimental designs are essentially the same as explained earlier in the book.

McMillan and Schumacher (1984) provide guidelines in the assessment of the quality of true experimental designs.

1. Was the research design described in sufficient detail to allow for replication of the study?
2. Was it clear how statistical equivalence of the groups was achieved? Was there a full description of the specific manner in which subjects were randomly assigned to groups?
3. Was a true experimental design appropriate for the research problem?
4. Was there manipulation of the independent variable?
5. Was there maximum control over extraneous variables and errors of measurement?
6. Was the treatment condition sufficiently different from the comparison condition for a differential effect on the dependent variables to be expected?
7. Were potential threats to internal validity reasonably ruled out or noted and discussed?
8. Was the time frame of the study described?
9. Was the design able to avoid being too artificial or restricted for adequate external validity?
10. Was an appropriate balance achieved between control of variables and natural conditions?
11. Were appropriate tests of inferential statistics used?

The following are the primary methods used in true experimental designs.

Randomized Pretest-Post Test Control Group Design

Following random selection of subjects and random assignment to either the experimental or control group, pretests are administered. Two experimental groups can also be used in this design, allowing for the testing of two methods/treatments (version 2). The treatment condition is introduced to the experimental group, and a follow-up post test given to each group. Groups are compared on the post test score to determine if the treatment had an effect. Essentially, the changes in mean scores on the pretests and post tests are examined.

Version 1

	Pretest	Treatment	Post test
Experimental Group (randomly assigned)	T_1	X	T_2
Control Group (randomly assigned)	T_1		T_2

Version 2

	Pretest	Treatment	Post test
Experimental Group#1 (randomly assigned)	T_1	X_a	T_2
Experimental Group #2 (randomly assigned)	T_1	X_b	T_2
Control Group (randomly assigned)	T_1		T_2

The Soloman four-group design is seldom used, but provides a good illustration of a way to test for the control and measurement of the main effects of pretesting and the interaction between pretests and experimental treatments. This design amounts to doing the experiment twice. If the two experiments produce consistent measurements, greater confidence can be placed in the findings. The model is illustrated below.

	Pretest	Treatment	Post test
Pretest Group#1 (randomly assigned)	T_1	X	T_2
Pretest Group #2 (randomly assigned)	T_1		T_2
No Pretest Group 1 (randomly assigned)		X	T_2
No Pretest Group 2 (randomly assigned)			T_2

Randomized Control Group Post Test Only Design

In this design, subjects are randomly assigned to either the control or experimental group. The researcher omits the pretest based on the notion that at the time of assignment the groups were equal. There is no interaction effect between the pretest and treatment. One group is exposed to leisure counseling, for example, and post tests are given to determine each groups' concept of free time. The design controls for but does not measure effects of history, maturation, and pretesting. This design, shown below, is useful when pretests are unavailable or too expensive to administer.

	Pretest	Treatment	Post test
Experimental Group (randomly assigned)		X	T_2
Control Group (randomly assigned)			T_2

Threats to Internal Validity of True Experimental Designs

ITEMS	Pretest-post test control group	Post test-only control group
History	?	?
Selection	+	+
Statistical Regression	+	NA
Testing	+	NA
Instrumentation	?	?
Mortality	?	?
Maturation	+	+
Diffusion of Treatment	?	?
Experimenter Bias	?	?
Statistical Conclusion	?	?

In this table a minus sign means a definite weakness, a plus sign means that the factor is controlled, a question mark means a possible source of invalidity, and NA indicates that the threat is not applicable to this design (and is also, then, not a factor). (Based on Leedy, 1985; McMillan & Schumacher, 1984; Isaac & Michael, 1985).

CONCLUSION

A research design is the process or method that will guide the investigator in the process of collecting, analyzing, and interpreting findings. Two types of research designs were presented: experimental and quasi-experimental. Experimental research deals with cause and effect. It involves the creation of an artificial situation in which events are manipulated. In a classical experimental sense, four components are present: comparison, manipulation, control, and generalization. Subjects are randomly assigned to treatment groups and a control group. Experimental designs are thought to provide the strongest evidence of proof. In a quasi-experimental design, subjects are not randomly assigned to conditions, but rather studied as the conditions occur naturally.

A number of internal and external threats to validity in experimental and quasi-experimental designs were noted. Traditionally, one group posttests (one shot case study) were used when experimentation was not possible. These studies are the weakest relative to the lack of control for internal and external validity. Quasi-experimental are weaker than experimental designs in terms of internal and external validity, yet can be controlled through the statistical application process. Quasi-experimental designs involve pre- and post-testing, which is very useful in leisure research. Strengths and weaknesses were noted for each of the designs presented. Importantly, in any study, randomization with careful control and considerations for external and internal validity will produce useful and meaningful research.

Chapter Five

Leisure and Survey Research

INTRODUCTION

In the preceding chapters we have provided an overview of the experimental methods that can be employed in leisure research. These methods offer the opportunity for doing basic research and increasing our understanding why people need recreation and how people enjoy recreation with respect to a variety of social and cultural variables. There is, however, another aspect of recreation research that is related to questions of decision making and planning. These aspects refer to the more fundamental aspects of the recreation industry and recreation practice. These decisions that professionals have to make are often quite pragmatic and the decision makers might not have the resources to conduct the experimental studies. In such situations practitioners can use well-tested evaluation and survey procedures to collect relevant data. The issues presented in the earlier chapters provide much of the foundation for the discussions that follow here. It is therefore critical for the reader to be able to understand the experimental methods before tackling the evaluation practices. It is also fair to remind the reader that there will be occasional repetition of the ideas presented in the earlier section since the survey method employs principles similar to the experimental methods. The evaluation method is geared toward gaining a good estimate of the attitudes, behaviors and attributes of the people who recreate and who are served by recreation agencies.

In the past several decades it has become increasingly important to know how the people in a particular constituency feel about a large range of issues. Groups from policymakers to political activists have recognized the need to have a clear understanding of the reactions of the "population" to a particular issue, product, candidate, or public or private service. There is an increasing dependency on data obtained through the process of public opinion polling. In many cases, the data are collected in ways that do not ultimately support the purpose of the research and consequently are not the best representation of the feelings of a specific group of people.

In the case of leisure and recreation, it is particularly important that the service providers have a clear understanding of the various attitudes and opinions of the people whom they are attempting to serve (Bannon, 1985). Private providers of recreation opportunities spend huge amounts of resources regularly in assessing the "market" for the service and then tailoring the service to that market. The same applies to local agencies, such as parks and recreation departments, which provide community-wide leisure and recreation services. To be effective, the administrators of such organizations must be able to design public opinion polls and become intelligent "consumers" of the poll results.

In many cases, lack of time and resources prevents leisure providers from conducting in-house polls extensively enough to provide community-level information. Occasional "user studies" conducted at specific facilities provide information about the people who use the services and resources but do not provide in-depth information about the entire community. However, it is extremely important for leisure providers to have such information for the purposes of short- and long-range planning. In many instances, service providers employ independent survey organizations to conduct community-level opinion polls. National organizations such as Management Learning Laboratories conduct polls specifically designed for assessing the leisure and recreation needs of a community. However, the service provider needs to be conversant in the specific aspects of a public opinion poll to be able to use the results effectively as well as critique the work provided by independent agencies.

This chapter lays out some of the fundamental aspects of the public opinion polling process, describing the history of this research trajectory, the various kinds of research, and the differences between public opinion polling and experimental research. Finally, the guiding principles of public opinion polling are discussed with particular reference to the field of leisure and recreation.

HISTORY OF THE FIELD

The period following the Second World War saw increasing interest in the study of the attitudes and opinions of large groups of people in order to better understand the reasons people behaved in specific ways. The effects of propaganda observed in Europe during the war motivated much of this research. There was an increasing recognition that human attitudes control behavior, and if it is possible to change attitudes, then it is also possible to control human behavior. This recognition laid the groundwork for attitude and opinion surveys.

Simultaneously, there was an increasing acknowledgment of the socio-scientific and psychological approach to the study of human behavior. This approach assumes that not only does attitude control behavior, but it is also possible to quantify human opinion, attitude, behavior, and beliefs and use the numbers as reliable and valid indicators of a person's opinions (Krathwohl, 1985). The work by expatriate European scholars such as Lazarsfeld established this socio-scientific, quantitative approach to the study of human behavior.

Along with the developments in the study of human behavior, there was an increasing awareness of the applications of statistical analysis to modeling and forecasting attitudes and opinions. This was the period when several innovative scales for the quantification of human opinions, attitudes, and beliefs were developed. Scales such as the Thurstone scale, the Likert scale, and Osgood's semantic differential scales were being tested and developed in response to the increasing need to develop measurement tools and the analytical sophistication to be able to accurately quantify attributes of human behavior (Moser & Kalton, 1972).

The effort to develop better methodology for the assessment of opinions and behavior got a boost with the establishment in 1945 of the American Association for Public Opinion Research (AAPOR), which became the forum for presentations and discussions about survey methodology. Set up as an interdisciplinary forum, AAPOR represented people from various fields who were all interested in exploring better ways of conducting human opinion research. This was accompanied and followed by the establishment of institutions devoted to the development of survey methodology with concentration on specific areas of survey research, such as sampling, questionnaire development, data collection methods, and data analysis. These methodological findings were adopted by the survey industry and applied to various substantive areas of public opinion polling. Thus, federal agencies such as the U.S. Census Bureau and private organizations such as Nielsen and Gallup began to use the methodological findings in their research.

Along with the need to assess general opinion, there was an increasing interest in assessing of the effectiveness of specific areas of public and private policy adaptation and development. This was most important in the area of educational research in the United States. With the development of specific innovations in the field of public education, there was a need to evaluate the effectiveness of the programs (Rossi, Freeman, & Wright, 1980). Specific tools had to be developed that could be repetitively applied to assess the ways in which specific educational methodologies were affecting students. The same principle was then applied to determine the effectiveness of a variety of programs and policies such as welfare and social security. This development of evaluation research led to the creation of the American Evaluation Association (AEA).

The evaluation emphasis was accompanied by research with emphasis on the assessment of the specific needs of target populations, such as the American disabled population. Results of the needs assessment could then be used in the development of policies and programs to fulfill unmet needs or the continuation of programs identified as meeting the needs of the population. With the increasing diversification of the American population, this research is becoming more important as different constituencies have different needs and often require different strategies.

In its current form, public opinion research has a variety of objectives. The goals of survey research include purely the methodological objectives of institutions such as the Survey Research Laboratory of the University of Illinois, or the more substantively focused goals of organizations such as the Management Learning Laboratories of Winston-Salem, North Carolina, which only conducts leisure and recreation needs assessments. These different objectives indicate the different emphases of research that have evolved over time, including methodological research on one hand and substantive research on the other.

The various directions of research have spawned different ways of conducting the research. There is the focus of basic research, where fundamental questions are addressed, and applied research, where the findings of basic research are used to investigate specific policy questions and programs. These two kinds of research were discussed in Chapter 1 to introduce the primary modes of doing research. It is now necessary to place the two kinds of research in the context of survey research and needs assessment. The next section elaborates on the similarities and differences between the two kinds of research, particularly from the perspective of the survey approach.

BASIC RESEARCH

The primary purpose of basic research is to investigate fundamental questions about ways of doing research, for example, about the way public opinion can be measured and interpreted. Within basic research in public opinion, there are two primary directions, the *methodological* perspective and the *substantive* emphasis. These two perspectives complement and support each other. In the specific area of leisure and recreation assessment, basic research has addressed questions of the ways in which leisure is conceptualized as well as changes in the perception of leisure and recreation. There has been little emphasis on methodology, which has been amply addressed by survey and public opinion research. This chapter considers the primary trajectories of basic methodological research.

Basic methodological research often starts with the question, what is the best way of finding out what needs to be known? This is indeed a question of method, since it is obvious that the quality and reliability of any data are only as good as the way in which the data were obtained. If the data collection method is flawed, the data becomes suspect and decisions made on the basis of the data may be misleading. However, data collection covers a lot of different aspects, and methodological research attempts to address all the different aspects of the data collection process.

Basic methodological research begins with questions of survey design with different refinements of the fundamental design proposed and tested. One-shot case studies of a sample of the population have been modified to include more elaborate designs that provide in-depth information that is time sensitive. This involves the notion of longitudinal research, where the opinions and behaviors of a group of people are tracked over a long period of time. This design can be of particular interest to the leisure and recreation provider since it is safe to anticipate time-dependent changes in the recreation needs of a constituency.

Basic research has paid a great deal of attention to selecting and reaching a representative sample. Since the purpose of most opinion studies is to estimate the attitudes of a population based on the responses from a small group, it is necessary to have a reliable and efficient sampling scheme that produces a sample representative of the population. Borrowing from basic research in statistics and probability, the researchers conducting basic methodological work have developed sophisticated sampling techniques to reach a variety of populations. With the increasing diversification of the American population, it is becoming necessary to reach a lot of different groups of people, some of which are difficult to locate. These problems arise in the case of leisure and recreation studies as it is becoming clear that people of different ethnicities, income levels, and ages have varying leisure and recreation needs. Consequently, it is necessary to be able to find representative samples of these populations. Basic sampling research has been able to devise such methods. Beyond the fundamental and ever-popular method of random sampling, sampling schemes include targeted sampling, network sampling, and sophisticated means of telephone random-digit dialing (RDD). Thus, one aspect of basic research has been the development of sampling solutions that can be applied to special circumstances.

A second area of basic research has been the development of efficient data collection procedures. In most attitude and opinion surveys, data collection involves the use of a questionnaire. The self-response questionnaire may be the only form of contact between the respondent and the researcher. On other occasions the researcher reaches the respondent through the mediation of an interviewer, who either calls the subject on the phone or visits the respondent in a face-to-face interview. In either case, there is the need to develop an effective questionnaire, and basic research has paid a great deal of attention to the development of an effective instrument of data collection.

There has also been a great deal of research to determine the ways in which the modus operandi of data collection can be refined. A significant amount of research energy (and dollars) has been spent in investigating which of the three major methods of data collection in the Unites States—phone, mail, and face-to-face meetings—is the best method, and how a mix of methods can lead to an increased response rate.

Finally, basic research has developed new forms of data analysis, where the sophisticated techniques of statistical computation have been mobilized to make the most sense of the data collected. With the increasing sophistication of study design there is a need to better analyze the data so that all the intricacies of the data can be unraveled. Particularly in the case of longitudinal surveys and in forecasting work analysis, such as path analysis, modeling and other tools of mathematics have been used to interpret the data that have been collected. This research has borrowed from a variety of traditions including statistics, mathematics, and in some cases biology and biostatistics.

The strength of basic research has been the development of methodology. Scientists were quick to realize that the policy decisions and answers to critical questions that were found through attitude and opinion research were only as good as the methodology used in collecting and analyzing the data. Weak or inappropriate methods of doing research often lead to flawed conclusions that can lead to significant costs later in the life of a program or campaign. Even in the most sophisticated research, there is always the possibility of errors arising from unforeseen circumstances (such as unexpected sampling problems, low response rate due to factors out of the researcher's control, and other issues that threaten to the validity and reliability of the method). Consequently, survey methodologists have stressed the need to properly design and plan the execution of a survey. In most cases, the findings of such methodological work are published and supplied to the public domain for further exploration and possible use in applied research. Indeed, the primary relationship between basic research and applied research is the way in which the applied researcher uses the findings from basic research to improve the quality of the research that has specific applications in different fields. While the methods are the same, the strength of applied research lies in the process of adaptation. As the next section explains, applied research has taken a variety of forms and has been conducted in different fields that have all borrowed from basic research and from each other to produce the most reliable and valid data possible.

APPLIED RESEARCH

A discussion of applied research is best organized around the specific areas where the findings from basic research have been extensively applied. The initial stages of the research may not necessarily distinguish between applied and basic research. The opinion polls conducted to study the voting behavior of Erie County, Pennsylvania, residents, for example, involved both applied and basic research. The application was predicting how the people would vote in the upcoming gubernatorial election. At the same time, specific research methods were applied to gain the most reliable data.

The application of survey research to study the opinions of people with respect to voting behavior and political attitudes has been a key application of the methods of survey research. Indeed, in the 90s, political polls have become a persistent fact of life in the United States. Political pollers use the techniques of telephone interviewing developed in places such as the Survey Research Laboratory of the University of Illinois to reap sizable profits as they continue to measure the political climate. This has been an area of applied research that has thrived and, if the current state of affairs is any indication, shall continue to thrive for years to come.

A second traditional area of applied research has been the counting of the American population. Once every decade the U.S. Census Bureau has the formidable task of producing a count of the population along with a detailed breakdown in terms of numerous demographic categories such as age, race, income, household composition, and marital status. This task has become increasingly difficult and often politicized (and open to political attack) because the findings of the census have far-reaching political implications in the redesign of voting zones and districts.

Additionally, the U.S. Census Bureau has to remain current with developments in new sampling techniques (indeed, the Bureau has a staff of excellent statisticians who continue to do basic research, and it funds basic research at academic research laboratories), and better methods of data collection and analysis.

Often, the Bureau has accessed the findings from the public domain to improve its own operations. For example, the Bureau came under significant attack following the 1990 count for undercounting hard-to-reach and transient populations, such as the homeless. It was evident that some of the methods used in sampling the homeless were inadequate. Consequently, for the year 2000 survey, the Bureau will be using methods of counting the homeless that were partly developed by the Survey Research Laboratory of the University of Illinois (see Johnson, Mitra, Newman, & Horm, 1993). This is an example of the ways in which an applied research institution such as the U.S. Census Bureau turns to basic research to improve its efforts.

Another set of agencies have the equally difficult task of providing ongoing counts of the media users in the country. Given the fact that American media depends on advertising revenue for its operations and profits, it is important for the media institutions to be able to count the number of people who are attending to their programming. In a competitive environment with an increasing amount of choice for consumers, there is a great need for accurate estimates of the total number of people tuning into a particular program. This number eventually translates to dollars, as blocks of audiences are "sold" to advertisers, and the media producer who can sell the largest audience block often has the most leverage with advertisers. Given this relationship, there has been growth and increasing sophistication in rating research, which is similar to the research conducted by the U.S. Census Bureau but is done much more frequently and with a far smaller sample.

Many different methods have been employed to gauge how many people are watching a program (as opposed to simply keeping the television on a particular channel) as well as the reactions of people to specific kinds of programming. The industry leaders in this area are the Nielsen and Gallup groups, who have been doing this kind of research for years. In fact, the Nielsen group has begun to diversify to other kinds of media use. In 1995 the Nielsen group reported their findings about the level of usage of the Internet. Using methods similar to those in their media rating research, the group was able to provide estimates that were considered to be more reliable than previous research in that area.

While groups such as Nielsen provide information about the number of people watching television (or using the Internet), they do not necessarily address the effects of media behavior in terms of people's purchasing habits, preferences, and trends. A large amount of applied survey research has been conducted in the area of market analysis to determine consumer preferences as well as to gauge the purchasing behavior of the American consumer. These kinds of surveys often provide insights into how to improve the services of a specific industry. It is now common to see short questionnaires at fast food restaurants eliciting consumer opinions about the establishment or the service. Similar surveys often accompany warranty cards, included with the purchase of household gadgets and appliances. Automobile dealerships often use techniques such as telephone follow-up to gauge the reaction of the consumer. The entire industry of telemarketing and telephone surveys for consumer products rests on the findings from basic research about the best ways of conducting population opinion polls.

Two other areas of applied research merit mention. Often research is conducted not for profit but for the design of public policy and programs (arguably, the U.S. Census Bureau does the same, but their research's use in profit generation is widespread based on the demographic maps that they are able to generate). With the development of innovative educational programs after the war, there was an increasing need to measure the effectiveness of the new programs. Consequently, there was a need to develop methods or identify existing designs and methods that would provide a way to analyze the efficacy of educational programs. This led to the growth of applied research in evaluation.

The primary goal of evaluation research is to measure the effectiveness of specific interventions in public programs. Thus, if a new textbook is adopted, it is necessary to evaluate the effects of the implementation. The greatest obstacle to this research is defining the criteria or measures of effectiveness. Often, attitudes and opinions are used for these measures. In other cases, changes in learning are used as the measure of effectiveness. In any case, it is necessary to adopt correct sampling procedures and methods of data collection. Basic research in survey methodology has provided insights in this direction, and evaluators often turn to survey researchers to provide the expertise necessary to develop the proper methodologies so that the appropriate attributes are evaluated.

Along with evaluation research, there has been development of the area of needs assessment. Here the goal is to assess the needs of a particular community with respect to a particular issue. Once it is possible to estimate needs of the community, it is possible to develop the programs necessary to address those needs. This form of research is gaining in popularity because limited resources make it necessary to develop programs that address the needs of the community. While the aim of this research is to gain information about the future needs of the community, the methods of composing the questionnaire and data collection are not much different from many of the other types of research methods discussed here. Here, too, the contributions of basic research are significant.

The attitude and opinion survey in leisure and recreation is yet another area of applied research. These surveys induce co-opting of all the sources mentioned above. Basic research offers the rationale and fundamental principles for leisure-related surveys, but the types of applied research discussed here also inform leisure research. In most cases, leisure research places a lot of emphasis on the opinions of the community served. Consequently, there is dependence on the methods of asking opinion questions. There is also a need for enumeration and description of demographics, similar to what the Census Bureau does. Very often, the findings from the leisure surveys are compared against the "standard" census information to verify the authenticity of the data collected. Also, similar to rating research, community leisure research attempts to develop estimates of the usage of facilities and services. Consequently, questions that arise in rating research often come up in leisure research as well.

Perhaps the two areas of applied research that have had the most impact on leisure-related research are evaluation research and needs assessment. Leisure departments are often interested in evaluating the effectiveness of their programs and services. In such cases, it is possible to apply some of the techniques and principles developed in the area of evaluation research to measure the effectiveness of specific recreation programs. At the same time, there is often a need to assess the future requirements of a community. Leisure research in this respect is closely tied to needs assessment, and the techniques of needs assessment have to be mobilized so that the agency can gain reliable information about the requirements of the community.

Leisure research thus draws upon a variety of traditions of applied research while benefiting from the findings of basic research. However, in spite of the different names and terms associated with leisure research (e.g., needs assessment, program evaluation, attitude and interest studies, community surveys), the fundamental approach is the same. Usually the goal is to obtain information about the attitudes and opinions of respondents with respect to leisure. These opinions may address existing leisure opportunities or future leisure needs. In most cases, the focus on gathering information about attitudes and opinions is supplemented by the collection of other, related information; however, attitudes and opinions remain the foundation of most leisure-related survey research. It is an interdisciplinary effort, and several different types of expertise need to be mobilized to conduct an effective leisure study and interpret the findings of the research. As in any type of well-conducted evaluation research and needs assessment, leisure surveys need to conclude with usable recommendations that constitute action statements useful for the operation of the agency. Given this framework, it is now possible to turn to the specific issues of leisure studies.

THE PURPOSE OF ATTITUDE AND OPINION SURVEYS

Research in social psychology has made it clear that human attitudes and opinions play a crucial role in determining the intention to behave in a particular way, and intention, in turn, largely determines behavior. This relationship is depicted in Figure 1.1. The work of Fishbein (1975) at the University of Illinois, as well as other social psychologists, demonstrates that if it is possible to understand the underlying attitudes and opinions of people about a set of issues, then it is possible to predict the kind of behavior they would participate in. More important, this approach suggests that by knowing the behavior of people, it is possible to make a set of judgments about their attitudes and opinions. Finally, the understanding of attitudes and opinions can lead to strategies by which attitudes can be modified through persuasion to alter behavior in a desired way.

In recent history, the study of attitudes and opinions has led to a large number of public communication campaigns with long-standing benefits. For instance, the relation between attitudes and behavior has made it possible to better understand why people do or do not use seat belts while driving. Studying opinions has also made it possible to devise specific messages aimed at an appropriate audience to encourage the use of seat belts. Statistics show that there has been a considerable amount of success in achieving the goal of increased seat belt use.

While these are relatively intuitive concepts, they are significant for several reasons. First, it is important to note that there is a homogenizing assumption at work here. In other words, it is assumed that people, in general, behave in similar ways. For instance, it is safe to assume that Americans generally have a positive attitude toward playing baseball and enjoying a day at the ballpark with the family. These can be considered common attitudes shared by a population independent of race, gender, age and income. Consequently, by studying parts of the population it is possible to arrive at conclusions about the way the entire population feels. This principle lays the foundation for the sampling assumptions discussed later in this chapter.

However, given the fact that people are not created equal, there are certainly situations where attitudes differ based on social, political, and cultural experiences. Thus, the attitude toward going to the ballpark to watch a game could well depend on the age and income of a person as well as past experiences of going to watch a baseball game. Some people have felt insecure at the ballpark, and some have had consistently good experiences, so their attitudes toward the activity will vary.

Therefore, in some cases, attitudes are not generalizable to a large population, but can only be applied to subsections of

Figure 5.1
Relation between Beliefs, Attitudes and Behavior

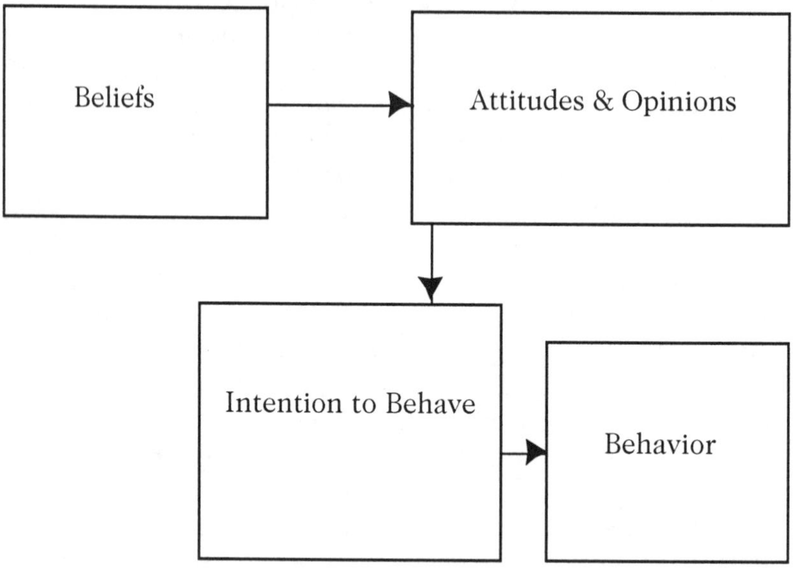

Beliefs → Attitudes & Opinions → Intention to Behave → Behavior

a population based on social, political, and cultural factors. This is often described as *demographics,* which refers to a variety of different allegiances a person has at any point in time. These variables include age, gender, ethnicity, income, and educational level. Some of these are static, such as gender and ethnicity, but others are liable to change, such as income and educational level. It is thus necessary to determine both the attitudes of the people being studied as well as their demographics, since the latter often has a determining role on the former.

There are thus two oppositional forces at work in the shaping of attitudes and opinions. On one hand there are centralizing tendencies where monolithic attitudes, opinions, and beliefs are held by large groups of people; on the other hand, there are decentralizing tendencies that tend to segregate people into different groups with different opinions, beliefs, and attitudes. However, there is always some variation in attitude between members of the same group. Thus, while it may be true that most Americans feel positive about the free market system, it is certainly possible that some feel *more* positive about it than others. In other cases, there might be a polarization of attitudes, where some feel positive about an issue while others would have a negative opinion, and, within these opinions there could be a certain degree of variation. Consequently, it can be assumed that attitudes vary within a population even if the modality is the same.

The combination of knowledge of people's variable attitudes and knowledge of the reason why attitudes vary (most often due to demographics) thus provides valuable information about the pulse of a group of people. Additionally, since attitude does determine behavior, understanding the variation in attitude, and the possible reasons for the variation, can provide useful insights into the way a group of people is feeling at any point in time. Consequently, it is no surprise that before national and local elections, there is a plethora of opinion polls followed carefully by the campaign professionals so that they can remain "on top of" the way the electorate is feeling about a specific candidate. Furthermore, this information becomes the starting point for the development of specific campaign strategies to either change the attitudes of the naysayers, create a positive attitude among the uncommitted, or strengthen the attitude of the supporters. Given the fact that attitudes play a crucial role in ultimate voting behavior, information about public attitudes and opinions is particularly useful for the planners of public campaigns in altering some kind of behavior.

Since knowledge of attitudes is an important forecasting tool, it is useful to the parks and recreation planning staff for several important reasons. First, the planning members in a park and recreation department can use the attitude and opinion information to gauge current feelings about the agency in the community. Information about the likes and dislikes of members of the community can be used productively to pinpoint the areas of discontent and correct the problems, and to identify the areas of satisfaction and ensure that the services eliciting the positive response are maintained and improved. For instance, in one community it was discovered that people were particularly concerned with the fact that an excessive number of nonresidents were using the facilities of the parks and recreation department. There was a negative attitude toward such usage, and this information about attitude assisted the planning department in strategizing to increase the opportunities of the residents to use the facilities. There are thus tangible outcomes of attitude and opinion surveys that play a crucial role in determining the way in which service is provided.

Second, attitude and opinion information provides valuable baseline information that can be used to better predict the needs of the community and translate existing attitudes and opinions to new needs for recreation. If there is a general opinion in the community that there is a lack of facilities for seniors, the astute recreation planner can relate the information with knowledge of the increasing number of elderly people in our communities today and predict that there will be a demand for facilities for older people a few years down the road. This conclusion can in turn translate to initiatives to construct facilities that would surely be less expensive to put up now than a few years hence.

In the case of leisure and recreation studies, the principal purpose of the attitude and opinion surveys is to gain an estimate of the community's opinion about a variety of issues related to leisure and recreation. Since it is impractical to ask every member of a population (consider, for instance, the task that would be faced by the recreation department in a city the size of Chicago or Dallas), it is necessary to use the survey methodology to gain the information that is needed. The outcomes of these surveys are similar to the results of a needs assessment or a program evaluation. In the case of a leisure department, the surveys yield important and useful information about the effectiveness of the service it is trying to provide to the community, as well as give the department a good indication of the needs of the community. Often these surveys are conducted in conjunction with a master plan being developed by an agency.

Collect Community Opinions

In most cases, the purpose of the leisure and recreation survey is to collect the opinions and attitudes of the community with respect to leisure and the facilities of recreation available to the community. The definition of community is critical here, because in most cases city or local taxes, which are paid by all the members living within the taxing zone, fund leisure and recreation departments. This includes people from all age groups with a variety of income distributions and, most important, different leisure and recreation needs and opinions. It is important that the opinions of the entire community be collected as opposed to opinions of specific subgroups of the community who might have specific positive (or negative) feelings about the department.

Thus, leisure and recreation surveys are unlike user surveys where the people using a facility or visiting an establishment are given a questionnaire. While those surveys are important and often provide valuable information, they do not reflect the opinions of the general body of people who are supporting the recreation and leisure department with their tax dollars.

Additionally, in the case of user surveys, an agency might gain comparative information about how a particular facility is being used. However, the fact that the user came to the facility in the first place indicates that he or she is interested in the particular facility or activity and is therefore positively predisposed to the particular activity the facility might provide. In such cases, the need for the facility at the community level often remains unknown. Consequently, a user survey might not expose the fact that the agency is providing a service that few community members have an interest in, and that a handful of community members are the only users of an expensive facility. In such cases, the agency can consider alternative ways of correcting this strain on resources and providing the opportunities in a different way.

It is important to note that the attitude and opinion survey is usually commissioned because of a larger planning need. It is rare that a recreation provider will embark on an expensive survey just for the sake of doing a survey. Most often the surveys are conducted to address an existing problem in a community to help the community plan for the future. In particular, at the end of the century, a large number of agencies are planning for year 2000 and beyond. In such cases, the surveys are commissioned to provide input for the agency. Yet the key point is that the input needs to be community-level input and not just reactions from the users. The community provides the data used to make plans for the future of the agency, which will serve the entire community and not just the regular users of the facilities. A user survey is too restrictive and focused to provide the bigger picture needed to plan for the future. Since specific plans have to be drawn up, it is imperative that all the members of a community get an opportunity to respond to the survey even if they never have used any of the facilities. Even nonusers often provide valuable information. The notion of "use" is a thorny concept, because a person might never visit a recreation center but still passively "uses" a park by driving past it on the way to work. Consequently, it is important to gather the information from all sources so that all members of the community are represented in the survey.

Representativeness of the Survey

Since the leisure and recreation study is implemented to identify the attitudes and opinions of the entire community, it is important that efforts be made to obtain the best representation of the community. This is a contested and often politicized issue. Often, a researcher is confronted with the fact (or belief) that minorities in a community are not represented in a survey conducted by a local agency such as a park and recreation department. The argument is that minorities often "fall through the cracks" of a survey, and their opinions are never heard. In one instance, representatives of the "inner city" of a medium-sized Midwestern city claimed that the opinion of the predominantly African-American community was never attended to by the local recreation provider.

The fundamental assumption of sampling is that every member of the community cannot be reached individually, so an estimate of community opinion must be developed for effective planning. Every member in the community should have an opportunity to be included in the survey. This opportunity to participate can be provided in two ways. In one case, the subgroups of a community are represented based on their proportion in the community. In other words, if there are 5,000 African-Americans in a community of 50,000 people, then 10% of the survey respondents should be African-Americans. Consequently, the opinion of the minority group will receive a relative weight of 10%. This has some far-reaching implications and associated problems. An example will help to illustrate the issue.

If, in a community of 50,000 people, a survey is obtained from 1,000 people, of which 100 are African-Americans and the rest are from the majority group, then for any opinion the "contribution" of the African-American community is only 10%. Thus, it is possible to argue that if there is overwhelming support for the construction of a new recreation facility, it is the overwhelming support of the majority, since the minor contribution of the African-American community becomes lost in the majority opinion. This is particularly true in cases where the minority is geographically concentrated. For example, even if all African-American respondents were to demand a new facility in a specific part of the city, the opinion of the remaining 90% would drown out that opinion.

Consequently, it is sometimes necessary to alter the probability of representation and give particular communities an advantage. In such cases, the part of the town with the minority community is given greater representation so that their voice can be heard. In the example here, the African-American community of 5,000 could contribute up to 500 of the 1,000 respondents, thus making up 50% of the respondents to the survey. This is no longer representative of the community in terms of its aggregate structure or the census proportions, but it provides the community an opportunity to express differing opinions.

Even in designs where there is no over- or under-sampling of specific population segments, it might turn out that the responses are not truly representative of the population. This could happen because of differences in the response rates from different segments of the population. For instance, if a particular ethnic group does not return the surveys at the same rate as another, then the first group would remain under-represented. In a similar way, if far more women respond to a survey than men, there would be an under-representation of men. This would happen despite the fact that the sample was selected in a random fashion. There are sets of statistical procedures that can be applied if such discrepancies are discovered. These procedures, such as "statistical weighting," are discussed later in the book.

In essence, these are questions of sampling, but they refer to issues that are more fundamental, and it is often important to consider them before embarking on a survey. One of the biggest problems with the process of conducting a survey is the inability to produce a design that is representative of the community, which means that any results would not be valid or reliable. These surveys are used to obtain estimates that become the source for making major decisions.

Obtaining Estimates

The aim of the whole process of doing a study is to obtain estimates of the population based on the small group of people surveyed in a community. The process of estimating is dependent on several factors, such as the definition of the goals of the study, appropriate sampling, and obtaining a high response rate. Since the results are estimates, this implies that there is some degree of error in the results. It is impossible to exactly measure the attitude of the entire community without obtaining the responses from all members of the community, and even that would be, at best, a snapshot of the community at a particular moment in time. Consequently, it is important to recognize the kinds of errors that enter into the estimation process as well as understand the statistical significance of the computation of the estimates.

Two principal kinds of errors enter into the computation of estimates. One source of error results from the sampling procedure. This is often called sampling error, and will be discussed in detail in a later chapter. However, it is important to recognize that this error is not due to any mistake in the process of conducting the study. This error is a part of the sampling process and is purely a function of the fact that opinions are being obtained from different subsections of the population. Naturally, if a study is done twice with two different samples, the estimates obtained from the two samples can be expected to be different. However, the critical question is how different. If the difference is too high, for instance, more than 5%, then it is possible to claim that one of the estimates is wrong. The sampling error is the measure of this error and is thus a way of gauging the quality of the sampling process. It is a necessary and unavoidable product of the sampling process and is now recognized as a part of the estimation process.

A second error, which is also often unavoidable and is more difficult to build into the estimate, results from incomplete responses from the sample. Even if it were possible to send a questionnaire to all the members of a community that a recreation department serves, a few people would not respond to the survey or not complete a telephone interview. The results of such a population survey would still be an estimate since there is no good way of inputting the responses of the missing people. There is no way of reducing this error other than encouraging all the members of a population or a sample to respond to the survey. This will be discussed in detail in the chapter on data collection, but it is important to note that this error plagues most surveys, and the results of the survey are not always qualified by the response rate. Needless to say, the estimates obtained in a survey where only 10% of the sample responded are far inferior to those from a study where 70% of the sample responded. It is far more difficult to compute this type of error. Usually, the only recourse is to argue that the percentage that responded is close enough to the demographic composition of the community and can thus be considered representative of the community, so that the estimates can be judged reliable.

Finally, the fact that surveys produce estimates opens up the issue of measuring the significance of the estimates and computing the probability that the estimates represent statistically significant relations. The following example illustrates this fact. Consider a community that is made up of 48% men and 52% women. Based on a survey it is possible to claim that the percentage of men varies between 45% and 51% (assuming a sampling error of plus or minus 3%) and the percentage of women varies between 49% and 55%. Suppose a survey is taken to see if there are any differences between men and women with respect to a particular activity such as aerobics. If it is found from the respondents that the average opinion about aerobics is more favorable among women than men, it is necessary to estimate whether that difference is due to chance and the composition of the sample, or if it actually represents a difference in the population. This is a process of estimation, and it is important to apply the correct statistical tools so that it is possible to claim that the estimate obtained from the sample can be extrapolated to the population.

The process of estimation thus depends on a variety of forces, and all of these forces act together to produce the best estimate. Finally, the process of estimation is also a function of the data analysis, and the data analysis needs to be thought about prior to data collection so that data of the correct kind are collected and remain available for appropriate analysis later.

Planning for Data Analysis

The process of data analysis is the last phase in most research. At this point, the analyst is ready to look at the results and see what the data say about the estimates of proportion, averages, and relations between different elements of the community. However, it is often at this point that the researcher realizes that some critical question was left out or a question was asked in a manner that does not lend itself to the kind of analysis that the researcher was trying to perform. For this reason it is terribly important to pay adequate attention to the kind of analysis the researcher should conduct prior to embarking on it. It is true that the results from a preliminary analysis sometimes indicate the direction of further research, but that does not mean that some analytic directions cannot be thought out ahead of time. This is the process of planning for the data analysis.

A key aspect of this planning is the development of the correct scales for the questions being asked. As discussed in Chapter 3, there are several different kinds of scales that can be used to measure attitudes, opinions, behaviors, and demographics. These different scales, the nominal, ordinal, interval, and ratio scales, offer different computational strengths. The scales on the lower rung often disallow the possibility of complex manipulations, while the higher-level scales can become too complicated for the measurement of simple attributes. Consequently, it is necessary to pay attention to the kind of analysis that might be performed on a particular question and devise the scale appropriately. Sometimes researchers create scales for ease and convenience in asking the question and then realize that the particular scale does not offer the opportunity for more complex analysis.

A second issue is also connected with the complexity of the questionnaire. It is necessary to attend to the design of the questionnaire and think about future analysis, which might call for data that might not have been collected at all. In such cases, there are no simple options because a piece of information necessary for the appropriate data analysis and estimation is not available. In some cases, though, the data can be approximated from questions that ask about similar concepts.

For instance, sometimes recreation agency administrators are interested in analyzing the interest in specific recreation activities based on length of residence in the community. However, if this analytical issue is not considered early in the design and planning process and the "length of residence" question is not asked, it will be impossible to do the analysis that is called for later. It may be possible to gain the information based on a related question, such as the age of respondents, by applying a standard formula to it, but that would undoubtedly be unreliable and inadequate. Consequently, it is extremely important that all questions be asked in the questionnaire so that appropriate data analysis can be conducted later.

Finally, the planning for data analysis also relates to the design of the questionnaire. Much attention should be paid to the production of an instrument that will make it easy to input the data into a computer file (if some automatic input system such as "scantron" is not used).

These are the various issues that need attention before the goals and objectives of a specific survey are developed. The fundamental concerns of collecting community opinions that are representative of the population and that lead to effective estimation through appropriate data analysis need to be kept in sight when conducting a survey.

COMPONENTS OF SURVEY RESEARCH

The survey research process that is applied to the needs assessment and the attitude and opinion survey of recreation and leisure activities should follow a set of steps and adhere to a set of fundamental aspects of all survey research. Most of the principles follow from the basic objectives of survey research and needs assessment. Each stage of the survey research process must be thought out carefully, since the aspects interact to provide the ultimate results. These aspects are discussed in this section.

Description of Objectives

One of the most important parts of a needs assessment or a program evaluation is the clear delineation of the objectives of the project. In broad terms, the objectives are to collect attitude and opinion information from a community being served by the agency in order to assess the needs of the community as well as gain an evaluation of the quality of service being provided by the agency. However, to conduct an effective survey, it is important to specify the goals in more clear and precise terms so that the survey can be conducted in a meaningful manner and an appropriate questionnaire instrument can be constructed to collect the relevant data.

Usually, the objectives of a leisure needs assessment cover four key areas. First, attention is paid to the specific activities offered by an agency and the facilities maintained by an agency. The objective of the survey often is to assess the level of interest in a set of recreation activities offered by the agency. Sometimes this objective is augmented with the additional concern for determining the future needs of a community. Since communities change with time, just as the opportunities for recreation change, it is important to be able to gauge both the current and future needs. Sometimes surveys are commissioned specifically to study the future needs of a community. This has become an important part of the survey process, particularly for surveys that are done in conjunction with the development of master plans for an agency. The current level of interest in leisure-related activities and the future need for leisure opportunities are often tied to the specific attitudes and opinions of the community.

The second broad objective of surveys is to assess the attitudes and opinions of the community with respect to leisure. Where specific information is sought about the way the members of the community feel about leisure and the agency that provides the leisure opportunities. The objective is to move away from the specific, use-related issues and deal with the more abstract feelings and opinions about leisure that exist in the community. For instance, within the first objective, it is legitimate to include queries about the level of interest in a particular activity such as aerobics; the second objective addresses the attitudes that the community has about aerobics, its benefits, and its drawbacks. Thus, the second objective is to go into further depth regarding the issue to better understand why there are specific variances in the level of interest in specific activities.

The third objective of leisure surveys is to obtain information about leisure-related behavior. While the first objective is to assess the level of interest, here the interest is in assessing the specific leisure-related behavior. At the simplest level, this is a question of attendance and participation. Even though the survey is meant to assess community-wide opinion, it is important to find out the level of participation to gauge what percentage of the community actually attends the activities organized by the agency. Also included are the issues surrounding the reasons for nonattendance and other behavioral factors that have a direct impact on the assessment of the agency.

A final objective of the assessment is to determine the demographic composition of the community being served. This information is often already available through the Census Bureau. However, it is imperative to add this to the objectives of the survey, since this will provide the anchor for comparing different demographic categories.

For instance, if the researcher cannot determine the gender, income, or age composition of the sample, it will be impossible to determine if there are any differences in attitudes across demographic groups. Inclusion of this as an objective also provides verification of the census numbers and reveals changes in the community. For instance, a survey conducted in 1996 or 1997 might not reflect the demographic information collected in the census of 1990 but might better match the annual surveys of the population conducted by the Census Bureau.

Additionally, by including the demographic issue among the objectives, it is possible to determine the accuracy of the representation of the sample by comparing the demographic information with the standard census information. For instance, if at the end of a needs assessment it is found that the proportion of people in the age group 34-41 is 15% in a particular community, and the census indicates a proportion of 25% for the same age category, there is reason to doubt the accuracy of one of the data sets. In most cases, the survey data would be deemed unreliable, simply because the census is generally considered the most reliable source of demographic information.

The overall objective of these assessments is to produce a final set of recommendations and suggestions based on the data. Characteristic of applied research, it is necessary that, at the end of the survey process, the researchers are able to work with the agency to produce a set of recommendations that the agency can use to revise its activities. This needs to be a well-articulated objective of these surveys, because the information means little until it has been interpreted, analyzed, and reported in terms of action statements that the agency can follow. It is necessary and important to define these objectives before embarking on the actual study.

Definition of the Population

It is also extremely important to be able to define the population of the survey in such a way that there is no opportunity for ambiguity. Very often, surveys do not accomplish their stated objectives, and the data are unreliable because the population has not been defined carefully.

First, it is important to note that the population is the entire community about which information is being sought. This is the group represented by the sample. Consequently, the selection of the sample is predicated upon the definition of the population. If the population is not well defined, then the sample selection will be ambiguous as well, and it will be difficult to gauge to what group the data apply. The definition of the population is usually made based on a set of demographic categories that can be determined using the survey.

In the case of leisure and recreation studies, it is necessary to consider the geographic location of the population under scrutiny. Since leisure and recreation providers often serve specific cities, towns, villages, and communities, it is important to restrict the population to the geographic area that the agency serves. It is this tax base on which the public recreation providers such as parks and recreation departments survive, so that geographic area becomes the best definition of the population. Using the tax base to determine the geographic spread of the population is often the simplest and broadest criterion for the selection of the geographic area, because it is the opinions, attitudes, and behavior of the taxpaying members of the community that ought to be most important to the agency administrators and the board overseeing the activities of the agency. However, this geographic definition is not necessarily easy to execute.

The thorniest problem with the geographic definition is determining an effective process of eliminating those people who do not belong in the geographic area. Since the recreation service areas do not necessarily coincide with the zip code boundaries or phone prefixes, a specific zip code area might include both the residents and nonresidents of the zone covered by a recreation provider. Since the sample has to be drawn on the basis of zip codes in the case of mail surveys, or on the basis of telephone prefixes in the case of telephone surveys, mechanisms must be built into the process to eliminate geographically ineligible people from the survey. In most cases this can be accomplished by asking a question in the survey about the geographic eligibility of the respondent, or by asking the respondent to indicate on a map of the service area the approximate location of his or her residence. Both of these methods help to identify respondents who should not have been included in the initial definition of the population. This is a problem in most large cities and metropolitan areas, where the dividing lines between the cities are relatively difficult to judge. For instance, in the suburbs of Chicago, one city merges into another seamlessly, and cities often share zip code areas, making this a particularly thorny problem.

In most community-level surveys of leisure and recreation issues, the geographic definition of the population is the most important factor, since the community, by definition, includes all demographic categories. Occasionally, however, it might be necessary to conduct surveys targeted toward specific parts of the population (it is important to note that this does not translate to a user survey). For instance, if the agency is planning on constructing a new senior citizen recreation center, there is a strong argument for doing a community-wide senior citizen survey (independent of usage) to determine the specific needs of that particular subgroup. Indeed, with increasingly diminishing resources, it might be necessary to do such targeted surveys to gather information about specific subgroups. With the growing availability of electronic relational databases, it is becoming simpler to produce targeted samples that represent specific parts of the population. It is possible to go to a private vendor, such as

Donnelley Marketing or Survey Sampling Incorporated, provide a detailed definition of the population, and have the vendors select a sample that best represents the population being surveyed. It is, however, a responsibility of the researcher and the agency to settle on the definition of the population that will best accomplish the goals set out as the primary objectives of the survey.

Development of an Instrument

Once the objectives of the survey have been defined and the population described in specific detail, it is possible to move to the next stage of the process—the development of an instrument that can be used to collect the data from the selected community. The issue of questionnaire development is taken up in greater detail later in the book; however, it is important to note here that this is a critical part of the survey process, since the questionnaire is the primary mode of contact between the researcher and the community. Consequently, ample attention must be paid to the development of an effective questionnaire.

It is also useful to clarify some of the problems surrounding the terminology applied to the questionnaire. In common parlance, several terms are used to describe similar concepts. For the purpose of this book, the term *survey* is used to refer to the kind of study being done (as opposed to *experiment*). The survey does not usually refer to the questionnaire or the sample. On the other hand, the term "questionnaire" refers to the instrument used to gather the data. This is indeed a tool, as the term "instrument" suggests, and often the terms "questionnaire" and "instrument" are used interchangeably. Finally, like any tool, the questionnaire/instrument can take different shapes when used for different tasks. Just as one can hang a picture by drilling a screw into the wall or by hammering a nail in the wood, the same task can be accomplished by different instruments depending on the method of data collection. Consequently, telephone, mail, and face-to-face surveys all use questionnaires although they may look different.

One other term that is often used is *interview*. This word refers to the situation where a respondent does not personally respond to the questions by checking boxes or writing out responses. In this case, the questionnaire is filled out by a third person—the interviewer—who uses a questionnaire to ask the specific questions and records the answers. Consequently, interviews conducted on the phone or face-to-face also require the tool of the questionnaire, but the respondent does not go through the process of "self-response," as in the case of a mail survey.

Independent of the nature of the survey, it is important that ample time and attention be devoted to the development of the questionnaire. One of the most important factors in the development of the questionnaire is the maintenance of content validity, ensuring that the contents of the questions indeed measure the concept being considered. Thus, if the concern is over safety in the parks, the question should measure exactly that and not a different construct. For instance, if in the initial research phase it is discovered that the members of a community have concerns about vandalism and violence in the parks, then a question about perceived safety should clarify that it is safety in terms of personal danger that is being measured, and not safety in terms of the security of the playground equipment. While post hoc tools such as factor analysis can check for internal consistency, the checks need to be conducted prior to the actual study, so that any possible problems can be overcome well ahead of the data collection process.

Following the development of specific objectives of the study and the definition of the population, the construction of the questionnaire is an important part of the survey process. This is perhaps one of the longest processes as well, since it is at this phase that copious checks need to be conducted to certify that all the different substantive issues are being covered, while ensuring that the questionnaire is attractive and short enough to gain a high enough response rate from respondents. Attention also needs to be paid to the composition and source of the cover letter that accompanies the questionnaire, since that is the most persuasive part of the survey, and the decision to return the survey (in the case of mail data collection) is often dependent on who signs the cover letter.

Data Collection

Once the questionnaire has been developed and the members of the community selected in a sample, it is possible to turn to the issue of data collection. The primary concern in data collection is the precarious balance between obtaining the most responses and not spending an inordinate amount of money. There are three primary modes of data collection—mail, telephone, and face-to-face interviews. There are advantages and drawbacks to each of these methods and these will be discussed in detail later in the book. However, what is important to decide while planning is the acceptable response rate. This ratio is usually defined as the proportion of eligible respondents who completed a questionnaire. Variations to that definition exist, but the common definition excludes ineligible respondents from the denominator. The goal of any data collection effort is to decide on a realistic response rate and then design the data collection effort to reach that goal. It is important to be able to settle on the expected and acceptable response rates. Years of research has shown that it is unreasonable to expect more than 35% of eligible respondents to send in a self-response mail questionnaire mailed only once to the sample. So if the agency wants to achieve a better response rate, a single-mailing survey design is not adequate. In this way, the decision about the mode of data collection is often made based on the acceptable response rate. A higher response rate requires an increased number of contacts in the form of multiple mailings, several callbacks, or repeated visits to the household. All of these increase the cost of the endeavor. Consequently, a balance is often struck between the data collection mode and the extensiveness of the efforts and the acceptable response rate. It should, however, be clear that while there are "acceptable" response rates, the goal is always to achieve a 100% response to eliminate any nonresponse bias.

Once the data collection method has been determined and the questionnaires have been sent out by mail or interviews have begun, it is possible to execute the data coding and analysis process.

Data Coding and Analysis

As the data come back to the researcher in the form of completed questionnaires, it is possible to begin the data entry process. There are three primary modes of data entry available now. The first method is the traditional process of entering the responses from a paper version of the questionnaire to a computer file. A second method is to use a "bubble sheet," which is filled out by the respondent and then electronically read or "scanned" to record the responses. A third method is to have the respondent's answers directly coded into a computer. This is most convenient in the case of phone and face-to-face interviews when the interviewer can record the responses using a computer-aided telephone interview (CATI) or a computer-aided paper and pencil interview (CAPI) system, respectively. All of these are reliable systems, and their merits and drawbacks will be discussed later, but it is important that the decision about the data entry process be made early because each format requires different kinds of start-up procedures. In the case of the scan process, it is necessary to obtain the scan sheets and other equipment (or resources) to do what is needed. On the other hand, if direct data entry is to be done by data coders, a different approach is called for. These are critical decisions that need to be thought about ahead of time in order to avoid time-consuming and frustrating problems later in the process. Furthermore, the process of data entry needs to be accompanied by a system of checks and verification to ensure that the data are accurately coded and the final data are clean. The chapter on data analysis presents a detailed discussion of the process of data coding and cleaning.

Once the data have been entered, they are ready for analysis. Many of the decisions about data analysis need to be made during the design of the study. The purpose of the study often helps to determine the data analysis needs. Some amount of basic descriptive analysis is required for all data sets. Measures of frequency of occurrence, central tendencies, and variances are necessary to make forecasts and predictions of needs or assessment of programs. Consequently, it is always necessary to have a measure of the percentage of respondents who show a particular interest in any activity, as well as measures of the average opinion and the deviation in that average. Decisions about specific advanced computations often need to be made based on the exact needs of the agency.

In addition, some things need to be done in the early phases of the research to facilitate the data entry and analysis process. For instance, some surveys use numeric notations for the columns in which the responses will be recorded in the data set. In other cases, the responses are precoded, so that a "strongly agree" response to an attitude statement is always recorded as a "5" and not a letter notation such as "a." This makes it easier for the data-entry person to record the response in the database; otherwise, the person would have to remember that a particular letter of the alphabet (or any other nonnumeric indicator) stands for a particular number. This can make the process error prone.

Thus, several issues in data entry and analysis are influenced by the earlier stages of the process, and it is important to keep sight of these issues when designing a study. Minor modifications can often make the data entry process smoother. Often, a well-done survey loses its strength due to bad data entry.

DIFFERENCES BETWEEN THE SURVEY AND THE EXPERIMENT

This chapter has elaborated on some of the fundamental aspects of the survey design as applied to the area of leisure research. As pointed out at the beginning of the chapter, the survey method plays a significant part in social scientific research in general, and leisure research in particular. This method has many components that are drawn from the traditions of experimental research as discussed in the earlier chapters. However, there are a set of fundamental differences between survey research and experimental research as well. It is important to understand and acknowledge those differences to be able to use the appropriate method in any necessary context. Sometimes, the purpose of the research requires an experimental approach, while at other times the survey method could be recommended. Therefore, the reader needs to be familiar with the differences between the two approaches.

At the fundamental level, the survey and the experiment differ based on the different purposes of the two methods. Simply put, the experiment (in the context of leisure and recreation studies) is an effective tool for basic research that attempts to prove a hypothesis or test the results of a specific intervention on general human leisure behavior; the survey, on the other hand, is aimed and designed to obtain accurate estimates of the leisure- and recreation-related opinions and behaviors of a specific population. This leads to differences at other levels.

Objectives

The primary difference between the two kinds of research is in the objective of the research. In the case of experiments, the research is often driven by a set of theoretical positions about leisure behavior or related sociological behavior, and the research is aimed at testing propositions about such behavior. In most cases, these propositions hypothesize the existence of a relation between key elements. Experiments are also often directed toward answering specific research questions based on theory. In these cases, specific questions are raised and their answers sought. Often these are not questions of policy or needs, but more basic questions about behavior and opinion that can shed light on the reasons people participate in specific leisure-related behavior. Finally, experiments often examine the effects of specific interventions on the leisure and recreation behavior of a group of people. This often amounts to measuring the differences between groups of people exposed to different conditions.

The survey, on the other hand, does not necessarily attempt to test broad questions of theory and principles of leisure behavior. These studies have the more modest objective of assessing the critical leisure-related attributes of groups of people, and the results from surveys are extremely useful for program planning and evaluation. The survey does not provide the opportunity of setting up hypotheses to be tested, nor does it provide the option of testing the effects of different interventions on groups of people. However, a survey, particularly one designed as a longitudinal study, can look at trends in a community and provide some insight into the ways that opinions change with fundamental changes in the composition of the community over time.

The primary difference between the survey and the experiment lies in the fact that the survey attempts to obtain the attitudes and opinions of the people in a community, while the experiment has the purpose of testing specific theoretical (and sometimes methodological) issues about a particular concept, which could be independent of the particular community and could be generalizable to a large group of people. This fact has an effect on the design and the way the experiment is put together and the survey is organized.

Design

One of the most important aspects of the design is the attention paid to the process of sampling. Representativeness of a particular community or a group of people is not necessarily the primary concern in the case of an experiment. Here the primary concern is with producing a design that best tests the hypothesis or answers the research question. The principle here is making the sample free of systematic error, which means that some degree of randomization of the subjects is needed to produce a pool with no obvious biases such as gender, age, and other characteristics that could act as confounding variables in the process of data analysis. In the case of the survey, the question of representativeness is critical, since the principal goal is to produce estimates, and without representativeness the estimates would be skewed. Consequently, extreme attention is paid to the process of sampling, with several different strategies used to produce a sample that best represents the opinions of the community being assessed. However, the question of bias is just as critical, because by excluding (systematically or accidentally) any particular group, the survey researcher becomes subject to possible criticism from reviewers who may examine the findings before they are made into policy.

A second area of design that illustrates the difference between the experiment and the survey concerns the question of cause and effect. In any social science research, it is relatively difficult to make an argument for pure causality. For instance, it is particularly difficult to claim that *because* the respondent is a woman, she is more likely to have an interest in aerobics. Such a statement attempts to establish a strict causal relationship between gender and interest in a particular program. Many other factors are likely to determine interest in a program such as age, number of children, program availability, and quality, etc. These confounding variables can complicate the causality argument.

In most cases, an experiment attempts to establish a causal relationship while a survey is content with demonstrating a relationship between a set of factors. Survey results can establish the existence of a strong relationship between two factors but are not used to make the claim that one causes the other. For instance, survey results could indicate a strong relationship between gender and interest in aerobics, but the data may also show that similar relationships exist between aerobics and age, availability, interest, and a set of other related factors. These relationships are not evidence of causality, but are nonetheless important findings that indicate trends in the data.

The fundamental issue of causality has an effect on the design of the experiment and the survey. In the case of the former, mechanisms need to be set up to eliminate confounding variables that may detract from the causality argument. The most common way of doing this is to use randomly assigned experimental and control groups, where the experimental group is exposed to a particular condition that the control group is not exposed to. Holding everything else constant, if a difference is observed in the data obtained from the experimental and the control groups, then it can be argued that the difference was caused by the intervention. That claim rests on the notion of control.

In the experiment, the design assumes a degree of control where the experimenter can manipulate the kinds of people included and the kinds of conditions they are exposed to. In the case of the survey, the only level of control lies in the selection of the sample. If the survey researcher desires, a sample can be stratified in such a way that there are an equal number of minority and majority groups. This provides some manipulation of the representativeness of a study but does not provide any *a priori* level of control over the project.

Additionally, the survey researchers cannot hope to adjust the living conditions of the people they survey. While the experimenter has the opportunity of bringing the selected people into laboratories and exercising the necessary control over their environments, the survey researcher reaches people in their "natural" environment and cannot manipulate the fact, for example, that inner city youth do not have access to a skating rink.

What the survey researcher is able to establish post hoc is the fact that there could be a strong demand for an ice skating facility among inner city youth, and this could be related to the absence of such a facility. However, it could also be due to the fact that the location of an existing ice skating facility is such that inner city youth do not have transportation to the facility.

In the absence of control, it is extremely difficult to pinpoint the true causal element. In brief, experimental research remains deterministic and reductionistic, attempting to determine how to reduce the perceived effects to a set of well-documented factors. On the other hand, survey research is much more exploratory and descriptive, attempting to identify the existing feelings of a community and studying trends over a length of time.

DIFFERENCES IN DATA ANALYSIS AND INTERPRETATION

While the design of an experiment provides the basis for making causal arguments, the process of making the claims depends on the way the data are analyzed. In the case of surveys, the analysis is often restricted to the computation of relationships using techniques such as the correlation coefficients. Such analysis does not establish a causal relationship but certainly shows with varying degrees of confidence and statistical significance the degree and the direction of the relationship between two variables. Here it would be illegitimate to go further with the data and attempt to establish causality, since the design does not support that level of analysis.

In the case of the experiment, the design allows for the analysis of causality with the computation of the regression equation which, in its simplest form, can establish a mathematical relationship between two elements. Using the equation, which in the case of linear regression would read $y = ax + b$, it is possible to predict a value for y knowing the value of x. For example, if x represents income level and y the amount of voluntary time that a person is willing to donate to recreation department activities, it is possible to predict with a great degree of precision the expected level of donation given knowledge of the income level of a person. Finally, if the experiment has been well done with appropriate control of the possible confounding variables, it is also possible to claim that the prediction holds independent of factors such as age, race, and gender.

In most cases, however, the relations are not that clean or well established. Regression analysis provides a good check on the authenticity of a relationship since it provides a test to show the amount of the variance in the dependent variable (x) that is explained by the independent variable (y). For instance, it is possible to claim that there is a degree of variation in the amount of time people are willing to donate to recreation department activities. The critical question is what amount of that variation is explained by the fact that the respondents have differing levels of income. If it were possible to claim that 100% of the variance in the amount of giving is explained by income level, it would make for perfect prediction. However, that is rarely the case, and regression analysis can show the actual percentage.

The data are thus interpreted and used in different ways. While survey data are useful for planning and assessment, experimental data are useful in establishing relations that can be used to explain the survey data. For example, if it can be established that there is a significant causal relationship between political attitude and attitude toward the conservation of open spaces and the environment, then strong support for open space conservation in a particular community could be claimed to be an indicator of political opinion. However, that can only be claimed if it is possible to find and establish such a relationship in the controlled and more precise experimental setting. In a similar way, if survey data across communities suggest a relationship between age and perception of community recreation, a good argument could be made for a series of experimental studies attempting to establish causality by controlling the other variables and testing to see if there is a deterministic relationship between age and perception of community recreation.

Thus, fundamental differences in purpose between experiments and surveys translate to a series of other differences. It is important to note, however, that these differences are not such that the two methods cannot complement each other. Very often, the experimental researcher has to turn to the survey specialist to see if the relationships established in the laboratory setting are reproduced in the real-life "field" environment. In a similar fashion, the survey researcher often provides the initial information that becomes the seed for further studies to examine whether trends discovered in the survey data are grounds for conducting experiments to establish causal relationships between variables that are obviously related.

The survey data produce recommendations and action statements supported with data that can be immediately used by an agency to revise its activities and plan for the future. Survey data address the evaluation and the specific needs of the community. Experimental data are much more abstract, laying down basic principles of behavior and possible reasons for the behavior. Such data are not necessarily specific to a community or a particular provider of parks and recreation facilities. Consequently, the data are used primarily to test for and establish grand relationships between different pieces of the puzzle.

In spite of the differences in purpose and design, both the survey and the experimental methods depend on correct and appropriate procedures. Keeping in mind that the data are only as good as the process of data collection, it is imperative the methods used in either kind of study be well reviewed and free of possible sources of bias. If that can be established, then the data can be trusted and decisions can be drawn on the basis of the data.

THE WHOLE PROCESS

Now that the differences and similarities between survey research and experiments have been established, it is useful to summarize the complete survey research process. While the segments of the survey process look different and represent different sets of activities, a flaw in any of the pieces will have a ripple effect on every other aspect of the study. Consequently, it is important for the team to meet frequently to see how the different parts of the study are progressing. Working knowledge of all the different pieces also helps in managing each of the pieces better. Thus, the head of sampling needs to be well aware of the data collection methods as well as the data entry and analysis projects to predict the amount of time the different tasks will take and to adjust the sampling activities to suit the needs of the other departments.

The next few chapters point out the fundamental issues that all sections of the survey team need to be aware of, expanding on the specific processes discussed here.

Chapter Six

Sampling for Leisure and Recreation Surveys

INTRODUCTION

In most cases, a leisure and recreation provider conducts a survey to assess the needs of the community being served or to evaluate the quality of the services from the perspective of the community. As in all communicative situations, one can get different results by asking different groups of people. For instance, if one were to ask people visiting swimming pools about their interest in water sports, it is likely that a positive response would be elicited, whereas asking the same question to members of the basketball league might not elicit the same response.

In addition, asking about the same thing in two different ways can elicit different responses. For example, by asking "do you have any interest in swimming?" one could get a different response than if the question were "given the increasing popularity of swimming, do you have any interest in swimming?" While both the questions concern the same activity, the second one biases the response to some degree, since respondents might not be very comfortable in disagreeing with something that is "increasingly popular."

As these two examples illustrate, it is extremely important to pay attention to whom the questions are directed, and how they are asked. The recommendations and policy decisions based on the data are only as good as the data, and the quality of the data is severely impacted by the way in which subjects of the survey were selected and the way they were asked the questions.

These two issues fall in the areas of sampling and questionnaire construction. Neither of these two processes is intuitive, and both require rigorous training and practice. This chapter will explore some of the principles used in the sampling procedure to illustrate the importance of *system* in the process of sampling (the word *system* is in italics to avoid future confusion with systematic sampling). We will discuss some of the common myths about sampling and how these "common sense" ways of thinking about sampling could be disastrous to the data. Finally, we will look at some common strategies that can be used to select samples for leisure and recreation attitude and opinion surveys.

Often, sampling and questionnaire design occur simultaneously in a study. However, these activities can also be conducted independently, and it is important to focus on sampling first, since this activity can require the assistance of outside specialists and could be a time-consuming process. It is important to complete both these processes in an efficient manner before initiating data collection.

SAMPLING BASICS

Four key aspects of sampling need attention (Sudman, 1976). It is important to consider the definition of the *population* that will be *represented* by the sample through a process of *randomization* that ensures, with a certain degree of *probability,* that the sample is indeed good.

Definition of the Population

In any survey, the first step to be taken is an attempt at defining in precise terms the population or the community of people whose opinions are sought. In most cases, this group is so large and diverse that it is impossible to ask each member of the group every question. Consequently, it is necessary to select a sample. However, unless it is clear who the population is, it is difficult to decide on the method to be used in selecting a representative group.

In the case of leisure and recreation surveys, the question of population definition can often be addressed by thinking of a set of common planning criteria. Agencies often have to restrict their services to specific geographic areas. For instance, if a city recreation department serves a particular set of zip code areas, then its population of interest in most cases is restricted to that set of zip code areas. Indeed, sending a questionnaire outside the geographic area of service could be considered an inappropriate use of survey dollars since the needs, attitudes, and opinions of the people outside the service area are of little interest.

A second criterion of defining the population is usage. If the objective of the survey is to obtain specialized information about the patterns of use of particular facilities, or attitudes and opinions toward programs from people who have been exposed to the programs, then the population can be defined as users and participators. This definition eliminates from the population those who do not use the particular facility. Such a definition of the population is also tied to the way in which usage is defined. The agency has to consider that question carefully before determining how the population is defined. In most attitude and interest surveys conducted for the purpose of evaluating existing programs or assessing future needs, the population is defined as every member in the geographic area being served by the agency. Distinctions between users and nonusers are often made post–hoc, after the data have been collected and a standard usage criterion has been established. In many communities, there are far fewer users than nonusers, and a master plan made only on the basis of the responses from users could be politically inappropriate, since the nonusers' opinions are equally important where the entire community is concerned.

In some cases, the definition of the population is tied to age. It is possible that an agency is interested in a particular age group and their opinions and attitudes. Given the fact that the latter part of the twentieth century is marked by an increasing number of "older" citizens in America, it is possible that agencies are interested in knowing more about the needs, attitudes, and interests of these people. In such cases, the agency has to clearly define the age categories so that the particular population can be targeted.

Most needs and evaluation surveys connected with planning and development are interested in the general population of the community being served. Since the tax base for most agencies comes from the residents of the recreation district, it is only right that every member of the community be given an opportunity to provide feedback to the agency.

Once the population has been defined, it is necessary to obtain a listing of the entire group so that it is possible to select subjects from the group. If the agency conducting the survey chooses to do its own sampling, it should recognize some of the common problems associated with population lists.[1] Although there is an increasing availability of electronic databases that list large populations, it is still difficult to obtain listings that are reliable and clean. The key questions that need to be asked about any list are as follows.

Are There Any Duplicates in the List?

Population lists often contain duplicates. A person's address can be listed under two different spellings of the last name, or a phone number could be listed twice, once under the business and again in the residential pages. Similarly, compiling a list from other existing lists can lead to duplication, because one person can belong to multiple lists and thus appear more than once in the master list. Duplication leads to violation of the probability assumptions associated with any sample. In simple terms, the fact that a name that appears more than once has a higher chance of being selected violates the fundamental probability assumptions. This can be avoided by looking for and eliminating duplicates. With the increasing use of electronic databases, it is now possible to do this more efficiently.

Are There Omissions from the List?

In many cases, lists are incomplete. Because of the time when the list was compiled, some members of the community may not appear in the list. For example, a phone book published in October will not contain the names, addresses, and phone numbers of people who moved into the community in November; their names will only be included after a year. That kind of omission is due to a systematic phenomenon. In other cases, there are random omissions without any particular pattern. These are less troublesome, since such random mistakes tend to "wash out" when a random sample is selected. However, if such an omission is discovered, it is necessary to correct it.

---

1. Increasingly agencies are turning over the survey process to trained professional organizations, such as Management Learning Laboratories, which have the right mix of talents to conduct an efficient survey. In such cases, the professional agency or its subcontractor could be responsible for the sample selection process. However, in any event, the agency personnel need to be aware of the issues associated with the selection process.

This is important because omissions also violate the probability assumptions. Just as duplication leads to a higher chance of the name falling into a sample, an omission leads to a nil chance of the member being included in the sample.[2]

Are There Ineligible Members in the List?

The question of ineligibility often comes up as well. This concerns situations where the population list contains names and addresses that are ineligible based on the definition of the population. This happens often in leisure and recreation studies because of incongruence between the way the agency defines its population and the way the listing agency defines the population. In one study, for instance, the population was defined by the area served by the agency. However, that area was not contained within well-defined zip code areas or city limits. Consequently, zip codes contained both eligible and ineligible populations. When the sample was selected, it was impossible to determine who was eligible without the time-consuming procedure of matching street addresses with street maps. In such cases, it is best to mail to both eligible and ineligible parties (unless the split is fifty-fifty, in which case attempts at cleaning the list should be made to avoid excessive mailing to ineligible populations), and then provide a screening question in the questionnaire to weed out the self-selected ineligibles. However, there are always some ineligibles in a population list, and this must be attended to when conducting the survey.

Is the List Accurate in Its Information?

Sometimes, in spite of one's best efforts, a list contains inaccurate information. In addition to omissions and duplication, there are other miscellaneous kinds of inaccuracies that need to be addressed. A list might have wrong addresses and telephone numbers. Samples selected based on such an inaccurate

2. In mail surveys conducted to assess the attitudes and interests related to recreation and leisure, the population lists are often obtained from utility agencies, departments of motor vehicles, and similar agencies which are relatively rigorous about maintaining complete lists with no omissions. If, however, the phone book is substituted for such lists, then an immediate problem with omission results because the book is dated and an increasing number of people are making their numbers "unlisted," thus voluntarily omitting themselves from the lists.

list would have mistakes that become expensive to resolve later in the survey. Two examples illustrate such problems.

In one case, a listing of all white-page phone numbers in the United States was obtained from a vendor. Delivered on CD-ROM, the list was searchable by a variety of fields, including zip + 4, city name, area code, and so forth. It was, however, discovered that many small cities simply did not appear in the listing. Often the phone numbers of the small cities appeared, but the city name referred to the closest large metropolitan area. In such cases, a geographically targeted sample selected on the basis of a village name would be quite inaccurate.

In another case, a vendor provided a sample based on a list that it maintains. While such lists usually have a 98% deliverable rate (i.e., the postal service is be able to find an accurate address in 98% of the cases), this sample provided a deliverable rate of only about 90%. This discrepancy was explained by the fact that the city consisted of areas with a high mobility rate. For instance, there might be an apartment house where the primary residents are students from a neighboring university, and every fall there is a change in the people staying at the addresses. Thus, while there is a physical address to deliver to, the person listed as the recipient is unavailable. In such cases, simply addressing the envelope with the name along with the designation "or present resident" would have corrected the problem. It is useful for the recreation agency to explore where such problems can occur and plan for it in advance.

Obtaining Representativeness in the Sample

Once the population has been defined, it is necessary to formulate a method by which a sample can be selected that represents the population. Representativeness involves a process by which all the constituencies in the population have a known chance of being selected for the sample. For instance, if a leisure agency services a community that has 70% white population and 25% black population, the sampling procedure needs to ensure that the sample contains the same proportions of the ethnic groups.

The same is true for other demographic criteria such as gender, age, income level, and household structure. The decennial census is often considered to provide the best estimates of the demographic composition of any population. Consequently, the test of representativeness lies in comparing the survey results with the census information to verify that the results are indeed representative and that the over- or under-representation of any particular group has introduced no systematic bias.

However, that determination can be done only after the survey data have been collected, when it is too late to correct any problems with the sampling procedure.[3] In some cases, however, the design may call for equal sample sizes from different constituencies. For example, if the population is 75% white and 25% black, a sample of 1,000 would yield around 750 white people and 250 black members. However, if the design calls for 500 of each, then the whites would be under-represented and blacks overrepresented. In such cases, the assumptions of representation can be corrected at the post hoc level. Assuming that the sample is representative of the population and there are no specific biases in the sampling procedure, it can be assumed that the sample will also represent the recreation-related attitudes, opinions and needs of the population.

Consider, for instance, a situation in a town where the primary sporting interest is softball leagues and tournaments. This interest is widespread, except among the senior citizens, who make up 20% of the population. In such a case, it is safe to presume that 80% of the adults have high to moderate interest in softball leagues and tournaments, while 20% have low to no interest in softball. If the sample is representative by age, and only 20% of the sample are senior citizens, then it is likely that only 20% of the respondents will express little to no interest.

Since recreation interests are often fundamentally linked to demographic attributes, if it is possible to obtain a representative sample from the demographic perspective, then it is quite likely that different leisure interests are being addressed. In general, any skewness or bias in the sample could be a reason for bias in the leisure interests of the sample. In the above example, if half the respondents were senior citizens, then the reported

3. In some cases when there is a lack of representation, a mathematical procedure of weighting the results can be done. Simply put, this involves giving a higher weight to the under-represented constituency and a lower weight to the overrepresented groups. In general, statisticians are suspicious of this procedure when it is used to correct for data collection problems. It is, however, a necessary procedure in some sampling situations such as stratified sampling.

level of interest in softball would have been inaccurate. It is important to note that while it is not possible to predict the levels of interest in leisure behavior (after all, that is why the study is being done in the first place!), it is certainly possible to compare the research data with the standard census information. That is often the *only* reliable standardized yardstick available to the researcher. Consequently, it is important for the researcher to be able to make the sample representative at least in terms of the census information. The rest often falls into place.

Mathematically speaking, the notion of representation is closely tied to the concept of probability. In a representative sample, it is assumed that every member of the population, independent of demographic category, has an equal chance of falling into the sample. Most often, a random selection process accomplishes this. By this procedure, every member has a known and equal probability of being included in the sample, and since this probability is known, it is possible to compute the population characteristics from the sample data with the assumption that no known biases gave any particular group a better (or worse) chance of falling into the sample.

Unless the sample is moderately representative, it is not possible to make predictions about the general population from which the sample is selected. Needless to say, a sample can never be exactly representative of the population. There are deviations from the population standards based on the laws of probability. However, a random sample selected from the population is often the best means of ensuring representativeness of the community, compared with samples selected in specific recreation facilities or public areas. For instance, if the population is defined as the people of the community, and the sampling procedure involves selecting everyone who attends swimming activities, the sample would represent the users of pools and not the entire population. Consequently, any decisions made on the basis of such a sample will not be generalizable to the population, and plans made on the basis of such data would be flawed. Thus, the notions of randomization and random selection are critical to the sampling process.

Randomization and Random Selection

The notion of random selection is closely tied to representativeness. By definition, a randomized sample is one where every member of the population has a known and equal probability of selection. Consequently, there were no biases in the list or the sampling procedure leading to an unequal probability.

A sample may be nonrandom due to problems with the population list or the sampling frame, and problems with the selection procedure. Some sampling frames have omissions or duplicates. These situations can occur when a leisure agency attempts to produce its own sampling frame.

For instance, if the frame is compiled from a list of attendees at a swimming pool and a list of users of the ice skating rink, then those who participate in both would fall into the list twice and would have a higher probability of selection. Another situation where the assumptions of randomness are violated is the case where the agency uses a suggestion box or other such method of data collection. In these cases, there is no control over the definition of the population and consequently no control over the sample. A suggestion box placed near a facility or at any public location could be used by anybody interested in filling out the survey, and it is nearly impossible to determine the probability associated with any of the responses received. Thus, while it may appear that the people who are putting material in the suggestion box are doing so at "random," the method violates the fundamental definition and assumptions of randomness.

A second way in which the assumptions randomness can be violated is through incorrect selection procedures. It is possible that a list is indeed complete and contains all the information about every eligible member of the population. If, however, incorrect procedures are used to select the sample from the list, then the resulting sample will not be random. For instance, suppose the leisure agency chooses to use the phone book as the sampling frame and selects 150 names at random from the book. If the sampler begins on the first page and then randomly selects 150 names from the first 50 pages of a 100-page phone book, then the procedure is flawed because the names in the latter part of the book had a zero probability of being included in the sample.

Thus, specific steps are needed to make the sample random and ensure that every member of the population has a chance of being selected in the sample. It is these conditions that will ultimately produce a representative sample, the data from which can be considered an estimate of the population characteristics. However, it is always important to note that the data collected from the sample constitute an estimate and nothing beyond that. The data can never amount to an exact accounting of the population description, because it is impossible to obtain the exact population description without collecting data from every member of the population.

Probability and Sampling Error

Since the sample is a randomly selected subgroup of the population, it is not expected to be an exact mirror of the population. It is assumed that the sample represents the population to a large degree, but it is an estimate that will differ from the true population measure by a specific amount. Indeed, the quality of the sample is measured as the sampling error, which reports the extent of error or "doubt" associated with the sample measurements.

When a population is large, as in the case of the American population or any general population like the members of a community or the service area for a leisure provider, it is possible to select multiple random samples from the population. Consider, for instance, a situation where the service area for a recreation agency consists of 100,000 people. It is possible to select 100 different samples from this population, each consisting of 1,000 members who are selected without repetition. Suppose the proportions of men and women are calculated from each of these samples. It is likely that the first sample has 51% men and 49% women, the second sample has 54% men and 46% women, and the third sample contains 48% men and 52% women. The question that the researcher or the agency administrator needs to consider is, which of these estimates is correct? The answer is that all are correct. These are accurate estimates of the population characteristics. Notice that the percentage of males varies between 54% and 48%. The midpoint of these percentages is 51%, and it is possible to claim that the percentage of men in the population varies between 54% and 48% or that the percentage of men in the community is 51% plus or minus 3%. The 3% represents the amount of error associated with the sample, and the probability that the estimates of population computed from the sample is within a certain degree of confidence, which is in this case is 95% or above.

In other words, it is possible to claim that the sampling procedure used gives us a 95% level of confidence that the estimates produced from the sample are representative of the population. Since it is impractical to select multiple samples as was done in this example, mathematical procedures are used to calculate the error associated with the sampling process. This error is often called the sampling error.

The extent of sampling error is the best measurement of the quality of the sample. The lower the sampling error, the closer the sample estimates come to the true population values. The sampling error depends on a variety of interrelated factors. However, two qualities of the sample help to reduce the sampling error. First, the bigger the sample, the lower the sampling error. When the sample and the population are identical, the issue of sampling error disappears, since the measurements represent the entire population. However, the relationship between sampling error and sample size is not strictly linear. The sampling error is large with very small samples, but beyond a particular sample size, the change in sampling error is small even with significant increases in sample size.[4] Consequently, it is important to observe a balance between the sampling error and the sample size, because a larger sample size always means increased cost.

However, even a large sample selected in a careless manner will lead to increased sampling error because of the biases introduced in the sample. Systematic errors in the sample can lead to the selection of a final subgroup that is far from representative.

In most surveys, the sampling error is reported as an important aspect of the data. It is important to keep in mind that the sampling error is a complex value that is often oversimplified. When the popular press reports poll results, there is often a number in small print that reports the sampling error. It is important to question how that number was computed and what

---

4. This will be discussed in greater depth later in this chapter, but suffice it to say that this relation between sampling error and sample size makes it unrealistic to go for specific percentages of the population because a higher percentage does not necessarily mean a significantly lowered sampling error.

exactly it represents. For example, is it the sampling error of a mean or a percentage? How was the sampling error computed? Was it estimated at the time of the sample size determination? In many cases these are the questions that a leisure survey coordinator needs to ask at the point of sampling. Since the sample is only an estimate, it is important to compute the probability that the sample constitutes the best estimate of the population.

These are all important considerations in the process of selecting a sample and need to be attended to before the actual sample design is conducted. Many of the assumptions behind the selection of specific kinds of samples are molded by concerns over the population, representation, and randomization and the extent of allowable sampling error. In most research involving the evaluation of existing leisure surveys and the assessment of future needs, the sampling error has to be maintained between 3% and 5%, that is, it needs to be less than 5% but the sample does not have to be so large that the error must be kept below 3%.

The process of sampling requires two principal steps. First, it is necessary to decide the kind of sample to be selected. This depends on the purpose of the survey, the kind of population that is being dealt with, the kind of data collection, and the overall goals of the project. Once this decision has been made, it is possible to move to the second issue, which concerns the process of sample selection. The next section discusses some of the kinds of samples that can be used in a leisure and recreation survey. While the administrator might not be directly involved with the process of sample selection, it is important for the administrator to be able to question the selection process based on some fundamental assumptions. Here attention is paid to the procedure to be used in selecting the sample. Several steps are involved in the sample selection process and it is important to be able to follow the procedures in a systematic fashion so that the selected sample is representative and retains the fundamental assumptions of the sample design.

TYPES OF SAMPLES AND SELECTION PROCEDURES

The type of sample to be selected is dependent on several factors. Principally, the type of sample depends on:

- Goals of the survey
- Population being studied
- Amount of funds available to conduct the survey (not just the sampling)
- Amount of time available to conduct the survey (not just the sampling)
- Level of difficulty in selecting the sample

The Simple Random Sample

Perhaps the most common form of sampling is the selection of a simple random sample. This is the kind of sample that is selected in most leisure and recreation evaluations. The fundamental assumption behind this sample is that every member of the population has the same probability of being selected, and that probability is simply the ratio of the sample size and the population size. In other words, if the leisure and recreation agency services a community of 100,000 people, then a simple random sample of 1,000 suggests that every member of the population has a 1 in 10 chance of being selected. Moreover, given the assumptions of randomness, this 10% chance of falling into the sample is independent of any preexisting conditions such as ethnicity, the amount of use of leisure services, and other demographic or behavioral characteristics.

The simple random sample is best used in leisure and recreation surveys that are attempting to collect aggregate information about the community. Master plans and other long-range planning activities usually need the input of the general population, independent of special leisure needs and interests. In such cases where average measures of opinions, interests, and needs are required, the simple random sample becomes most appropriate. It is, however, not the best kind of sampling technique if specific comparisons are to be made between different sections of the population. That is, however, not a common condition for leisure and recreation administrators.

When the leisure agency is interested in the opinions of the general community, it is not necessarily interested in statistically comparing differences in needs between demographic categories. What is more important is obtaining a representation of the different ethnic and other demographic categories so that the administrators can support their results as representative of the community they are serving. Thus, if a community of 100,000 consists of 7,000 African-Americans, then a simple random sample of 1,000 ought to contain at least 70 African-American members to adequately represent that proportion of the community.

In many cases, the simple random sample is also the least expensive of all the different sampling procedures. It is cheaper, because it can be done in a single pass through the sampling frame. It does not call for any complex manipulation of the frame and thus takes less time, too. Since the process can be automated (particularly with use of the computer), it is faster as well. Finally, the simple random sample can be used in almost any kind of data collection strategy. There are no specific sampling assumptions that require particular data collection methods. The simple random sample can be used to produce a subgroup that is amenable to the various data collection technologies.

The process of selection of the simple random sample can be divided into two parts. First is the development of a clean and complete sampling frame free of the problems discussed earlier in this chapter. The actual process of randomization and the selection of the sample follow. Before the time when sampling frames could be computerized, the process of randomization involved sequential numbering of the elements in the frame and then the selection of a set of random numbers from standardized random number tables. This was followed by the selection of those cases corresponding to the random numbers selected. While this is a sound method, it is increasingly unnecessary to go to these lengths. Indeed, a majority of sampling frames have been computerized and are available in digital formats. Once the frame is computerized, it is possible to apply a standard randomization function to select a subgroup of the frame. Many standard statistical analysis computer packages come with built-in simple random selection procedures. All the user has to do is to instruct the computer about the sample size, and the computer does the rest. In most cases, the random number generated by the computer is a "pseudorandom" number; the computer's clock value at any instant is used as a seed number and then put through a computational procedure to produce the random number.

A variation of the simple random sample is the systematic random sample. Here the need for the selection of a set of random numbers is eliminated by the selection of a random starting point and a fixed interval. Thus, if a list of the 100,000 members of the community is available, and a sample of 1,000 is desired, it is possible to select every tenth person in the list. However, given periodicity of the list (e.g., the list could be arranged in alphabetical order), if one were to start at the very first name, there is a possibility that some degree of bias could be introduced because every tenth name could have some similarity. In order to avoid such bias, a random starting place is selected. For instance, in the list of 100,000, a random number of 9,503 could come up, and the systematic selection procedure would start at the name 9,503 with every tenth name selected until the entire list is exhausted. This procedure can also be programmed into a computer; given an electronically formatted sampling frame, any database program would be able to accomplish this procedure.

Alternatives to the Simple Random Sample

While the simple random sample serves the needs of representativeness, randomness, and the other criteria of sampling, there are occasions when the sampling needs are different from obtaining an aggregate representation of the population. The study design could call for objectives much more specific, where the leisure services administrator needs to have detailed information about specific constituencies with needs that may be particularly different from the average needs of the community. In such cases, alternative sampling techniques are required to ensure that the specific study needs are met. The following examples illustrate some of these alternative needs:

- An administrator might need to find out if there are differences between the leisure needs of a particular minority community and the majority of the community he or she serves.
- An administrator might need to know the specific needs of a particular neighborhood within the community he or she serves.
- An administrator might need to know the needs of a section of the community that is narrow, such as disabled people.

All of these needs call for different sample designs, and often the specific design precludes the possibility of getting general information about the community. In other words, a sample design meant to elicit information about the differences between different sections of the community would not necessarily yield any information about the overall needs of the entire community. However, there are three kinds of sample design that can accomplish such tasks.

Stratification

The process of stratification involves dividing the population into specific groups and then using the categorization as the beginning point for the sampling process. The sampling process itself could be a random sampling within each category or stratum, or a more complex sampling procedure within the strata. The resulting stratified sample is one that helps to determine the difference between groups. In most measures of difference, a fundamental assumption is that the sample sizes of the groups are comparable. Thus, to test for a statistically significant difference between groups, it is important that the number of people from each group be equal or close to equal. For a simple random sample, that is not the case. As shown in the earlier example, in the case of a sample of 1,000 from a community of 100,000 with 7% African-Americans, only 70 of the 1,000 members would be African-Americans. In that situation, it might be possible to gain an estimate of the needs of the minority community, but it would be impossible to arrive at specific issues of difference between the minority and the majority.

This calls for stratified sampling, where the population is divided into the specific strata of interest and equal-sized samples are selected from each stratum. In the above example, if the interest is in looking at statistically significant differences between the minority and the majority, there should be 500 members selected from the minority and 500 from the majority. This would reduce the error associated with the estimate of the differences between the groups. What is lost, however, in this scheme is the ability to obtain any aggregate results for the total community. In order to make the sample sizes equal, the probability of selection of a member of the minority is radically increased to 500/7,000 while the probability of selection of a member of the majority is sharply reduced to 500/93,000, leading to an over-representation of the minority and an under-representation of the majority. Consequently, any estimates for the total based on this sample would be incorrect.

This is precisely why it is extremely important to determine the goals of the research prior to selecting the sample. Due to the rigorous needs of statistics, it is sometimes impossible to obtain two goals using the same sample. Comparisons between disproportionate groups become extremely difficult when a simple random sample is selected, while estimates of totals are often difficult to obtain from a stratified sample.

The selection of the stratified sample also requires some prior knowledge of the population. For instance, in trying to select a stratified sample of minority and majority members of the community, it is important to be able to identify who the minorities are in the population, put them in a different list, and then select equal samples from the two lists. If that information is not available ahead of time, then complicated procedures of screening need to be adopted. However, in cases where the groups are nearly equal in number, as in the case of gender, these problems disappear since the simple random sample yields nearly equal groups.

In terms of ease of sampling and cost, the stratified sample can be more time consuming to select and more expensive as well. This is primarily due to the fact that it takes a good amount of time to separate the strata in the frame before sampling. Barring that, it takes a sizable amount of resources to oversample from the population in order to obtain equal sample sizes.[5]

Cluster Sampling

The primary goal of cluster sampling is to identify specific groupings where people of similar types can be found. Additionally, it is often the case that people of similar types are rare enough that to identify them through a process of simple random sampling would be terribly expensive. For instance, if the

---

5. If the frame cannot be separated out at the beginning, then to obtain the 500 minority members it would be necessary to sample nearly 7,000 members of the community (7% of 7,000 is 490). However, this also means that the majority would need to be subsampled to retain only 500 of the 6,500 majority members. This makes the sampling procedure terribly expensive.

administrator of the leisure and recreation department is interested in obtaining opinions of the youth, it is possible to do a simple random sample and, depending on the nature of the community, obtain the necessary sample size to get a representative group of youth respondents. Thus, if the community has 10% of its population between the ages of 11 and 18, and the administrator wants a sample size of 1,000, the agency would have to mail 10,000 surveys or make 10,000 phone calls to obtain 1,000 youth respondents. This situation calls for cluster sampling.

In cluster sampling, it is assumed that there are geographic areas or other such clusters where the probability of finding people of the kind sought is increased. For example, most metropolitan areas have specific neighborhoods that are predominantly populated by specific minority groups. Thus, if the administrator of the Dallas Parks and Recreation Department is seeking to determine the needs of the Asian community, it might be possible to identify neighborhoods with a large percentage of Asians and conduct a simple random sample within that neighborhood. The danger associated with such a plan is that it is possible that other Asians in other parts of the city would be missed by this sampling procedure. While that is a drawback, the trade-off lies in the fact that cluster sampling makes it possible to reach people who would otherwise be almost impossible to identify. In the example of the youth, the clusters are schools in the community. These are places where the youth gather and thus are ideal clusters to sample from.

Selecting a cluster sample is a two-step process. In the first stage, the clusters of interest are identified. Then the sample is selected from within the cluster. An important measure associated with cluster samples is the degree of homogeneity within the cluster. Given the assumptions of clustering, it is expected that homogeneity is relatively high within a cluster.

Network Sampling

Sometimes leisure and recreation decision makers need to gather information about specific populations that are scarce and hard to reach. With the increasing concern over the opportunities available to the disabled and with the aggressive adaptation of the Americans with Disabilities Act, there is a need to know what the disabled have to say about leisure and recreation needs and opportunities. However, this is a small population that is often difficult to reach. In a recent study, only 7% of respondents indicated that they were disabled, which would require a subgroup size of 35 in a sample of 500. Needless to say, there are more than 35 disabled in the city, and the simple random sample cannot yield all the respondents. In this case, the option of clustering is also unavailable (unless there are specific services limited in number of where most of the members of this population go to). However, this is an ideal situation for attempting network sampling.

In network sampling (also called "snowball" sampling) a few members of the limited population are identified and then questioned to see if they know of other people with similar characteristics. It is likely that one disabled person might know of others in the community, and thus a network can be established by which a much larger number of members of the particular community can be reached. This strategy can be used with ethnic groups, special interest groups, and any subgroups of the community who have a high probability of interacting due to similar interests (e.g., hobby groups, special sports groups, and so forth).

Determining the Optimum Sample Size

In addition to maintaining the randomness of the sample, making sure that the sample is representative, and deciding on the kind of sample to use, the practitioner has to answer another key question about the sample—how big does the sample have to be? Before answering this question, it is necessary to dispel a myth about sample size. The sample does not need to be a particular percentage of the population. Too often, leisure service administrators demand that a 10% sample of the population be used. The fallacy of this approach becomes clear when the following examples are considered. If the population of a community is 100,000, a 10% sample would yield 10,000 members, which is far more than what is necessary to obtain good estimates; on the other hand, if the community consists of 200 members, a 10% sample would yield 20 members, which is grossly inadequate. Thus, it is unnecessary to think of samples as percentages.

The starting point of answering the question of sample size lies in the issue of error. As indicated earlier, the practitioner needs to obtain an estimate of the population attitudes and opinions from the sample. Needless to say, if different samples are selected, different estimates will be obtained. These estimates will differ by a certain percentage, and the measure of sampling error is expressed as a function of this percentage. If the samples are too small, then the sampling error will be large. In other words, several samples of 50 members will vary greatly in their estimates compared with several samples of 500 members. It is possible to compute the error size based on the sample size and vice versa, but as stated earlier the error that is considered tolerable in social science research is 3-5%. This means that if the agency finds that 75% of the sample is interested in golf, then the planner should be able to claim that the 75%, plus or minus 5%, of the population is interested in golf.

Consequently, the sample size is determined by the amount of allowable error. In most cases, a sample size of 500 or more results in an error of 5% or less, and a sample size of 650 often produces errors small enough even for populations that are much larger than the sample size. It is assumed that a random sample has been selected and no biases have been introduced in the selection process. This, however, is a simplification of a set of very complex computations and assumptions.

In brief, the computation involves two assumptions. First, it is assumed that the sampling error is 5% or less. Second, it is assumed that the variable being estimated will have a half-and-half split. Thus, to estimate the sample size to obtain a 5% error on the estimate of gender (which is often a half-and-half split), a size of 650 is generally adequate. However, if the estimate is of a measure where the split is 70/30, the sample size estimate needs to change as well. The tricky part is the fact that the proportions (such as half-and-half or 70/30) are not known ahead of time, and the best "guess" is often used to estimate the sample size.[6] The issue here involves the prediction or "guessing" of

---

6. The sample size can be measured using the following formula:
sampling error = square root of [(p)(1 minus p)/(sample size)] where *p* is the probability that a condition exists. For instance, if the condition is smoking, then *p* could be 30% (the proportion of the population that smokes). In most cases, since the actual value of *p* is not known prior to the survey, it is assumed to be 50% for the purposes of estimating sample size.

two related criteria. Since the sampling error is related to the probability that a particular attribute will be found in the population, to be able to "guess" the sampling error, one needs to guess the probability of finding the attribute in the population. The following example will help to illustrate the case and demonstrate the futility of using preexisting tables and "guidelines" to obtain convenient sample sizes.

Consider a questionnaire that has two questions, one asking the respondent's gender and the other asking whether or not the person smokes more than a pack of cigarettes a day. It can be guessed that half the population is male and the other half is female, thus producing a 50/50 split with respect to the first question. Using the formula for computing sampling error, it is evident that a sample size of about 650 would produce an estimate of gender within an error of about 3%. As for the other question, let us for a moment "guess" the proportion of the population who smoke more than a pack of cigarettes a day to be 15%. Now we have an 85/15 split, and using the formula for sampling error and sample size, a sample size of 650 would yield a relatively low sampling error. Indeed, it would be possible to obtain a sampling error of 3% for a sample size far smaller than 650. However, to estimate gender, it is still necessary to have a larger sample size. Indeed, based on a simple calculation, it is evident that it is safest and most conservative to assume a 50/50 split and select the sample size needed to estimate sampling errors based on that larger sample size.

However, these arguments become partly moot in view of the relation between sample size and resources. Sample size is also determined by the resources available to do a study. In ideal conditions, responses should be obtained from all members of a population. However, in a large metropolitan area, it is inadvisable to try to conduct a survey with every member of the community. Consequently, it is necessary to strike a balance between how much in the way of resources can be spent to obtain what level of error. The goal is to minimize error as well as costs. This requires that the difficult decision about sample size be made early in the design process. Sometimes the community is so small that every member can be contacted, and in such cases that should certainly be done. In other cases, there are enough resources to go beyond the bare minimum of 650, and a bigger sample size should be considered. However, it is inadvisable to do a study with an inadequate sample since even after considerable expense the results could be flawed and unreliable.

In summary, the sampling process starts with a clear description of the population, obtaining a reliable list, and the determination of acceptable error. Following this, several methods can be used to select a random sample who will be contacted for the survey. In some cases (as in a community of 200 people), this could mean that all the members of the population are contacted, while in other cases cost determines the possible sample size. All these issues go into defining what the final sample is and who is actually contacted in the study.

Chapter Seven

Questionnaire Design for Leisure and Recreation Surveys

It is important to bear in mind that the only contact between the sample group and the leisure agency (or the research group hired to do the survey) may be the questionnaire sent out to each household or individual. The success of the data collection process and the reliability of the collected data are dependent on the content, structure, and format of the questionnaire sent by mail.[1] Until the potential respondent fills out the survey and sends it back to the researcher, the process is incomplete. Consequently, it is necessary to follow a set of guidelines when preparing a questionnaire to ensure a high response rate (Dillman, 1978). Moreover, it is critical that ample attention be paid to the way in which the questions are worded. Inappropriate wording of questions can lead to biased results.

ASKING QUESTIONS

It should be clear by now that the survey process is an interrelated set of activities where every step impacts the following step. Thus, the identification of the goals of the survey often determines the population of interest, which in turn determines the sample selection process. The sampling, in turn, is affected by several aspects of the way in which questions are asked.

Essentially, the process of asking questions involves three primary considerations: the data collection method to be used, the different kinds of questions to be asked, and the precise

---

1. The mail survey is used as the key example here and in all discussions because that is the most common way of collecting attitude and opinion data concerning leisure and recreation. However, the same principle applies to other forms of data collection—face to face, telephone, and via the Internet.

wording of the questions. These issues are interrelated as well.

Methods of data collection can be divided into two broad categories. The first involves the use of an intermediary who poses specific questions to the respondent and then records the answers. This method uses trained interviewers. Interviews are usually conducted face-to-face or by telephone. The respondents do not usually get to see the questionnaire in these situations; they only hear a question and a list of possible responses (in the case of closed-ended questions), and their responses are recorded either by hand by the interviewer or by computer.[2]

The second form of data collection involves the self-response system, where the respondent receives the questionnaire and then responds to it by circling numbers, checking boxes, or writing out long answers to specific questions. The primary method used for this form of data collection is the mail delivery system, where the respondent receives a questionnaire by mail and then responds to it and returns it to a central address. Alternative methods of self-response data collection are emerging in which the delivery system is computer based.[3] This method of data collection depends to a large degree on the cooperation of respondents and their willingness to return the completed questionnaires in a timely fashion.

The primary distinction between these data collection methods lies in the fact that they require two different kinds of questionnaire formatting. In the case of the interviewer questionnaire, the format is most suitable for the interviewer to read from, with the necessary directions for skipping from one question to another or maintaining a question flow that is appropriate for the specific respondent. In the case of the self-response questionnaire, much greater attention needs to be paid to the way in which the questions are laid out on paper and to the

---

2. There is an increasing use of computers in data collection. Most professional survey organizations now maintain some form of computer assisted telephone interview (CATI) system, where the interviewers simply punch in the answers, thus producing a data set as the study progresses. In face-to-face situations, interviewers are equipped with portable computers and use a computer assisted personal interview (CAPI) system.

3. There has been a growth of computer-based surveys, particularly on the Internet and the World Wide Web, where users can access computer forms and questionnaires that they can fill out and send back to a central computer address. The primary problems with this method are that computer availability is still restricted to less than 50% of the American population and there is no good way of keeping control over the sample.

specific directions given to allow the respondent to answer the questions easily and without too much confusion. In the case of needs assessments and attitude and opinion surveys related to leisure, the primary method of data collection is self-response. Consequently, we will concentrate on this method and the way the questionnaire needs to be laid out.

Once the issue of data collection has been resolved, it is necessary to decide upon the broad areas that need to be covered in the questionnaire so that all the goals of the survey are met. The specific questions emerge later in the process. Following are lists the key areas that need to be covered in the attitude and opinion survey.

Existing Level of Interest and Participation

A set of questions should address the level of interest that community members have in the existing facilities and activities of the agency. This requires an extensive examination of the various activities provided by the agency. These can either be organized in alphabetical order or in some groupings, such as "general activities," "fitness and exercise," and "trips," that seem logical to the respondent. These questions are designed to determine the current levels of interest and thus provide valuable baseline information to the planner (see Figure 7.1).

Future Needs

A second set of questions should address the future needs and perceptions of needs of the community. These could vary from the need for future land acquisition to the desire for better maintenance of facilities. Here, too, an extensive list must be developed, and respondents can indicate their perceived level of need for each item in the list. There is a trend of also asking the community about the manner in which they would want to pay for the additions and renovations. This provides an element of realism to the questions, and the respondents will have to think about the costs as they produce a wish list (see Figure 7.2).

Figure 7.1
Measuring existing level of interest: Examples of questions used in the assessment of leisure interests

RECREATION INTERESTS

Listed below are many different types of recreational activities that can be enjoyed year round. For each activity, please indicate whether YOU would have an interest in participating in that activity. It is possible that you might not have all the activities and programs available to you in Any City, but please indicate whether you would have an interest in the activities if they were available.

	No	Yes	Don't Know
VISUAL/GRAPHIC ARTS, CRAFTS IN GENERAL	1	2	8
Ceramics/Pottery	1	2	8
Painting and Drawing	1	2	8
Sewing	1	2	8
Quilt Making	1	2	8
Photography	1	2	8
PERFORMING ARTS IN GENERAL	1	2	8
Dancing	1	2	8
Theater	1	2	8
Music	1	2	8
SPORTS, ATHLETICS, & AQUATICS IN GENERAL	1	2	8
Aquatic Aerobics	1	2	8
Baseball, Instruction	1	2	8
Baseball, Leagues	1	2	8
Baseball T-ball	1	2	8
Basketball, Instruction	1	2	8
Basketball, Leagues	1	2	8
Basketball, Open Play	1	2	8
Bocce	1	2	8
Floor Hockey	1	2	8
Football, Touch	1	2	8
Figure Skating, Instruction	1	2	8
Ice Skating, Indoor Open	1	2	8
Ice Skating, Indoor Lessons	1	2	8
Ice Hockey, Leagues	1	2	8
Golf, Lessons	1	2	8
Golf, Tournaments	1	2	8
Golf, Leagues	1	2	8
Gymnastics, Instruction	1	2	8
Indoor Playgrounds	1	2	8
Laser Tag	1	2	8
Open Gym	1	2	8
Roller Blade (in-Line), Instruction	1	2	8
Roller Blade (in-Line), Course	1	2	8
Roller Hockey	1	2	8
Running	1	2	8
Skateboarding	1	2	8
Soccer, Youth	1	2	8
Soccer, Adult (indoor and outdoor)	1	2	8
Softball, Instruction	1	2	8
Softball, Leagues	1	2	8

Figure 7.2
Measuring future needs: Examples of questions used in the assessment of future needs

IDEAS FOR NEW RECREATION AND SERVICES

The Any City Parks and Recreation Department has several ideas for improving and increasing recreation services and opportunities. For each of these listed below, please circle the appropriate number to indicate your opinion.

	Should this be done?		
	Yes	Not Sure	No
A multipurpose center in general containing the following:			
ample parking	3	2	1
arts and crafts room	3	2	1
auditorium	3	2	1
basketball courts	3	2	1
card tables	3	2	1
computer facility	3	2	1
dance studio	3	2	1
gymnasium	3	2	1
indoor track	3	2	1
kitchens	3	2	1
latchkey after-school programs	3	2	1
modern equipment	3	2	1
pool tables	3	2	1
racquetball/handball courts	3	2	1
recreation center	3	2	1
retired people's activity area	3	2	1
showers/lockers	3	2	1
skating areas	3	2	1
swimming pools	3	2	1
teen drop-in center	3	2	1
video arcade	3	2	1
walking/jogging areas	3	2	1
weight room	3	2	1
Bicycle paths	3	2	1
Botanical Garden	3	2	1
Culture Bus Tours to areas of interest	3	2	1
Football fields	3	2	1
Jogging trails	3	2	1
Lighted fields and walkways	3	2	1
Nature Center with focus on the environment	3	2	1
Nature preserves	3	2	1
New basketball courts	3	2	1
Playgrounds with equipment	3	2	1
Soccer fields	3	2	1
Softball/Volleyball courts	3	2	1
Tennis courts	3	2	1
Walking trails	3	2	1

Personal Opinions

There must also be a section that asks personal opinion questions. Ample research has been done on the ways in which personal opinion questions should be asked. It is now the convention to use specific opinion statements and then ask the respondent to indicate his or her level of agreement with each statement. The list of statements needs to be developed carefully, and the wording of the statements must be clear and precise. The personal opinion section yields specific perception data that can be correlated with other information collected in the survey (see Figure 7.3).

Figure 7.3
Measuring personal opinion: Examples of questions used in the assessment of public opinions

PERSONAL OPINIONS

The Any City Parks and Recreation Department (ACPRD) would like to obtain your personal opinions about a variety of issues. Please circle the number that most closely reflects your attitudes.

	Strongly Agree	Agree	Disagree	Strongly Disagree	Not Sure
I believe the facilities maintained by the ACPRD are safe	4	3	2	1	8
In general, the facilities that I have visited satisfy my needs	4	3	2	1	8
The ACPRD is responsive to community recreation needs	4	3	2	1	8
The ACPRD needs to have more organized activities where the ACPRD staff play a leadership role	4	3	2	1	8
When I sign up for recreation activities the registration process flows smoothly	4	3	2	1	8
the park facilities I visit are clean and well maintained	4	3	2	1	8
The ACPRD needs to keep certain facilities open longer hours	4	3	2	1	8
The quality of leadership provided by the ACPRD is good	4	3	2	1	8
The ACPRD's staff is courteous and helpful	4	3	2	1	8
I feel the ACPRD needs more staff to run all its activities efficiently	4	3	2	1	8
I prefer to organize my own recreation as opposed to the ACPRD providing it for me	4	3	2	1	8
I feel the ACPRD is a significant part of the recreation activities in Battle Creek	4	3	2	1	8
The ACPRD is an important provider of recreation for me	4	3	2	1	8
Transportation to programs and facilities is a problem	4	3	2	1	8
Park facilities are easily accessible within my neighborhood	4	3	2	1	8
I am aware of the recreation programs and activities the ACPRD offers	4	3	2	1	8
the ACPRD does a good job of advertising its recreation programs and activities	4	3	2	1	8
The ACPRD needs to promote itself with the use of signage at special events so the community is aware of its involvement	4	3	2	1	8
There is a need for more activities for people with disabilities	4	3	2	1	8
The ACPRD should seek more private sponsors	4	3	2	1	8
There has been a general decline in women's sports in Battle Creek	4	3	2	1	8
The ACPRD should provide a centralized source of information about all recreation opportunities in Battle Creek	4	3	2	1	8
The ACPRD should attempt to reduce the duplication of recreation offerings in Battle Creek	4	3	2	1	8

Figure 7.3 Cont.

The ACPRD should consider expanding the linear park	4	3	2	1	8
The ACPRD offers enough special events	4	3	2	1	8
The ACPRD has received an unbiased media coverage	4	3	2	1	8

Behavioral Information

An additional section should deal with specific behavioral issues of the community. These include the question of time availability to determine how much time members of the community have for leisure-related activities, and when that time is available. Additionally, the planners might be interested in finding out how often the community members use any facility. This provides valuable usage data that can distinguish users and nonusers. In many cases, the agency has some indications of why the facilities are not being used, and this section can include a question about the reasons for nonuse of the agency's facilities and activities. Because nonuse often has to do with lack of information about the agency, it is a good idea to include in this section a question about the way(s) in which the community learns about the agency. A list can be developed and the community response obtained with respect to the various methods of information delivery. This is also the section where questions about competition can be included. This section thus provides a profile of the community and its leisure-related behavior.

Goals

There is increasing interest in assessing the community's perceptions of the goals of a leisure-providing agency. With all the changes in society and popular culture, and with the emergent social concerns about youth violence, drug abuse, unsupervised children, endangering of the environment, and a general decline in the quality of service in many industries, the public perception of the role and efficiency of leisure agencies is changing. Moreover, since needs assessments and attitude and opinion surveys are often parts of a large-scale planning process, it is useful to solicit the community's opinions about the long-term goals of an agency. Here, too, a set of goal statements can be developed and respondents can rank them as they see fit (see Figure 7.4).

Figure 7.4
Measuring goals: Examples of questions used in the assessment of goals

GOALS OF THE ANY CITY PARKS AND RECREATION DEPARTMENT

The Any City Parks and Recreation Department is in the process of defining its future goals and mission. Some of the possible goals that have been identified have been listed below. Please rank each goal statement between 1 and 7 where 1 represents "very important" and 7 indicates "least important," to indicate your opinion about the stated goal.

Goal							
Improved maintenance, modernization and operation of facilities and parks	1	2	3	4	5	6	7
Construction of new facilities	1	2	3	4	5	6	7
Greater involvement in addressing social issues (at-risk youth, drugs, etc.)	1	2	3	4	5	6	7
Providing equitable recreation opportunities for all sections of the population	1	2	3	4	5	6	7
Increase public awareness of the programs offered by the department	1	2	3	4	5	6	7
Concentrate on athletic activities	1	2	3	4	5	6	7
Expand its operations to include programs and activities beyond athletics (such as music, art, drama)	1	2	3	4	5	6	7
Concentrate on neighborhood-based programs	1	2	3	4	5	6	7

Demographics

By convention, this is the last part of the questionnaire and includes questions about gender, age, and income. These three characteristics are essential to planning decisions. Additionally, questions about marital status and ethnicity can be included. In most cases, it is advisable to use the categories used by the Census Bureau so that comparisons can be made between the data collected in the attitude and opinion study and standard census data.[4] This section can also contain questions that seek information about the respondent's household in terms of number of adults, number of children of various age groups, and length as well as location of residence in the community. This last piece of information can be collected with the use of a map on which respondents can indicate their locations. All of these pieces of information make up the valuable demographic data that are essential for planning purposes.

Once the question categories have been formulated, one can begin to put together the final questionnaire. The primary development in the process of questionnaire construction, particularly in terms of the precise wording of questions, has been the use of focus group research to make the questionnaire suitable to the specific community and research needs. There is an increasing recognition that focus groups offer the opportunity to collect information that can be extremely useful in the construction of questionnaires. The next section points out some of the key issues in the use of focus groups in the process of questionnaire design.

FOCUS GROUPS FOR QUESTIONNAIRE DESIGN

Since the questionnaire needs to address a variety of topic areas, ranging from attitudes and interests to demographics, the researcher might not have a detailed understanding of the specific concerns and appropriate questions for a particular com-

---

4. This is an important issue and is often missed by the planner. For instance, if the age breakdown in the questionnaire is 17-21, 22-26, etc., these will not match the standard census categories, making comparison impossible at a later time. It is much better to use the census categories when devising the questionnaire. This same principle applies to questions of ethnicity.

munity. In such conditions, where the researcher lacks "local knowledge," focus groups are particularly effective. Focus group discussions have been used in a variety of settings. For example, focus groups have been used to collect information for market research, for obtaining student perspectives in academic settings, with managers and teachers, and with community groups (e.g., Fisher, 1993; Ryan, 1993; Kramer, 1993; Twombly, 1992; Doty, 1991; Bloch, 1992; Lengua, 1992; Pryor, 1992; Carey and Smith, 1992; Krugman and Johnson, 1991; Cannon, 1991). These studies used focus groups primarily to gather qualitative information about specific issues from unique groups of people.

Goldman and McDonald (1987) have proposed the use of focus groups in the process of questionnaire construction. They point out five primary uses of focus groups in this application: (1) identification of terms and phrases that community members use in talking about services, (2) development of answer categories that reflect real-world perceptions, (3) development of meaningful response categories, (4) selection of a set of rating dimensions, and (5) generation of a battery of descriptive statements that become the basis of segmentation analysis. Morgan (1988) also makes the same argument in pointing out the usefulness of linking focus groups with surveys. The two primary areas of advantage in this context are assisting in item and scale construction and augmenting the information collected in past surveys. The use of focus groups helps in designing a questionnaire that best fits the community while retaining an overall generic structure.

There are two direct ways in which focus groups help to make a questionnaire specific to a community. First, focus groups provide community-specific input about the various recreation issues that are of importance to the community. Second, focus groups help in the design of a final instrument that is appropriate for the specific leisure program being studied. A third, indirect benefit is the intrinsic value of the focus group in providing a public relations channel for the recreation provider. Focus groups can increase awareness about the recreation opportunities in the community and publicize the survey, thus increasing response rates for the final mail questionnaire.

Three different kinds of groups can be used. Gatekeeper/stakeholder groups are made up of the staff and board members of the recreation agencies that are being studied. Special interest groups represent particular recreation interests in the community. Finally there are groups of randomly selected members of the community who represent the overall feelings of the community. Figure 7.5 lists some examples.

Figure 7.5
Example of Focus Groups used in Questionnaire Development

A. STAFF GROUPS
Park District Staff
Recreation Center Staff
Maintenance Staff
Board Members

B. SPECIAL INTEREST GROUPS

Senior Citizen Groups	City Council
Grandmothers' Club	Small Business Groups
Optimist's Club	Community Theater Groups
Baseball Leagues	Volunteer Bureau
Junior Women's Leagues	

C. GENERAL PUBLIC GROUPS
Invited Open Public Meeting
Small Private Citizen Groups

Each group serves different purposes. Staff and board members provide useful information about the activities offered by the agency, and provide useful organizational and institutional information concerning the ways in which the recreation providers reach out to the community. Special interest groups can provide in-depth discussions about specific needs of the community in terms of specialized recreation and leisure opportunities. Finally, the general public groups may provide information that is relatively unclouded by institutional or special interest concerns.

The method of recruiting the groups is largely decided by the nature of the groups. For staff and board members, no separate recruitment efforts are needed, since all staff and board members are invited to attend the group meetings. Special interest group members can be sent letters of invitation to attend the focus groups, and the general public can be informed about group meetings with press releases that invite community members to attend. For most focus groups there is rarely need to randomize the sample.

Focus group meetings should be kept informal. The role of the moderator is simply to facilitate the discussion. As suggested by Goldman and McDonald (1987), Krueger (1988) and Morgan (1988), usually only one moderator should direct the group discussion; however, when the groups become larger than four to six people, a second moderator can assist to make a useful discussion. The focus group meetings should last between 60 and 90 minutes. An outline of issues to be discussed should be drawn up by the moderator. The issues can include general attitudes toward the recreation provider, assessment of specific current activities provided by the recreation provider, future needs for recreation activities, ways of financing such activities, and a closing discussion of any other issues the members of the group might want to address.

Overall, focus groups assist in three specific ways in designing the interests/needs section of the questionnaire. First, the discussions help draw out unique needs of the community by focusing on issues that are not typically addressed by a standardized set of items. Second, the groups assist in narrowing down unmanageably large lists that include items that are irrelevant to the community and the provider of recreation. Finally, these groups help to develop a taxonomy of items targeted at the community by the use of terms that are easily recognized within the community.

The focus group discussions help in similar ways with respect to the design of the attitudes and opinions part of the questionnaire. First, these discussions help focus on concerns that are unique to the community. These concerns are invariably connected with the leisure interests of the community, which are examined in other parts of the questionnaire. Thus, the focus groups help to reinforce the interest-related items with the attitude items.

The focus groups also help in wording the attitude questions in terms of the local vocabulary, not only in terms of names of specific activities and facilities but by using a language that is closer to the linguistic culture of the community. For example, it is a matter of deciding whether to use terminology such as "reciprocal recreation activities" or "shared leisure programs." This will assist in better comprehension of a questionnaire item by a respondent in the community.

Finally, focus group discussions help to bring out the history of the community and thus help in constructing questions suitable for the specific community and perhaps completely irrelevant to other communities. For example, in one community it was found that the leisure provider used to conduct competitive activities for teens. This was discontinued for several years, but a focus group was able to point this out, resulting in an attitude question about these activities.

The success of focus group administration in the area of leisure needs assessment depends on two main factors. First, there must be ample interest in the community to provide input toward the needs assessments. Since the group recruitment is conducted on a purely voluntary basis with no incentive or coercion, the success of the group depends directly on the level of interest and awareness in the community. This suggests that it could be useful to have some incentive to attend focus groups. In some communities, the interest is so low that focus groups simply do not happen because of lack of attendance.

The second criterion for success lies with the moderator or moderators of the focus groups. Most focus group advocates point out that the moderator plays a relatively passive role in the focus groups. For example, in describing the role of the moderator, Krueger (1988, p. 73) says,

> The moderator exercises a mild, unobtrusive control over the group. The discussion remains on track and, when irrelevant topics are introduced by participants, the moderator carefully and subtly guides the conversation back on target.

However, in the case of leisure needs assessment, the moderator often has to be more obtrusive to keep the groups focused on issues. In many instances, special interest focus groups become forums for airing complaints and grievances about recreation providers. This tendency needs to be checked to keep the group focused on the matter of helping design a questionnaire. Also, at least one of the moderators needs to have a clear grasp of the substantive issues of recreation to guide the discussion along useful channels focused on recreation issues and not irrelevant discussions. Morgan (1988, p. 50) points to this in saying that "high involvement [of the moderator] also has the ability to ensure that a desired set of topics are covered."

QUESTIONNAIRE WORDING AND FORMATTING

Once the focus group discussions have been completed, it is possible to construct the actual questionnaire. Several different issues need to be kept in mind in formatting and writing the final questions.

One important decision that needs to be made concerning the way questions are worded is the choice between open-ended questions and the closed-ended or multiple-choice questions. The first kind is a question that can be answered in several different ways. This is similar to the "essay" question in an examination, where no predefined answers are provided. The multiple-choice question, on the other hand, provides a set of possible responses, and the respondent is asked to choose one (or more). Occasionally this "forced choice" is supplemented with the "other (specify)" response choice, where the respondent need not choose from the existing categories and can specify another choice. This strategy works well with questions about recreation activities, where some respondents might not find their activity of interest within the supplied responses. The different question formats are illustrated in Figure 7.6.

Figure 7.6
Examples of Different kinds of questions

Open-ended question

In general, what are your opinions about the courteousness of parks and recreation staff?

Closed–ended question

In general I think the parks and recreation staff are courteous (circle the appropriate number).

Strongly Agree	Agree	No Opinion	Disagree	Strongly Disagree
5	4	3	2	1

Closed–ended with "other" option

In general I think the parks and recreation staff are (circle all the numbers that apply):

Courteous	1	Polite	4
Helpful	2	Other (specify)___	5
Well–informed	3		

In the case of the open-ended question, attention must be paid to the "openness" of the question and the multiple ways in which the question can be interpreted. Unless respondents all derive the same meaning from the question, different respondents will have different kinds of answers. While variation in responses is expected and natural, it should depend on differences in attitude and behavior, and not on the question wording or interpretation. The open-ended question also poses a significant coding problem since the answers are diverse and no systematic method of attaching a numeric value to the responses can be developed prior to receipt of the responses. In most cases, the coding processes involves the use of elaborate coding schemes that attempt to find similarities between responses and then attach a numeric value to comparable responses. This is a cumbersome and time-consuming process, and it is error prone as well as subject to the biases of the coders. Often this process results in unreliable coding because multiple coders have interpretations of the responses, resulting in the need for tests of intercoder reliability, which, if low, can lead to the need for recoding.

The closed-ended question does not pose such coding problems. Responses are often precoded with numbers, and these numbers often refer to specific and unproblematic concepts, resulting in little coding difficulty. There are two broad kinds of closed-ended questions that can be used in an attitude and interest survey. First, questions may have responses ordered in some fashion. These questions, which can capture a range of possible attitudes, are often fashioned after the Likert scale and are thus called Likert-type scales. These items often use a five- or a seven-point numbering system, where the lower numbers refer to the absence or negative presence of an attitudinal item and the higher numbers refer to the presence or positive attribute of an attitudinal item. For instance, in a Likert-type five-point scale, the statement could refer to the safety of public facilities and the respondent could be asked to "strongly agree," "agree," be "unsure," "disagree," or "strongly disagree" with the concept expressed in the statement. Each of the five responses is given a numeric value, with "5" attached to "strongly agree" and "1" the value for "strongly disagree." Consequently, at the point of analysis, it is possible to compute a mean value for the scale and make some judgments about the aggregate feeling of the community. For example, a mean value of 4.5 would suggest that the respondents feel relatively safe in the facilities.

While these ordered responses can provide information about the extent of feelings and attitudes, there is often a need to elicit information about specific options available to the respondent. For instance, it is often necessary to look at the various ways in which information is disseminated by a recreation agency. One of the ways to accomplish this is to have the respondents check the options that are provided. Here the options do not fall on a continuum, and the average value would be meaningless since the numbers are merely labels. For instance, in asking about how the respondent gets information about an agency, the question could provide a set of options such as "newspaper," "quarterly brochure," and "flyers in schools," and these options could be numbered 1 to 3. A mean of 2.8 is irrelevant in this case, since the numbers do not measure the extent of any attitude but merely the presence or absence of an attribute. This type of question also lends itself to the use of the "other (specify)" option since the researcher could easily have missed a possible source of information about the agency.

Overall, there are several advantages and disadvantages to both open-ended and closed-ended questions.

Open-ended questions:

1. They elicit detailed information.
2. They empower the respondents, offering them the opportunity to expand on their thoughts and responses.
3. They can probe deeper and are not restricted to specific options and responses categories.
4. They are very difficult to code.

Closed–ended questions:

1. They make coding easier because there are predetermined response categories.
2. They appear less intrusive because the respondent does not have to divulge detailed information.
3. They are less empowering because the respondent does not get the opportunity to expand on specific issues.
4. They provide standardized and easily comparable results.
5. They can use standardized terms particularly in the response categories.

6. It is possible to ask a larger number of questions in the space restrictions of a questionnaire.
7. The responses of these questions are open to detailed statistical analysis.

Given these advantages and disadvantages of the two kinds of questions, it is common for attitude and interest surveys to use a combination of open- and closed-ended questions to elicit different kinds of information. The closed-ended questions provide information on issues that needs to be coded and analyzed to test for statistical differences and correlation. Issues of internal, external, and construct validity can be tested with the closed-ended questions. On the other hand, open-ended questions provide the opportunity to elicit detailed information from the respondent. Often the open-ended question can be as short and direct as "Additional comments:". More detailed and specific questions can address specific needs, attitudes, interests, opinions and behaviors of the respondents.

Once the combination of questions has been determined, it is necessary to pay attention to the specific ways in which the questions are worded and asked.

Factors to Consider in the Wording of Questions

Several different conventions can be used in the construction and wording of questions. However, the fundamental important issues are clarity, directness, parsimony, and ease of interpretation. All the constructs that make for effective communication are applicable to the questionnaire. This is the primary form of contact between the respondent and the researcher or research team, and for the instrument to be of maximum benefit, it has to appeal to the respondent and be easy for the respondent to understand and react to. In view of this, the following factors need to be considered when an instrument is put together (Dillman, 1978; Bannon, 1985).

Will the Words be Clearly Understood?

Many questionnaires use words that are confusing, vague, unclear, and complicated. This can make it difficult to answer since the respondent will not be able to interpret the question. In such cases, the use of simpler wording that is more conversational will make the question more accessible to the respondent. Figure 7.7 illustrates the use of appropriate an inappropriate wording in a question. Focus groups help in this respect because they often expose the exact terminology used in a specific community as well any linguistic patterns in the community.

Figure 7.7
Will the words be clearly understood?

Inappropriate

The Parks and Recreation Department should attempt to encourage people to take part in *self-directed* independent activities in the *passive areas* of the parks.

Strongly Agree	Agree	No Opinion	Disagree	Strongly Disagree
5	4	3	2	1

Appropriate

The Parks and Recreation Department should attempt to encourage people to participate in their own recreation activities in the open areas of the parks.

Strongly Agree	Agree	No Opinion	Disagree	Strongly Disagree
5	4	3	2	1

Are Abbreviations Being Used in the Questions?

Questionnaire designers may use unusual abbreviations and technical concepts that are familiar to the agency staff but completely foreign to the community. For instance, a term such as "zero-depth pool" might mean a specific kind of swimming pool to the agency planners, but when used in a question, the term should be clarified. Similary, an abbreviation such as ADA (Americans with Disabilities Act) might be familiar in the trade but might not be as clear to the community. In such cases, abbreviations should be explained (as demonstrated here) by providing the full form in parentheses.

Do the Questions Seem Vague?

Sometimes the questionnaire designer is unclear about the specific issues that are of interest. There may be a general area of concern and the planners decide to construct a question about the area. This often results in the production of a vague and ill-formed question that can mean different things to different respondents. People interpret the same term in different ways depending on their personal experience. Most often, this vagueness is seen in the personal opinion questions. Unclear statements are provided, and the respondents answer in different ways simply because they interpret the terminology in different ways. An example of this can be found in questions about the perception of the long-term goals of an agency. A statement such as "the agency should be involved with social issues" is an unclear statement because the concept of "social issues" could vary widely between respondents. A set of examples in parentheses can help to focus the question, thus providing uniformity of interpretation.

Another way in which vagueness creeps into questionnaires is in the construction of the response categories. In closed-ended questions the strength of the question lies in how well defined the response categories are. It may be difficult to distinguish terms such as "rarely," "occasionally," and "regularly," just as it is difficult to define these terms with respect to the use of recreation facilities. A more precise way to classify the frequency of attendance is "about once a month," "about two or three times a month," "about once a week," and so on, thus narrowing the categories.

Does the Question Have Built-in Bias?

When agency staff administer internally produced assessments, they have certain expectations and personal opinions about the issues they would like to find out about. This often leads to biased questions. Such questions are worded such that respondents are forced to answer them in a manner that might not accurately reflect their feelings about the issues, but in a way that might be "conventional." Similarly, biased questions lead the respondent to say what "the researcher wants to hear" rather than providing a true reflection of his or her feelings and attitudes.

Bias can happen in many different ways. For instance, the question might be biased toward a particular behavior. For instance, in asking about the usage of agency facilities, a question that says, "Hundreds of people attended the pools this summer; how many times did you attend?" obviously puts the respondent on guard and can easily lead to a convention–based answer rather than the truth. Bias can also take the form of overly positive (or negative) terms and definitions to describe behavior. Thus, the statement "There have been many injuries due to rollerblading. Do you think we need a new rollerblading facility?" is worse than stating "Is there a need for a new rollerblading facility?" where the negative comment about rollerblading is simply removed.

In most cases, bias can be removed by a careful review of the questionnaire by an outside group. Questions produced by independent researchers who come in as consultants in a community are often free of bias since they have fewer preexisting notions and expectations about the community. The best way to reduce bias is to rephrase questions to eliminate unnecessary terms that could lead the respondent to answer in a predefined manner. This is primarily a semantic issue. By striving to remaining objective, many of the problems of questionnaire bias can be avoided.

Does the Question Seem Objectionable?

Some questionnaires contain items that might be unpalatable to the respondent. Most often, this applies to personal questions of behavior and demographics. Without the proper rationale, respondents will refuse to answer questions of private belief, behavior, and allegiances. Thus, questions of sexual behavior in a recreation needs assessment will probably not yield responses from the community. Potentially objectionable questions can be made less so by providing a context for the survey. In a community recreation needs assessment there is no relevance to questions of sexual behavior, but a questionnaire about AIDS and its risks could ask questions about sexuality and yield truthful responses. Similarly, questions of personal background, such as race, income, and religion, can be objectionable since respondents might feel that such questions probe too deep. However, in recreation studies these are often important questions, and the best way to pose these questions is by providing categories that are not too precise. For instance, instead of asking a respondent to report annual income, it is better to provide a set of categories such as, "less than 25K," "26K to 35K," and so on, where respondents can indicate which group they belong in. Such strategies help to make the questions appear less intrusive.

Does the Question Ask about Two or More Issues?

This is perhaps the most common problem with novice questionnaire writers. Very frequently, items ask about two different but related issues, leading to confusion on the part of the respondent and ultimately resulting in unreliable data. This happens most often in the personal opinion questions unless the writer is particularly careful. For instance, a questionnaire item such as "I feel that the agency staff is courteous and well informed about leisure activities" might seem legitimate, but the respondent would be faced with a dilemma since courteousness and being well informed are two different attributes; it is possible that one can be courteous and uninformed or vice versa. In such cases, the response becomes ambiguous and unreliable since at the end of the study the planner will not be able to distinguish the two concepts, leading to incomplete planning information. The simplest way to correct such double-barreled questions is to split them up into multiple questions, each addressing a specific construct the agency is interested in. An example is given in Figure 7.8.

Is Too Much Knowledge Assumed?

In many cases, researchers assume too much about the respondents. Assumptions may be made about their level of knowledge, their behavior, and their overall awareness of the issues that the researcher is interested in. This could lead to either inappropriate answers or missing information. This often happens in the case of leisure questionnaires since the authors of the questions are leisure professionals who might know a lot about the specific field. However, the questionnaire goes to members of the community at large, and many of members will not know of the specific activities or even the existence of the leisure-providing agency. Indeed, it is not unusual for 75% of a community to never have attended any leisure and recreation activity or facility provided by an agency. In view of this, any assumptions about the community can be detrimental to the survey.

Figure 7.8
Double-barreled questions

Inappropriate

The facilities owned by the Parks and Recreation Department are *safe* and *well maintained*.

Strongly Agree	Agree	No Opinion	Disagree	Strongly Disagree
5	4	3	2	1

Appropriate

Break down into two questions:

The facilities owned by the Parks and Recreation Department are *safe*.

Strongly Agree	Agree	No Opinion	Disagree	Strongly Disagree
5	4	3	2	1

The facilities owned by the Parks and Recreation Department are *well maintained*.

Strongly Agree	Agree	No Opinion	Disagree	Strongly Disagree
5	4	3	2	1

Is There an Appropriate Time Reference?

In asking questions of behavior, it is often necessary to find out the level and extent of a behavior to assess the need for a particular facility. In such cases, it is imperative that appropriate time references be provided to the respondents so that they can assess the extent of a behavior within a period of time. Such time references also provide the researcher with a better tool for the planning activities since they can project usage over specific periods of time. Consequently, asking a question such as "How often do you use the swimming pool?" yields much less information than asking, "How often have you used the pool in the past 12 months?" One has to be careful, however, about how precise the time reference is. It is better to keep the reference broad enough so that an accurate assessment can be made about the period. It is better to ask about a month than a week, but it is also better to ask about one year than three years.

In addition, it is better to ask about the past month or year than a specific period of time such as "between May 1, 1992 and April 30, 1993." Such specific time periods may be difficult for the respondent to recall. If such questions need to be asked, then some reference needs to be provided, such as: "The year the Olympics were held in Atlanta, how often did you play basketball in the neighborhood park?" Here the respondent can relate back to a special event and thus answer the questions in a more informed manner.

Can the Responses be Compared with Standard Information?

Perhaps one of the most frustrating experiences in leisure needs assessment is the collection of large amounts of information with little indication of the validity of the information. It is possible to compare the demographic information with experience, particularly the census. However, to do so, the response categories need to match the categories of the standard database. For instance, if the response category for age in the census is "between *x* and *y* years," then the needs assessment should also use the *x* and *y* limits so that the results are comparable. Consequently, it is imperative that the standard information be consulted before the questions are written and the data collected.

Other Issues of Questionnaire Construction

Once the wording of items has been resolved, it is possible to move on to the final stage of creating a questionnaire, where it is formatted in a way that makes it easy on the respondent. It is important to note that the way the questionnaire looks has a lot to do with how readily the respondent answers it and sends it back. Consequently, attention needs to be paid to a variety of issues, ranging from the ordering of questions to the amount of blank space provided in the questionnaire. The following are some of the conventions that can be followed.

The Questions Need to Be Ordered in a Logical Fashion

The order in which questions are presented impacts the response rate. It is advisable to place the personal demographic questions at the end of the questionnaire. This makes the questionnaire appear less intrusive. It is always a good idea to begin the needs assessment questionnaires with a set of questions about leisure behavior, where respondents can simply indicate their behavior with respect to leisure and their needs for specific recreation and leisure activities and facilities. This is often followed by the personal opinion questions, which are slightly more intrusive.

Within the group of personal opinion questions, it is often a good idea to have "reverse" questions. Sometimes respondents fall into a trend of either agreeing or disagreeing with similar questions. Thus, a bank of questions about the safety and security of parks could elicit similar responses. However, if within such a bank there is a question that would reverse the trend of responses, then the respondent is forced to pay attention to the questions and not fall into a repetitive trap.

For instance, placing the statements "I feel safe in the parks" and "There is a high level of threat to security in the parks" next to each other would force the respondent to pay attention to the questions and not simply respond with agreement or disagreement since it is unlikely that a respondent would agree to both statements. Indeed, if they agree with the first then they probably disagree with the second statement and vice versa. Thus, the ordering of questions has a lot to do with the way the responses are elicited. The personal opinion section is followed by the more personal questions about leisure time availability, personal demographics, and household information. This has been the convention in most questionnaires, and increasingly people expect this pattern, which makes the questionnaire appear less intimidating.

The Questionnaire Must Be of Reasonable Length

In most self-response mail surveys, a long questionnaire is undesirable. Any questionnaire that is longer than eight to 10 pages (8.5 by 11 inches) could find its way into the trash can. Long questionnaires are more demanding in terms of the respondent's time and are consequently avoided. It is also possible to think of the questionnaire in terms of the time it takes a typical person to fill it out. Anything that takes more than 20 minutes is undesirable in the case of community needs assessments. Attention needs to be paid to keeping the questions of reasonable length so they do not become too demanding on the respondent.

The Questionnaire Should Be Easily Readable

Very often, in an effort to pack a large number of questionnaire items within a reasonable number of pages, researchers are tempted to use minute type and clutter the questionnaire with too much printed information. This becomes a burden on the respondent since the questionnaire simply appears unappealing and confusing. It is thus a good idea to allow enough white space in the questionnaire, with ample margins at the top, bottom, and sides, and enough space between question items so that the material is easily readable. Sometimes techniques such as the alternate shading of lines are used to distinguish question items. Efforts need to be made to make the instrument attractive to the respondent.

This is connected with the issue of the cover letter. In most cases, mail surveys such as community needs assessments are delivered by mail and are accompanied by a cover letter. This is the first piece of communication that the respondent encounters, and attention needs to be paid to this document so that it is appealing and the respondent is persuaded to answer the questions. Additionally, the cover letter should stress the issues of confidentiality and anonymity when they apply. The cover letter should be signed by a recognizable public official and should use an official letterhead to legitimize the survey to the respondent. Figure 7.9 provides an example of a good cover letter.

All these efforts provide the link between the questionnaire elements and the factors that are critical to the data collection process. As indicated earlier, in most cases the method of data collection used in the community surveys is mail. The alternatives available to the agency are data collection by telephone interviews or by face-to-face interviews. Each of these methods has its strengths and weaknesses, and it is beyond the scope of this book to enter into a detailed discussion of these.[5] Suffice to say that the mail data collection system provides a cost-effective way of collecting information from the community.

---

5. For a detailed discussion of these factors, the reader is urged to look at the comparison offered by Dillman (1978) in his book on the total design method.

Figure 7.9
Cover letter: Example of cover letter that can be used with a questionnaire

Dear Any City Parks and Recreation Department Resident:

Our mission is to provide high-quality recreational opportunities for the residents of the Any City Parks and Recreation Department. In order to fulfill that mission, we need to know what the citizens of the community think of current recreation opportunities and what activities might be provided in the future. The City has authorized a survey conducted in order to help determine those recreational needs and interests.

Your name has been chosen as part of a randomly selected group of Any City Parks and Recreation Department residents to represent the opinions of the community. Please help us by completing the enclosed questionnaire. Your answers and those of others participating in the survey will be recorded and analyzed. Your survey responses will be strictly confidential and anonymous.

This survey will help us only if you complete it–so please take the time to answer the questionnaire. We have tried to keep the survey as short as possible. You will find a postage–paid return envelope enclosed in which to mail your completed survey. For your efforts and cooperation in returning your survey, enclosed you will find a ***two for one coupon for one of our facilities.***

Thank you for your help!

Director

Chapter Eight

Data Collection in Leisure and Survey Research

INTRODUCTION

Designing a study, selecting the sample, and constructing the questionnaire are the principal initial phases of any needs assessment or program evaluation phase. The power of the survey then depends on the way in which the data collection is attempted. The quality of the data is primarily dependent on the way in which the data collection is accomplished and the effort put toward contacting every member of the sample. In general, there are three primary modes of data collection: a face-to-face format, a telephone interview format, or a mail data collection system.

This chapter will explore the advantages, disadvantages, and practical considerations of each of these methods. It is, however, important to note that there are also situations when the methods can be combined to achieve the best results. The issue of results is critical to the data collection process. As in the case of study design, sampling, and questionnaire construction, specific criteria can be used to determine the quality of data collection. These include the reliability of the data, the validity of data based on interviewer characteristics, and, most important, the response rate.

Earlier, there was a detailed discussion of reliability and validity in Chapter 3, where the questions of content validity and other kinds of validity and their tests were considered. However, while all those issues are important in the case of survey research, there are additional concerns such as response rate. Unless the response rate is high, the survey data collected are of little value. Consequently, it is useful to consider this issue before looking at the various kinds of data collection and the details associated with each.

RESPONSE RATE

The key aspect of the data collection process is setting up a system that will yield the largest response rate. In explaining this idea, we will use the example of mail data collection because that is the most common data collection method used in leisure and recreation research. However, all the concepts associated with the mail process are applicable to the other forms of data collection. The primary difference lies in the categories of dispositions, which could be slightly different in the various modes.[1] In all cases, however, response rate (RR) is defined as: RR = (total completed questionnaires)/(eligible sample). When multiplied by 100, this rate can be expressed as a percentage.

The numerator is the count of the total number of completed questionnaires. Certain criteria need to be set to determine when a questionnaire is considered complete. Often, respondents will not answer all the questions in the questionnaire. However, if at least a third of the questionnaire is completed and the demographic information is provided, it can be considered a completed instrument. When a questionnaire is considered "completed " should not be an area of debate, but should be determined on the basis of specific and well-established criteria for a particular study. Two approaches are usually recommended.

First, a questionnaire can be considered complete if a certain portion of it has been completed. This method is insensitive to which portions have been completed. For instance, if the cutoff is set at half the questions and the questionnaire has only a few demographic questions, none of which have been answered, then the response does not provide any cross-reference information. A second approach uses a set of key questions strategically chosen within the questionnaire as the criteria for determining the completeness of the questionnaire. If all of the key questions were answered, the questionnaire is considered complete. This is a far more stringent method for determining completeness, but should be used whenever the research goals

---

1. For example, in the case of phone data collection there may be disconnected or unlisted numbers, which cannot be the case for mail data collection.

require that specific questions be answered. The researcher can also consider using a combination of these two approaches.

The denominator in the above formula refers to the total number of eligible members in the sample. Eligibility is a key criterion and needs to be well defined. Often eligibility depends on geographic location. As indicated earlier, a key aspect of study design is the determination of the population. This also determines the question of eligibility. Thus, if the population is defined by a particular age category, then only those community members who are in that age category are considered eligible. Similarly, if only the people in a particular neighborhood define the population, then anyone outside of the neighborhood is ineligible. Also, members of the sample who have moved are considered ineligible, and this is easily determined by counting the number of questionnaires returned as undeliverable by the mail system. Usually, the sampling process attempts to eliminate any ineligible members by targeted sampling with respect to location, age, and other possible eligibility criteria. However, even in the most carefully selected sample there may be some questionnaires that are undeliverable, and they need to be removed before computing the response rate (RR). The following example illustrates the way in which RR can be computed:

Total sample selected	1,000
Total returned by post office as undeliverable	12
Total considered outside of the geography by zip code	350
Total completed and geographically eligible	475
Total eligible (1,000-[12+350])	638
RR (475/638)	74.45%

It is important to note that simply dividing the total number of completed interviews (475) by the total sample (1,000) would yield a lower RR (47.5%), which would be an incorrect representation of the response rate. A low response rate indicates that a section of the people who received the questionnaire did not fill it out and return it to the surveyor. This *could* mean that the nonresponding members of the sample represent a section of the population who have a common characteristic. On the other hand, if a large number of the nonrespondents are ineligible, i.e., not members of the population being studied, then their nonresponse is no cause for anxiety. As in the above example, out of the 525 members of the sample who did not respond, 350 were not even a part of the eligible population; consequently, their lack of response is of little importance to the validity of the study.[2]

Perhaps the biggest challenge to the agency/researcher conducting the mail survey is obtaining a "high" response rate. Just as the sample size is a nebulous number and is dependent on several competing factors (cost, allowable error, etc.), the appropriate response rate is also dependent on many considerations.

Although the notion of the response rate is extremely important to the study, very few leisure and recreation surveys (or other surveys) report their response rates. These numbers are often not clearly stated in reporting the results of a survey. Thus, national organizations such as *USA Today* and Cable News Network (CNN) that conduct large-scale surveys of political opinion usually report only the sampling error based on the number of completed interviews, which leads the reader to assume that a thorough data collection effort was conducted to achieve the highest possible response rate. However, a low response rate has two primary consequences.

On one hand, low response rates introduce nonresponse error, which is far more difficult to compute and estimate than the sampling error. The computation and correction of nonresponse error requires the imputation of the missing responses and making estimates based on the existing responses. This, too, is an inaccurate process and cannot legitimately be applied in the case of missing responses (imputation is best done with incomplete responses). Consequently, a low response rate leaves the researcher guessing about the people who did not respond. In some cases, it is possible to argue that if the respondents are similar in demographics to the overall composition of the community, then there is little fear that missing responses are significantly different. While that may be true, it is still at best an assumption and the reasons for the nonresponse remain a mystery.

---

2. Such cases of high ineligibility, however, involve a cost factor that the researcher needs to be careful about. The eligibility criteria need to be settled *prior* to sampling, and the ineligible population should be eliminated from the initial population list.

This is the second consequence of a low response rate. Since the reasons for the low response remain unclear, it poses an image problem for the leisure organization. It can be argued that the very fact of a low response rate could be connected with the appraisal of the provider. For instance, in one needs assessment at a medium-sized Midwestern city with an active recreation department, the first mailing yielded a response rate of 10%. Since such a low response rate was unacceptable, a second mailing was commissioned. However, one of the problems associated with the department was lack of visibility. Although the department made significant contributions toward the enrichment of the leisure experience and opportunities, it failed to advertise its efforts very well. As a result, many residents probably did not even understand where the mailing came from and simply threw away the questionnaire.

Low response rates also pose a political challenge for a tax-supported body such as a recreation department. In the end, the department is responsible to the people of the community, and the constituency can easily raise the questions of validity and reliability associated with low response rates. When thousands of dollars of public money are spent doing these surveys, an inadequate response rate can raise some very troubling and legitimate questions about the process.

Continuing the example of the city with an initial 10% response rate, it was found that even with the low rate, a sample size was obtained that was ample to make predictions within the 3% to 5% sampling error, and the 10% of the sample who responded were similar to the census figures in terms of demographic composition. Arguably, some projections of recreation need could have been made on the basis of the 10% who responded. It was also, however, decided that such a strategy would be disastrous for the image of the agency and that a second mailing would have to be conducted.

However, such low response rates are not that common, and usually response rates obtained in the mail data collection process associated with leisure and recreation studies are well within the accepted industry levels of 25% to 35%. Yet that is an arbitrary convention based upon experience. Simply put, the best response rate is 100%, and anything less is a compromise. However, different data collection methods provide different response rates, and as we discuss each data collection method, we will discuss the associated conventional response rate.

One of the most important considerations for survey researchers is finding strategies to boost the response rate. As pointed out earlier, low response rates have a number of unpleasant consequences, and since it is impossible to predict the response rate, researchers are often taken by surprise when data collection efforts result in unacceptably low response rates. The primary recourse at that point is to repeat the data collection effort, often at great costs of time and money. However, methodological research suggests some strategies that can be used to boost response rates, including repetition of data collection efforts and the offering of incentives to the respondents. The ways in which these two strategies are applied vary with the different modes of data collection and are discussed later. However, suffice it to say that attempting to reach people in a repetitive fashion can encourage respondents to eventually answer the questions. Similarly, offering respondents a reasonable incentive might gain their cooperation in answering questions.

MODES OF DATA COLLECTION

Several different strategies fall to the process of data collection. In general, these strategies can be divided along two axes: (1) the communication technology of data collection and (2) the communication strategy applied to data collection. The first criterion deals with the communicative technology that is used to reach respondents. Currently there are three primary technologies that are commonly used—face-to-face meetings, printed questionnaires sent by mail, and the telephone. There is also an increasing use of electronic communication technologies such as electronic mail to collect data. On the other axis, data collection can be divided based on the communication strategy—self-response or interview. Needless to say, some of the technologies are more conducive to self-response while others can only be done in the interview mode. Thus, any discussion of data collection needs to consider both axes of differentiation.

Self-response versus Interviews

Before entering into a detailed discussion of the specifics of the three modes of data collection, it is important to point out a fundamental distinction between the data collection processes. There are essentially two primary styles of data collection. In the case of telephone and face-to-face contact, there is the intervention of a third person or an interviewer in the data collection process. The respondents do not have to read or see the questionnaire; rather, the questions are read to them, and they answer by selecting categories offered by the interviewer. The respondent has fewer burdens because he or she does not have to pay attention to skip patterns in the questionnaire or any other distractions that the formatting may pose. Moreover, the question of readability does not apply, since someone else is reading the questions aloud for the respondent. This makes the interview process more valuable for conditions where there are potential problems with respondent literacy. Thus some conditions demand the use of the interview process.

Perhaps the biggest downside of the interview process is intervention of the interviewer. Unless the interviewers are good (there are hardly any studies with a single interviewer!), the data are unreliable. The two primary reasons for this arise from the fact that the introduction of the interviewers brings in a set of "human" variables. First, there needs to be extensive training so that the interviewers are sensitized to the way in which questions should be articulated so that all the interviewers are asking the same questions. Furthermore, in the case of complex responses, the interviewers need to be trained to record the correct response. An example will clarify the issue.

Say there is a question in the survey that asks about the reasons why the respondent might not be a regular attendee of the recreation department's activities. Among the various precoded choices are two responses—"The facilities are not safe" and "Getting to the facilities is difficult." Now consider a respondent who says, "It is so unsafe, I can never get there." How should this response be recorded? In most cases, a probing question ought to be asked to see if "it" refers to the facilities or the buses one could use to go to the facilities. If the latter is the case, then it is of little relevance to the specific recreation survey, and the primary reason for nonattendance is that "getting to the facilities in difficult." However, if "it" refers to the facilities as well, perhaps both responses are legitimate (and both should be recorded, since such questions are often designed to accept multiple responses). However, with multiple interviewers there must be some degree of reliability that the various interviewers will interpret the responses in a similar manner.

A second issue connected with interviews is the fact that interviewers are often tempted to "interpret" a question for the respondent. While probing for clarification is a legitimate task of the interviewer, interpreting questions or response categories (unless they are well defined and standardized) leads to contamination of the data. For instance, a common question category is the level of interest in various activities provided by a recreation department. The possible response categories could be based on a five-point scale ranging from "Lots of interest" to "No interest." If a respondent were to say, "Oh, I go there once a month—would that be low interest?" the interviewer should not answer the question but probe the respondent to clarify the response and put it in one of the five categories. This is important because different interviewers could answer the question raised by the respondent in different ways and thus yield different results. Some of these problems can be identified by observing the interview process and later computing intercoder reliability to check the degree of agreement between the interviewers. Many of these problems disappear in the self-response questionnaire, as in the case of a mail survey.

In the self-response questionnaire, the respondent is the one who reads and answers the questions. This requires specific literacy needs and puts the burden on the questionnaire designer to make the survey well formatted so the respondent will desire to answer the questions. This process also puts a burden on the respondent, because he or she will have to make the extra effort to take the questionnaire to the mailbox and arrange for its return. Although there are strategies to facilitate the process, it is still something the respondent has to do. On the other hand, there is little room for error in this process because the respondent has the questions and categories laid out in clear terms. As long as the questions are readable at the level of the intended respondent, it has to be assumed that the respondent is truthful and is able to interpret the questions in a standardized manner.

Finally, with the increasing linguistic diversity in the United States, the self-response questionnaire often needs to be translated. It must be anticipated that there is a potential body of respondents who might speak a second language.

However, these remain the primary two modes of data collection, and several different questions need to be asked in deciding on the mode to use. These include the following:

- Is the particular kind of research—its goals, population, and questions—suitable for a particular mode of data collection?
- Are enough resources available to use the selected process?
- Is there enough time to complete the selected process?

The discussion of each of the modes of data collection will be built around these concerns.

Telephone Interview

As indicated earlier, telephone surveys can be used in situations where the respondent cannot be sent a self-response questionnaire. Moreover, if the questions are of a particular kind then a phone survey may also be more appropriate. The research shows that respondents are moderately honest in phone surveys, but are less honest in face-to-face surveys and are most honest in mail surveys. Thus, if the researcher is interested in asking sensitive questions about private matters, then a high level of honesty is desirable. At the same time, it is possible that matching the interviewer with the respondent (e.g., a male interviewer with a male respondent) can lead to a high level of candor, which allows the option of asking questions that might not be possible to include in a mail questionnaire.

Phone data collection costs more per completed interview but can be implemented and completed more quickly than mail mode. The higher cost is associated with the technology, the paying of interviewers, and the need to supervise the interview process. However, given a heterogeneous population such as a community in the case of leisure and recreation research, phone data collection yields a greater response rate compared with the mail process and about the same response rate as the face-to-face interview.

There are increasing concerns about the use of telephones for survey data collection. The concerns are related to the interpersonal communication aspects of phone data collection process as well as to changes in the technology of telecommunication. At the interpersonal level, the American population, in general, is becoming "oversurveyed." With the increasing awareness of the importance of consumer surveys and market analysis, as well as the ease with which listed phone numbers can be obtained, more households are getting phone calls from people wanting to do surveys. This can lead to an increasing resistance to phone interviews.

Almost as a challenge to this increasing tendency for phone solicitation, the American household now has a variety of technological gadgets available to control the flow of phone calls. Survey researchers are increasingly frustrated by the use of answering machines connected to a phone line. Often the answering machine is used as a "call screening" device, so phone interviewers might never have access to an adult in the household. Other technological options such as "caller identification" add to the potential respondent's ability to refuse to complete an interview. These developments make it more and more difficult to maintain the high response rates that phone data collection is known for.

Sample Selection

In telephone data collection, the sample consists of telephone numbers. The most common form of a sample of telephone numbers is the simple random sample. The assumption in this case is that every member of the population has an equal and measurable opportunity to fall into the sample. As in the case of all samples, it is necessary to start with a complete listing of the population. For instance, if the recreation provider is interested in considering the needs and attitudes of an entire city or village, the surveyors have to obtain the most complete listing of the telephone numbers of the community. The obvious place to start is the local telephone book.

The telephone book, however, has two glaring shortcomings as a complete enumeration of the population. First, it is often dated. Telephone books are published only once a year, but telephone numbers are issued, changed, or withdrawn over the entire year. Thus, there is always a section of the population who will not be included in the population listing and consequently have zero probability of being included in the sample.

The second problem is voluntary omissions, where members of the population request that their phone numbers not be listed in the phone book. The concern about the phone book being a "dated" list can be less problematic, since it can be argued that there is no necessary pattern in the movement of people and the issuance of new phone numbers. However, the concern over unlisted phone numbers is more critical, because it can be argued that specific categories of people are the ones who choose to have their numbers left out of the phone book.

For instance, it is not unusual to find that single women living by themselves, doctors, lawyers, and other professionals choose to have their numbers left out of the phone book. Needless to say, the loss of these people from the sample can have an effect on the validity of the survey data. Additionally, this tendency has continued to grow, and in larger metropolitan areas the unlisted rate can be as high as 35% to 40%, suggesting that a very large section of the population is being kept out of the data collection process.

Finally, there is some relation between social and economic characteristics and telephone coverage. Particularly in larger cities, the issuance and withdrawal of telephone numbers is often related to the ability to afford a telephone connection. Consequently, when phone numbers are disconnected, the reason could be connected with demographic issues that are of critical import to the recreation provider.

Based on these problems with telephone data collection, a strategy has been developed that helps to preserve the probability assumptions of the simple random sample and also provides a mechanism with which the people who would be lost in a directory-based sample have a chance of being included in the sample.[3] The procedure rests on the assumption that phone numbers are issued in a sequential manner. For example, using the prefix (the first three digits of the seven-digit phone number) 123, the phone company usually begins to issue phone numbers starting with 123-0000 and attempts to fill the 10,000

---

3. The directory-based sample is one in which a simple random sample of phone numbers is selected from the white pages of a phone book.

numbers before moving on to another prefix. (It is, however, not true that the next prefix would necessarily be 124.)

Although there are often holes within this numbering scheme (e.g., it might be that 123-0002 and 123-0004 do not exist), by and large the phone company attempts to fill the numbers in these banks of thousands. Given this fact, it is possible to identify the prefixes in a city and then randomly select a set of four numbers corresponding to phone numbers within that prefix. Thus, if a city has five prefixes and a sample of 1,000 is desired, it is possible to select 200 strings of four-digit random numbers and produce the sample of phone numbers. This process is often called random digit dialing (RDD).

While in theory this is a sound process, in practice it could be a nightmare. After the selection has been completed, the researcher could find that none of the numbers actually exists because by chance only nonexisting numbers were selected. This would mean a return to the drawing board and reselection of phone numbers. Because of the problems associated with the pure four-digit RDD process, modifications have been made to the selection process.

Two-digit RDD is the most popular form of selection. In this case, the phone book is first used to select a phone number; this is followed by randomization of the last two digits by replacing them with a two-digit string of random numbers. For instance, if the selected phone number is 123-4567, then the randomized number could be 123-4578, where "67" has been replaced by "78." This process increases the probability of finding a working number at the randomized location, since the number uses not only the prefix, but also the first two digits of an existing phone number, which makes it more likely that there is another working line in that bank of numbers. In other words, if 123-4567 is a working number, then 123-4578 is much more likely also to be a working number than 123-3489. Two-digit RDD thus reduces the likelihood of reaching nonworking numbers and increases the possibility of reaching numbers that are not included in the phone book.

The biggest drawback with the RDD process is the fact that it leads to the dialing of nonworking and nonresidential numbers. In most surveys related to leisure and recreation, the objective is to reach households to gain an understanding of the attitudes and opinions concerning leisure. Consequently, reaching nonresidential numbers is useless. However, the RDD process leads to the generation of nonresidential numbers, causing unproductive dialing. In most metropolitan RDD samples, it is likely that about 40% of the numbers selected in the RDD process will be nonworking and that only about 60% of the working numbers will be residential. Thus, if one were to select a sample of 1,000 phone numbers by a RDD process, it is possible that only about 360 of these are actually working residential numbers. But these residential numbers include numbers that were not listed in the original sampling frame (i.e., the phone book), and the researcher and the agency are assured that a representation of the population will be obtained.

This suggests that careful attention needs to be paid to the percentages as a RDD sample is designed. Some estimates of percentages can be obtained from the local telephone companies, but better estimates are available from companies in the business of doing sampling. Companies such as Survey Sampling and Genesys often provide such figures to assist samplers in determining the sample size. There are no predetermined guidelines that can be used to make this determination. It is always advisable that data specific to the target population be obtained before determining the sample size because of the differences between different population clusters as well as differences caused by changing demographics and consumer patterns (e.g., more people are unlisted, just as more home businesses are cropping up).

If, for example, 1,000 working residential numbers are desired in a city such as Chicago, it is safe to start with 2,778 numbers using the RDD process (the reader is encouraged to verify this sample size). Additionally, it is important to remember that the sample must be bolstered to account for unreachable phone numbers, computer numbers, fax numbers, and other such numbers where an interview cannot be attempted. The use of RDD thus requires a large number of dialings, albeit many of short duration, simply to verify that a number is working and residential.

There are several alternatives to the RDD process for designing a telephone data collection process. Two of these are worthy of mention. The first involves the Mitofsky-Wakesberg process, which requires the careful maintenance of accurate records of dialing results to eliminate banks of phone numbers that have a lower likelihood of containing residential phone numbers. Thus, if it appears that a majority of numbers in the 123-45XX bank of numbers are business numbers, then it makes sense to stop calling numbers within the 123-45XX bank. However, this determination is made in a stepwise fashion and is an involved process; if done without enough care, it can easily reduce to a poorly conducted straight two-digit RDD process. With the increasing use of phone surveys, the Mitofsky-Wakesberg process has gained a lot of attention, and a variety of modifications of the process were devised.

The second variation to the RDD sample is the telephone book-based sample. In some conditions, it is possible to use the directory-based sample and not lose a lot of validity and reliability. This is primarily true in the case of communities that are relatively small and stable. For instance, small towns and villages, particularly in the rural parts of the United States, tend to have lower mobility rates and fewer unlisted phone numbers. In such cases, it is possible to use the telephone book–based sample and still obtain good results. This is, however, a decision that needs to be made in an informed manner. It is possible to obtain mobility figures by researching the annual census updates, and if the mobility rate is low, it is unlikely that many new numbers will be missing from the phone book. Also, a local telephone company can give a sense of the unlisted rate in the community. If that is deemed to be small as well (e.g., less than 5%), then a directory-based sample can be used. Finally, with the increasing appearance of electronic phone books (e.g., some companies that put out CD-ROMs that claim to list all white-pages phone numbers in the United States) and the quarterly updates that are available, the process of selecting the directory-based sample (or the RDD sample) is becoming simpler and simpler.

Once the sample has been selected and the phone numbers identified, it is possible to work out the details of the data collection process.

Hiring and Training Interviewers

Because the success of the phone interview is directly dependent on the quality of the interviewer, it is imperative that an agency spend the time to find professional interviewers. As a rule, it is better to avoid the use of the recreation and leisure department staff to conduct the interviews. Even if the questionnaire is written in an unbiased manner, those involved with the survey can inject biases into the data collection process that could contaminate the data. For instance, if the parks supervisor is involved with the telephone interview process, questions concerning the parks would have special significance to the person, and unforeseen (or planned) biases may be introduced that would make the data unreliable (e.g., the supervisor may probe the respondent too much to try and obtain a favorable response).

Consequently, it is critical that the interviewers be hired from a pool of people trained to conduct phone interviews. With the increasing use of the telephone for data collection, it is now possible to find, particularly in larger metropolitan areas, people who have developed an impressive range of skills in interviewing. However, in all cases, certain criteria need attention in the hiring of interviewers. Agency administrators in charge of hiring interviewers are well advised to consider the following parameters:

- *The ability to read the questions clearly and fluently*, particularly in cases where the interview might be conducted with persons with special hearing difficulties (and in a community survey, it is likely that a proportion of the sample will be so affected) or with people who might not follow the language well.
- *A quality of voice that is distinct and well articulated, particularly when heard over the phone.*
- *A quality of voice that does not greatly interfere with those of other interviewers* who could be working in close proximity in an interview center.
- *The ability to "ad lib" and respond to questions posed by the respondent.* Although there are specific scripts set up to respond to the standard questions, there might be occasions when the interviewer has to respond to special questions raised by the respondent.
- *The ability to generate some degree of comradeship with the respondent* so that the respondent will be willing to stay on the phone and complete the interview.

When these conditions are present in an interviewer, it is likely that the person will require less training and will be able to conduct interviews smoothly from the beginning.

Some training, however, must be performed, since the interviewer will be dealing with a specific topic area that he or she might not be familiar with. In such cases, it is important that the interviewer obtain some orientation concerning the questions being asked, the general area of recreation and leisure, and the terms associated with the industry. This is study-specific training and should be ample to get good interviewers started. It is, however, advisable that some form of training manuscript be developed that the interviewer can refer to after the training is over and the fieldwork begins. Finally, a question-by-question (Q-by-Q) training of the interviewer is imperative so that the person is clear about the exact wording of each of the questions, the response categories, the logic of the organization, and the reason a particular question is being asked. Q-by-Q training should never be circumvented, and the initial time investment often helps to save a lot of time later in the process.

While the interviewers are being hired and trained it is possible to develop some of the procedures and protocols to be followed when the telephone interview is being conducted.

Setting up the Phone Call Protocol

The phone protocol involves several different factors, and each factor needs attention for the successful implementation of the data collection process. In the case of leisure and recreation surveys, it is advisable that independent interviewers conduct the actual interview process. However, unless the interviewers already belong to a telemarketing or similar organization, they will have to be provided a space from where the phone calls can be made. Also, it is wise to hire one or more supervisors to oversee the data collection process.

Centralization is the key to the space question. The interviewers should be provided a central place with multiple phone lines so that they can all be observed and supervised at the same time. While the centralization process can lead to some degree of interference between the interviewers, that issue should be addressed in the training and planning. It is not a good idea, for instance, to seat all interviewers around a seminar table in a conference room with multiple telephones. It is necessary to provide each person with a small desk and some degree of privacy, perhaps using portable dividers to create cubicles. Avoid arrangements where interviewers can do the surveys from their homes, or even spread out across an agency office in different rooms. Such separation and distance from the supervisor can lead to spurious interviews, as well as frustration on the part of the interviewer if he or she does not have easy access to a supervisor who can answer questions.

Once the place problem has been resolved, it is necessary to decide on the time of the interviews. In most general population surveys, it is better to use the evening hours to conduct the survey. The daytime hours are often unproductive because many households will have no one at home. However, some amount of daytime calls need to be conducted in the early part of an RDD survey to eliminate the working nonresidential numbers from the sample pool. Consequently, it is important to schedule interviewers in such a way that the bulk of the phone calls can be conducted in the evening.

Once the phone call has been made and someone has answered the phone, it is possible to decide whom to interview. In most cases, the "a most recent birthday" method is used, where the interviewer asks the person to list the people living in the household by their birthdays, and then the adult over 18 with the most recent birthday is selected for the survey. This proves to be one of the random ways of choosing a respondent when a random household has been reached.

It is, however, important to recognize that reaching the household can be a long and laborious process. In many cases, the respondent will refuse to cooperate with the interview; in other cases, some device like an answering machine or fax will be reached, or sometimes the call may simply result in a busy tone. Indeed many possible dispositions can result from a call. In some cases, these are final dispositions, and the phone number can be dropped from the sample.

For instance, if on the first call attempt a recording saying that the number has been disconnected is reached, then it is safe to drop it from the sample. If, on the other hand, the first attempt results in a busy tone or a refusal, then provisions need to be made to call the number back. It is critical that some standardized criteria be set up for the callback process. If this is not done, it is difficult to maintain many of the probability assumptions associated with the sample.

For instance, if there are no standards set up, one interviewer may decide to call each number only once, and another may keep trying a number until an interview is completed, albeit with an irate respondent. An automatic bias is thus introduced into the process, because the first interviewer reaches the most "cooperative" of the population who might have had some experience with the leisure and recreation department, while the other interviewer obtains a better representation of the community. To avoid such pitfalls, it is necessary to determine the number of callbacks that should be attempted.

In most "quick and dirty" phone surveys, such as those following campaign speeches, State of the Union addresses, and political debates, no callbacks are attempted. A number is tried once, and if no response is elicited, it is not called back. This is not advisable for more carefully conducted surveys, the results of which can have far-reaching planning and policy implications. On the other end, research organizations are involved in sensitive surveys about health, social behavior, and crime, where it is imperative that every member of the population have a fair chance of being reached. In such cases, it is not unusual to use up to 10 callbacks to reach the respondent.

Clearly, there is a significant difference between one and 10 callbacks as far as the response rate is concerned. In the first case, the response rates are dismal (although the pollsters rarely report the response rate, but simply report the sampling error, which provides incomplete information); the latter produces response rates of up to 97% and 98%. Thus, the agency commissioning its own telephone survey of the community will need to decide on the number of callbacks. The "industry standard" for local government agencies varies between three and five callbacks (or four to six dialings of each number). After the set number of callbacks, the telephone number is given a final disposition and removed from the sample.

As should be clear from this discussion, with a sample of 1,000 and four callbacks, there is a need to keep good records of the ongoing disposition of each phone number. Often, the same interviewer does not call the same phone number back, so different interviewers need to know the disposition of a number at the beginning of a new shift. If the disposition is such that the respondent has refused twice, the supervisor might need to designate a more experienced interviewer to the number in an attempt to convert a persistent refusal.[4] On the other hand, there

4. Indeed, there are experienced interviewers who advertise themselves as "refusal converters" who can cajole and charm a respondent into giving an interview even after several previous refusals.

could be respondents who are willing to be called back at a particular time or actually set up an appointment. Such special requests on the part of the respondent need to be followed. Consequently, it is necessary to keep good records of the call outcomes. This can be done using a relatively standardized form, often called the Interview Record Form (IRF). When kept in a centralized location, this form can provide an interviewer new to the number ample information about the status of the last call and the action needed on the next call. The IRF can easily be adapted from the example provided in Figure 8.1.

Figure 8.1
Interviewer Record Form (IRF)

Name of Survey Organization Study #________
Address of Organization Project #________

ID# 100067
Phone Number: 555-555-1212

Call Attempt Record

Attempt	Outcome	Interviewer #
1.	______________________________	________
	______________________________	
	______________________________	
2.	______________________________	________
	______________________________	
	______________________________	
3.	______________________________	________
	______________________________	
	______________________________	
4.	______________________________	________
	______________________________	
	______________________________	
5.	______________________________	________
	______________________________	
	______________________________	

While paper is the older way of keeping records, and IRFs used to be attached to the paper-and-pencil questionnaire, there is an increasing shift toward the use of computer-assisted telephone interview (CATI) systems. These systems vary from simple computer routines that allow the recording of the responses on a standard database system to more complex, multisystem networked programs that allow for great complexity. It is important for the agency to be aware of these systems, because they can often make the interview process more efficient and less error-prone since the interview and the data entry are happening simultaneously. However, if the interviews are being done in-house, then each interviewer needs to be provided with a computer where the responses can be directly logged into the CATI system. This can become expensive, making it more feasible to contract the work to independent agencies that already have a CATI system in operation. Needless to say, it is desirable to have *as high a response rate as possible*, and there are several strategies that can be adopted to reach this goal.

Self Response—Mail

Mail data collection uses the self-response system, where there is no intervention between the respondent and the agency. The respondent receives the material in the mail and is expected to answer the questionnaire and send it back. Needless to say, this is a tricky process, since the respondent might have little incentive to cooperate. Moreover, there are no "refusal converters" to cajole and charm the reticent respondent. Consequently, obtaining a good response in a general population mail survey often requires the production of a well-formatted and attractive questionnaire that is easily read and free of complications. In such cases, the respondent might pay more attention to the questionnaire and feel like responding to it rather than getting rid of it.

The Mailing Process

The way in which the mailing is conducted often helps to determine the response rate. Agencies should always consider the use of a first-class personalized mailing, where the name of a respondent appears on the address label. Too often households receive direct mailings addressed to "Resident," and such mail automatically finds its way into the wastepaper bin. Personalized mail has a greater possibility of being attended to. The questionnaire itself needs to be simple and accessible, and the cover letter should make a clear appeal to the respondent as to why it is important to complete the questionnaire and return it. The cover letter often plays a critical role in this process. If an agency that is highly visible in the community is attempting to gather information about community needs, then a cover letter signed by the agency director might be recognized and elicit a good response. On the other hand, in large metropolitan areas, where the specific administrators are not household names, it might be better to have the cover letter signed by the city mayor. In that case, the respondent might feel a greater need to return the questionnaire.

The return process should also be made as simple and effortless as possible. There should be a postage-paid, self-addressed return envelope accompanying the survey. Often, the questionnaire can be designed in such a way that the respondent merely completes the instrument, folds it, and puts it back in mail. The key is to make the entire process simple and easy without placing an undue burden on the respondent and without introducing any hurdles (such as having the respondent buy a stamp to send the questionnaire back). Using these procedures on the first mailing often helps to increase the initial crop of returns.

The mailing itself needs to be coordinated in a way that all respondents receive the questionnaires at about the same time. If the sample consists of 8,000 or 10,000, this could be a formidable task, since it would involve the stuffing of that many envelopes with the questionnaire and return envelope, sealing the outgoing envelopes, and carrying them to the post office. These tasks can be contracted out at a relatively low cost and that is sometimes the best option for an agency. However, it is important to ensure that all the mailings happen within a short period of time so that there is no bias introduced by the fact that different people receive the mailing at different times.

If the strategy is to use a single mailing of the questionnaire, then the data collection process concludes here, and the agency has to wait to see how many among the sample return the completed questionnaire. Depending on the quality of the questionnaire, and the amount of interest in the issues in the community at large, the response rate on a first mailing could vary between 10% and 35%. If the response rate is over 25%, it is possible to consider this to be adequate and proceed with the data analysis. If the response rate is lower than 25%, it is necessary to consider other strategies to boost the response.

It could be true that the nonrespondents are similar in some fashion, and thus the lack of response from this possibly homogeneous group could lead to a high level of nonresponse error. To a certain degree, comparing the respondents against standard census information can test this proposition. If the census reports that the percentage of African-Americans in a community is 15% and the needs assessment shows that only 5% of the respondents are African-American, there is certainly a problem of nonresponse error, since the African-American section of the sample will be under-represented. In such cases, new mailings could be needed. However, this should be anticipated as early as possible and special efforts made where lower response rates can be expected.

Follow-up

If time and resources permit, the best way to boost the response rate may be to do some form of a follow-up to the first mailing of the questionnaire. It is sometimes difficult to predict if a follow-up will be required. Yet to organize and conduct a follow-up mailing in the course of a study is a relatively daunting task. Consequently, it is a good idea to plan a follow-up, make the necessary preparations, and not do it if the response rate is favorable instead of scrambling to put one together in the middle of a study.

For any kind of follow-up, multiple records of the sample need to be maintained. In other words, if the agency plans to buy a set of address labels for the mailing, it is always better to buy multiple sets of labels at the beginning. Since the mail sample is selected in a random fashion, the computer program that produced the random sample might not be capable duplicating it later. Sometimes the sample can be maintained as an electronic file from which future labels can be printed. Multiple sets of questionnaires need to be printed as well, so that they are available when needed.

It should also be clear that follow-ups are conducted with the same sample. Some leisure and recreation boards have demanded that the follow-up be conducted with a fresh sample. This is simply incorrect, since that would not be a follow-up but an addition to the original sample size. Thus, if the first mailing consisted of 5,000 cases, of which 500 responded, yielding a response rate of 10%, the second mailing needs to go the same 5,000 (minus the 500 who responded, if they can be identified), out of which another 500 might respond, thus doubling the response rate.

If the second mailing went to a different 5,000 and 500 responded, the total number of responses would still be 1,000, but that would come from a sample size of 10,000, thus not changing the response rate at all.

Any follow-up procedure requires a careful control of the mailing process. This procedure is often called *sample control.* It is certainly not cost-effective to do a follow-up with the entire sample, since a proportion will have responded to the first mailing. Consequently, a coding system using identification numbers needs to be devised to control the sample as completed questionnaires are returned. The identification number on the questionnaire (often placed in an inconspicuous area of the instrument) needs to be matched with the identification number on the sample file so that the people whc have returned the questionnaire can be eliminated from the follow-up procedure.[5] Clearly, the process of sample control adds a cost component to the needs assessment, which is only a part of the extra costs involved in a follow-up.

There are several different follow-up processes that can be adopted, and the choice often depends on the amount of time as well as resources available. It is important to note that each follow-up adds to the cost of the project as well as to the length of the process.

Typically, a single mailing is followed by a reminder postcard to nonrespondents. This can be done within two weeks of

---

5. This process often calls into question the issue of anonymity and confidentiality. It is certainly possible for an agency to match a respondent with a questionnaire and thus obtain sensitive information about a particular citizen. However, in most cases, the needs assessment is contracted out to an external survey organization, where the respondent information is zealously guarded by the sampling section of the organization. If an agency decides to do the needs assessment in-house and incorporate some follow-up procedures, it is the ethical responsibility of the agency and its researchers to maintain the confidentiality that is promised in the cover letter.

the mailing of the original questionnaire. The postcard simply reminds nonrespondents to fill out the questionnaire and put it back in the mail. This is enough incentive to get some nonrespondents to cooperate. The postcard can be followed in two weeks by a second mailing of the questionnaire. Sometimes people receiving the instrument have the intention to respond, but misplace the questionnaire. The second mailing of the questionnaire offers them a second chance at responding. This three-mailing procedure is perhaps the most common method used in mail surveys.

Variations can include a phone call in place of the postcard. There are two key considerations in using the phone reminder. First, it assumes that working phone numbers are available for all members of the sample. This might not always be the case, since people are increasingly using unlisted numbers and phone numbers can change before they are updated in the phone book. Additionally, it can be very tedious to collect the phone numbers of thousands of sample members unless they can be found electronically and printed out in a usable format.

Another concern with phone follow-ups is the extent of information that can be obtained. It makes little sense to contact potential respondents on the phone merely to remind them to send in a questionnaire that they could easily have misplaced. If it is possible to find a potential respondent, then it is far better to obtain a completed interview over the phone. This suggests that the phone follow-up could transform into a phone interview. Consequently, the person doing a phone follow-up needs to be cross-trained as a telephone interviewer so that reliable data can be collected from people who agree to do the phone interviews.

These procedures help to boost the response rate so that any bias associated with nonresponse error can be minimized. However, in addition to these mailing-related procedures, another way to increase response rates is to simply increase the awareness of the community about the forthcoming survey.

Promoting the Survey

Community surveys are unlike surveys of special populations, where a population might have some intrinsic interest in the issue being surveyed. For instance, surveys of professional groups such as doctors, lawyers, university professors, or leisure professionals are often less complicated because the group will have some degree of interest in the subject and will often feel responsible to respond to the questionnaires. As a result, there is a lesser problem of low response rate. In the case of the general population, for mail surveys of recreation needs and opinions, there is no compelling reason why the recipient would be interested in returning the questionnaire. Consequently, generating some degree of "hype" in the community is a good way to produce the necessary interest. This can be done by placing newspaper stories about the survey, by putting out press releases, by inserting information about the survey in the general mailing of the agency brochure, and by placing stories in local and community radio and television broadcasts. These methods produce a certain degree of awareness of the survey as well as of the agency, and when the questionnaire reaches the homes, people might pay greater attention to it and be encouraged to fill it out and return it.

The response rate is thus dependent on a variety of factors that apply at every stage of the survey. Incorrect definition of the population and sloppy sampling could have an effect on the response rate; those receiving the sample could simply be ineligible, and if that rate of ineligibility cannot be determined, a lower response rate will be reported. The response rate is also dependent on questionnaire wording and layout. The focus group discussions should also be used to increase response rate by seeking the assistance of the participants to talk to their communities and encourage members to respond to the questionnaire when they get it. Thus, the response rate is not simply dependent on the number of mailings or the nature of the follow-up, but on a network of factors that all lead to the final conduct of the survey.

Alternative Forms of Data Collection

While the telephone interview and the mail survey represent the two most common forms of data collection employed in community-wide surveys for leisure and recreation needs and evaluation, other forms of data collection can also be attempted. The most common of the alternative forms is face-to-face (f-to-f) data collection.

In the f-to-f scenario, the sample consists of neighborhoods (or census tracts), blocks within tracts, and finally individual houses within blocks. With the increasing sophistication of the information available to researchers, it is possible to create maps of blocks that pinpoint individual dwelling units and can thus be used for sampling purposes. Once the sample has been identified, trained interviewers are sent to the houses where they conduct the interviews. In some cases, a procedure similar to CATI, called computer assisted paper and pencil interviews (CAPI), is being used by interviewers to enter responses directly into a computer system.

It is expected that interviewers will return to households a predetermined number of times (much like the callbacks in the phone data collection) before considering a dwelling unit to have been finalized. Given the direct contact with households, f-to-f interviews often yield response rates as high as 98%.

Several factors make the expensive method of f-to-f data collection attractive. First, f-to-f data collection is the most effective form when some type of cluster sampling has been adopted. If it is known that a particular section of the population is concentrated in a particular geographic location, then it makes sense to send f-to-f interviewers to such locations to collect data. To some degree, the process used in youth surveys (a common component of mail leisure and recreation surveys), with coordinators traveling to schools and distributing questionnaires in the assembly hall and collecting them at the end of a period, is a variation of the f-to-f system, except that in the f-to-f system the interviewer acts as the mediator between the respondent and the questionnaire.

This direct contact is the second reason the f-to-f process is often the best way to collect data. As agency administrators know, there are in most American cities pockets where the minority and the underprivileged have been segregated. These are people who might not have a permanent address or a phone number, and thus these are people who are unable to voice their opinions through the more formal channels of telephone and mail data collection. Yet these are members of the community and in many instances irate and angry minority community members representing the "inner city" feel that leisure service providers pay little attention to their needs. Often this is because the traditional channels of collecting information are ineffective. In these situations, supplementing the primary mail sample with a cluster sampling of the neighborhoods and using face-to-face data collection is perhaps the only procedure available to gather the necessary information. Although the process could be expensive, it is the only way to obtain a representative sample of the community.

Another situation where f-to-f data collection is the only possible procedure is when the data collection needs to be supplemented by other collections, such as physical samples, or when the collection of opinions and attitudes needs to be corroborated with descriptions of the household that can only be obtained by observation. This is the reason many medical surveys are conducted face-to-face, since the opinion data often must be supplemented by the collection of physical evidence such as blood or other bodily fluids. There have been surveys where the interviewer was accompanied by a trained phlebotomist who followed up the interview with the collection of a blood sample. While this might not arise too often in the case of the leisure and recreation survey, it is an illustration of special conditions where the f-to-f method seems most appropriate.

The primary disadvantage with the f-to-f method is cost. Given the fact that interviewers have to travel to the respondents and often go back a number of times, the f-to-f method is an expensive data collection process. It also takes longer since there is more work involved, part of which consists of simple transportation. These two factors need to be kept in mind when considering use of the f-to-f process.

Other forms of data collection that are emerging include the use of electronic mail and other procedures that use the Internet as a possible tool for data collection. There are, however, two primary concerns with the validity of these processes. First, it must be recognized that Internet access is uneven and, as surveys have demonstrated, is used primarily by people of a particular age group (young to middle-aged) within a specific income range, and the users are mostly male. Thus, it would be difficult to obtain a good representation of the general community.

The second problem with on-line data collection has to deal with sampling. Given the fact that it would be easy for a respondent to provide duplicate responses, the sample integrity might be compromised and unknown biases can creep in. It is, however, possible to use the Internet as a supplemental system where the respondent provides the response to the mail questionnaire by using the Internet. Thus, it is possible to provide an Internet address on the questionnaire to which the responses could be e-mailed. In a similar fashion, a World Wide Web site can be designated where the respondent can find a copy of the questionnaire and respond to it electronically. These are relatively new options that need to explored and researched before being instituted as a standard part of the data collection process.

Combining Methods

A well-designed survey could use multiple methods to get the best representation and response rate without unduly increasing cost. A scenario is described here that requires strict sample control and planning. A combined method could begin with a mailing of questionnaires with the option of an electronic response to an Internet address. After about two weeks the nonrespondents (both mail and electronic mail) could be reached by a follow-up phone call, and an interview could be conducted with those who can be reached by phone. This process would also yield a list of respondents who could not be reached by phone, but for which the post office did not return the mailing as undeliverable, suggesting that it is a deliverable address without a phone. All or some such remaining members of the sample could then be reached by f-to-f contact. This procedure would ensure wide coverage and, with appropriate numbers of callbacks and returns to the households, a good response rate as well.

Needless to say, this would be an expensive procedure, and very often the overall data collection process ends up being a compromise between response rate and cost. While a concerted approach such as the one above could yield a high response rate, agencies could easily argue that it is not necessary to spend a large amount of money to boost the rate by a few percentage points. That choice needs to be made with the awareness that there is no response rate as good as 100%. Anything less is already a compromise and will have an effect on the quality of the data.

Chapter Nine

Preparing for Data Analysis

INTRODUCTION

Once the data collection has been completed, it is possible to move on to the final stage of the survey process—data analysis. The term "data analysis" conjures up a variety of images, from the of basic counting of information and categorization into small groups to very complex manipulation of data to investigate trends and analyze relationships. The key is, however, being clear about the specific needs of the agency and the reason the data collection was even attempted. Generally, the two broad goals of a data collection effort are to assess the future needs of the community and to evaluate the current opinions and levels of satisfaction of the community. Based on this information, the agency should be able to make a set of informed decisions and move on with the process of creating a master plan, strengthening areas of weakness, or identifying areas where a need is developing.

The survey process is a pragmatic affair requiring particular actions at the end to make the effort worthwhile. It is not a process of abstract research to find out the opinions of the population and then conduct elaborate statistical manipulations to test the relationships, differences, and other mathematically reducible trends in the data. Needless to say, these could be required to answer the pragmatic questions raised by the agency, but the research should be driven by the questions, and data manipulation should not become the goal.

This dichotomy is the difference between the statistical/academic approach and the practitioner/pragmatic approach. While both approaches have their merits, it is important to be able to use the appropriate approach at the correct time. Witness, for instance, the situation where, as an academic, a college professor doing work for an agency requested that printouts be produced for cross-tabulating every question with every other one. This resulted in multiple stacks of several feet of computer printouts that had to be carted from the computer center to the agency office in a van and that was perhaps eventually thrown away. This completely useless venture at the cost of several forests was driven by the legitimate academic desire to look at all the relationships. The pragmatic approach is to consider the goals of the survey and then use the appropriate analysis to make judgments about the data. It is thus important to be able to make this distinction when beginning the data analysis process. It is crucial that the goals of the analysis be clarified before the manipulation begins.

To briefly summarize, the goals of most leisure and recreation surveys can be categorized as follows:

- Investigate the current level of interest in the specific activities and facilities provided by a recreation provider.

- Investigate what future interests the community might have in terms of specific recreation needs.

- Investigate the opinions of the community with respect to the efficiency and the sufficiency of the leisure services available to the community.

- Gather all relevant demographic and behavioral data that can be used to better understand the composition of the community, its time availability, and the ways in which time is spent by the community.

The first three goals require a particular direction of analysis, while the last goal calls for a slight modification of the analysis. However, these goals certainly do not require complex mathematical modeling and other advanced statistical procedures, which would simply be irrelevant to the task of fulfilling the goals.

Before moving on to the kinds of analysis, it is necessary to review some fundamental notions about the data and scales to assist in the understanding of the analysis.

REVIEWING THE BASICS

As discussed previously, the final instrument is often a complex product using a variety of questions of different types incorporating different kinds of scales to provide answers. Closed-ended questions offer the respondents a limited set of responses to choose from. In many cases, these options are precoded, and the data entry personnel do not have to remember specific code numbers. For instance, if it has been decided that men are to be numbered as "1" and women as "2," those are the codes that will be used consistently throughout the study. Needless to say, in some cases these are arbitrarily assigned numbers, while in others, the numbers have to be selected carefully.

The discussion in Chapter 3 on different kinds of scales used in survey research explains the need for specificity in the coding process. In summary, data coding, either precoding by building the numbers corresponding to responses into the questionnaire, or postcoding by assigning numbers to response categories at the time of data entry, is essential to the process of data analysis. It is inefficient for computers to tally alphabetical responses, and it is far better to have a numeric code associated with each response. However, the specific number associated with each response often depends on the type of scale being used in the questionnaire.

The notion of scale has major implications on the limits and scopes of the data analysis and the way in which it is conducted. Although the nomenclature used for the types of scales was discussed earlier in the book, it important to consider how the different scales are associated with survey research and how the choice of scale can impact the data analysis. A simple example will illustrate the point. To find out someone's gender, you ask (if you cannot hear or see the person, such as in the case of a mail survey) if the respondent is male or female. You might then attach the number *1* to the women and *2* to the men. You can then count how many *1*s there are and how many *2*s there are among the respondents. Ultimately, you can claim that there were, say, 200 *1*s and 250 *2*s among the 500 respondents, and 50 people did not answer the question. You now know that among those who answered the question, 44.4% are *1*s, or women, and 55.6% are *2*s, or men. And that is usually the extent of the analysis. It is meaningless to compute an average and say that the average gender is 1.56, because the number 1.56 is of no value here—gender can only be *1* or *2*. The situation is quite different in the case of questions where the respondent is responding on a continuum from "strongly agree" to "strongly disagree." Here it is assumed that if the average response is 4.5, where *5* stands for "strongly agree" and *1* stands for "strongly disagree," then it is likely that the average attitude is on the positive side. Moreover, in this case, the policymaker would also gain from knowing what percentage of the respondents said *5*, how many said *4*, and so forth. Different scales need different forms of analysis and provide different opportunities. It is thus useful to consider the options provided by some of the common scales used in these surveys.

At the lowest level is the nominal scale. The options on this scale simply assign names to categories, and there is no relationship between the numbers. Thus, in the case of gender, the two categories *male* and *female* are mutually exclusive and giving the number *8* to males and *547* to females would have no impact on the data analysis. In the end, the agency would still be interested only in knowing what percent were *8* and what percent were *547*. The same goes for categories such as race, where the numbers associated with the categories are meaningless and are simply used to organize the population into groups. In questions about leisure and recreation needs, questions that deal with specific options fall into this group as well. In the example in Figure 9.1, the fact that people cannot attend activities due to "lack of information" or "lack of parking" can be gleaned independent of the numbers attached to the categories.

This scale thus provides a particular kind of information and does not allow the option of conducting some level of analysis, except that of counting. It is certainly possible to count the number of respondents listing any of the options for a particular question. It is, however, meaningless to compute averages or conduct higher-level analyses for this scale.

The next level of scale is the ordinal scale. In this case, responses represent mutually exclusive categories, but there is a relationship between the numbers. This is not a commonly used scale in leisure and recreation surveys, but it could be useful for asking questions to establish some ranking of the respondents. Questions about income, for example, could be asked in a way where the ordinal scale is used.

Figure 9.1
Example of a nominal scale: Questions used in the assessment of leisure behavior

*There are many reasons why people can not, or do not, participate in activities sponsored by the Parks and Recreation Department. Please indicate the reasons you have for **not** participating (circle all that apply).*

Getting to the facilities is difficult..1
Inconvenient timing of events..2
The facilities are crowded..3
Lack of information..4
Lack of security..5
Lack of parking..6
Lack of appropriate staffing..7
There are no programs for people with special needs..8
Not Interested..9
Better private facilities elsewhere..10
The user fees are too high..11
Level of crime at the facilities..12
Poorly-maintained facilities..13
Lack of rest-room..14
Activities do not interest me..15
I do not have the time..16

There are also several reasons why you might have visited the facilities, or participated in activities and programs. Please indicate the reasons you have for attending (circle all that apply):

They are affordable..1
The facilities are well maintained..2
The staff is courteous..3
There are innovative programs..4
The leadership is good..5
The facilities are in the neighborhood..6
The special events are held there..7
No other provider..8

As another example, suppose a question asks respondents to indicate their level of expertise for a particular skill. The responses are arranged in such a fashion that the group that is most skillful is far more advanced than the second group, which is only slightly more advanced than the third group. Now, it is possible to assign numbers to each of these groups. However, it is important to note that although there is a relationship between the numbers vis-à-vis the fact that group 1 is better than group 2, which in turn is better than group 3, the difference in skill between groups 1 and 2 is different from the discrepancy between groups 2 and 3. This inequality is a critical element of the ordinal scale, where the computation of an average is just as difficult as in the case of the nominal scale. Since the numbers are not equidistant on a scale, the average of 2.5 and the average of 1.5 are vastly different, and without a clear notion of the way in which the scale is established, the numbers may be quite meaningless. On the other hand, the computation of frequencies of occurrence is quite appropriate with the ordinal scale.

These problems disappear to a large degree in the case of the third kind of scale, called the interval scale. This is one of the more commonly encountered scales in leisure and recreation surveys. This scale is also often called a "Likert scale," after the person who devised it, although a pure Likert scale is far more complex and rigorously produced than the garden version seen in questionnaires. Consequently, it is better to refer to these as "Likert-type" scales.

The most popular example of such a scale is one where the respondent is asked to express a level of opinion about some statement. Consequently, a Likert-type scale requires two components. There must be a statement of action, opinion, hope, interest, need, or anything else that can be put in the form of a single clear and unambiguous statement. Second, the respondent must be given a limited set of choices to express the level of interest, agreement, etc. with respect to the statement. It is further assumed that the respondent's feeling can be placed on a psychometric scale, where a number such as *1* could stand for a low opinion, while a higher number such as *5* (in a five-point scale) would represent a high opinion. It is also assumed that the difference in opinion represented by the distance between the numbers *3* and *4* is equal to the difference in opinion expressed by the distance between the numbers *2* and *3*. Clearly, these assumptions are open to argument. Yet research and experience have demonstrated that it is possible to obtain accurate and reliable information about people's opinions using such scales.

Suppose there is a single statement followed by a five-point scale that contains a neutral point of 3 in the middle.[1] Now depending on the responses, it is certainly possible to compute the frequency of each of the responses. Thus, it would be pos-

---

1. It is important to note that there is a growing tendency among scholars and researchers to abandon the midpoint and use four-point scales, with a different number such as *8* provided as a "do not know" response. This response is then discounted from the final analysis. However, a counterargument could be made that lack of information or knowledge does not necessarily presuppose a lack of opinion. Thus, to discount the neutral opinion is to force people to have opinions when they might not. Given this, it is important to consider the implications of the even-numbered scales. If one is to be true to Likert, then the five- or seven-point scale is recommended.

sible to find out what percent of the people responded with "strongly agree," what percent said "disagree," and so forth. However, it is also possible to compute an average. Thus, if the mean (rounded to an integer) for the statement is "4," it would provide the basis to claim that the average opinion of the population is on the positive side of the scale. Moreover, since it is possible to compute the mean, it is also possible to compute higher-level statistics. What is lacking in this scale is the presence of an absolute zero. In other words, it is very difficult to assign absolute measures of attitude. Stop and ask yourself whether there can be a zero attitude corresponding to a box with zero elements in it. However, there are times when it is necessary to measure the complete absence of an attribute.

In such cases, the ratio scale is used. This is the same as the interval scale, except that there is a well-defined zero point. Thus, the distances between the various points are proportional, and there is the starting point of zero. The point on the scale that has the value "3" is thus defined with respect to the starting point of zero, and is thus specifically related to the other points on the scale. This scale, however, is not used often in leisure and recreation surveys.

Variables: Independent and Dependent

As indicated earlier in the book, there are two principal kinds of variables that any researcher must consider at the point of data analysis (at the time of study design there are many more variables that have to be considered). These are the independent and dependent variables. In the case of an experiment, an independent variable is one that the researcher can manipulate. In a leisure and recreation survey, where there is no manipulation, the independent variable can be interpreted as any variable that can be expected to have an impact on another variable. The variable that is affected by the independent variable is called the dependent variable.

Consider a question in the survey that asks the respondent to show his/her level of interest in aerobics. Such questions often use an interval scale, and the response falls in the range from great interest (5) to no interest (1). It is then possible to compute the percentages for each response, as well as the mean and standard deviation. However, it may be argued that it is there could be a difference in interest based on gender.

Thus, men might have a lesser interest in aerobics than women. In that case, the researcher is arguing that gender is an independent variable and the level of interest in aerobics is the dependent variable, and further computations can be conducted to examine the relationship between the two. Thus, the independent variable often determines the changes in the dependent variable.

In the case of leisure and recreation surveys, it is often enough to establish a relationship between the two types of variables without assuming the existence of a necessary causal relationship. It is difficult to claim that gender "causes" a higher level of interest in aerobics, but it is certainly valid to claim that there is a statistically significant relationship between the dependent variable, interest in aerobics, and the independent variable, gender.

In leisure and recreation surveys, the standard independent variables are demographics, which includes gender, age, income, race, household characteristics, and place of residence within a recreation service area. Other factors such as equipment available for recreation and the reasons for not using public recreation facilities, can be constructed as independent variables. The primary dependent variables deal with attitude, interest in current activities, need for future activities, and other questions that directly concern the issues of recreation.

However, in a survey, it is often possible to alter the scope of independent and dependent variables. For example, it can often be argued that a particular attitude, e.g., the perception of park safety, can have an effect on a behavior, e.g., the number of times one visits parks. In that case, the attitude can be considered to be the independent variable and the number of times the behavior is performed the dependent variable. The key is the way in which the two variable are related. Whenever one variable can be argued to have a "controlling" potential, it can be considered the independent variable, and the one that it is "controlled" is the dependent variable.

Thus, every question in an instrument is a variable. Usually, an instrument is designed in such a way that items whose responses are not expected to vary (i.e., are not variables) are not included in the questionnaire. Thus, in a leisure survey questionnaire, one will usually not find a question that asks the respondent if he or she is taxed for the use of public recreation facilities. Except in very special circumstances, the answer to the question is not a variable quantity, because everyone is taxed, and all the respondents would respond with a "yes." This is unlike an attitude question that asks about the respondent's feelings about the quality of recreation received for his or her tax dollars. Needless to say, it is expected that there will be a good amount of variation in that response. Consequently, every question in the survey is a variable, and it is possible to use any question as an independent or dependent variable if grounds exist to propose a theoretically sound relationship to one or more other variables.

SETTING UP THE DATA FOR ANALYSIS

The starting point of the data analysis procedure is the returned, completed questionnaire. As discussed earlier, it is necessary to establish some criteria to determine what is considered a completed questionnaire. The next step in the process is the translation of the questionnaire data to a computer-readable format. This consists of two stages. First, it is necessary to visually inspect the questionnaire for obvious problems that suggest that the questionnaire might have been completed in a frivolous manner and the respondent did not pay adequate attention to the process. If there are lines drawn across questions, frivolous remarks next to questions, and a general appearance that the questionnaire has not been taken seriously, it is safe to discount it from the data set. That is, however, not to say that such an act should not be noted, since it might provide valid (although not statistical) information about the feelings of one member of the community about the recreation services.

Before proceeding further, it is important to assign an identification (ID) number onto the questionnaire. Sometimes, after the data entry has been completed, it might be necessary to follow up on a wrong entry. For instance, if in the initial pass of data analysis it is discovered that there is a respondent with the gender *3* (which is not a possible response because gender can have only two possibilities, *1* or *2)*, this signifies a mistake in data entry. In such cases, it is important to return to the original questionnaire and see what the actual response was to make the necessary change. It is impossible to find that information without access to the identification number.

Having completed these steps, it is possible to move on to the question of data entry. It is presumed that the data to be entered are numeric data obtained from the coded questionnaire. Data entry is not possible until the data have been coded. As discussed earlier, the coding process involves the translation of the responses to the questionnaire to a numeric format. Regardless of whether the questionnaire is precoded or whether postcoding is conducted after all the questionnaires have been collected, it is imperative that the coding be completed before the data are entered. It is recommended that the questionnaire be precoded so that there is consistency in the codes assigned to each response. Once the coding procedure has been satisfactorily concluded, it is possible to move on to the data entry phase.

In most cases, independent of the software used for data entry, the product of the data-entry process needs to be standardized. Many of the problems with data entry arise from the fact that data are entered in an inconsistent fashion, leading to future problems with analysis. The fundamental principles in data entry are as follows:

- Every variable needs to have a separate column. In cases where a variable needs more than one column, the necessary number of columns must be reserved for it.

- Every questionnaire, identified by the ID number, needs to have a separate row. In cases where there are several questions, it is possible that one questionnaire will take up more than one row, in which case every variable is identified by its row as well as its column.

- There should be no empty spaces in the file. All missing information should be coded in a predetermined manner.

If these principles are followed, then a "flat file" or matrix of numbers will result that will have a standardized format. [As shown in Figure 9.2, the data set is made up of a file where every questionnaire occupied two lines (or rows) and first of the two lines started with the identification number of the questionnaire. Thus, Line 1 of the file starts with 0001 in the first four columns. Thus, columns 1 to 4 of the first line for each questionnaire are reserved for the identification number. The 5th column of the first line is reserved for the first variable that is the first question in the instrument. Thus, all spaces up to the 65th column of the first line are reserved for specific variables. The second line starts with another variable, and the columns in the second line are reserved for different variables until the last question of the questionnaire is reached. A new line with the ID number "0002" begins on Line 3, and the pattern continues. Also, note that any missing value is coded as a "9" so that there are no empty columns in the data set.[2]

Figure 9.2
Example of data set
(numbers in parentheses are column numbers)

```
ID (1-4) Q1(5) Q2(6) ................................ Qn (65)
000123 ........................................................ 4
000233 ........................................................ 3
000322 ........................................................ 5
000413 ........................................................ 2
```

These are some of the fundamental issues that need to be considered in the data entry. At the end of the process, a simple visual examination of the data set will illustrate aberrations where the columns spill over or lines are shorter than expected. Such discrepancies are immediate flags indicating that there is indeed a problem with the process.

---

2. This example assumes that the data entry is done using a standard word processor or editor where the line "wraps around" after the 65th column. If that is not the case then the entire questionnaire can be entered into one line.

Chapter Ten

Data Analysis

With the availability of easy-to-use software, the process of data analysis is becoming increasingly simple. Major computer software developers now routinely include statistical tools in their standard spreadsheet programs. Moreover, there is specialized software primarily for data analysis, and some computer programs are customized for the statistical analysis of data collected in leisure and recreation surveys. However, these tools are useful only if the practitioner knows the kind of analysis that needs to be done to answer specific questions (Jaeger, 1990). Very often, data analysis is done in an aimless manner. That kind of analysis serves no clear purpose. On the other hand, when the goals of analysis are set in a clearly articulated manner, the analysis can be a useful and exciting task.

In general, analysis has two goals: the exploratory goal and the functional goal. The first goal of analysis is to explore the data. In this stage, every question in the data set is individually analyzed to discover the various trends in the data. This phase has to be conducted before any further analysis can be performed. The next stage involves the functional goal, where the analyst is interested in getting answers to specific questions from the data. For instance, the exploratory phase might have indicated that 75% of the respondents were interested in swimming, but in the functional phase the coordinator of the swimming programs might be interested in knowing whether the interest is among the youth or the adults of the community. This "functional" question can be answered by cross-referencing the swimming question with specific demographic questions.

Both the stages are critically important and often share similar analytical tools. This chapter explores some of the key statistical tools that can be used to fulfill the exploratory goals of the analysis, some of which can also be used for the fulfillment of the functional goals. The discussion of statistical analysis in this chapter is necessarily brief and introductory. For a fuller understanding of the concepts represented here, the reader is encouraged to consult standard statistic texts.

DESCRIPTIVE ANALYSIS

Any form of data can serve a descriptive purpose. Given the fact that surveys are conducted to obtain the best and most reliable estimate of the population's beliefs, attitudes, and behaviors, it is particularly important to consider the ways in which the characteristics of a population can be described on the basis of the data collected from the sample.

At the most fundamental level of description are counts. The best example of a count is the decennial census. Every 10 years, the Census Bureau engages in the daunting task of compiling a reliable count of the American population. Along with that, the Bureau counts different characteristics of the population, such as gender, race, household income, and other parameters that help to describe the American populace.

In many ways, leisure and recreation surveys provide similar data. To begin with, leisure surveys contain a set of questions about the demographic characteristics of the respondents. It is thus certainly possible to count the number of men, women, income brackets, and other demographic characteristics of the sample, and then project from that to the population after incorporating the sampling error in the count. However, surveys also contain valuable belief, attitude, and behavior questions, often using interval measurement scales such as the Likert-type scales. Thus, it is possible to obtain counts of the number of people with different attitudes. Thus, in Figure 10.1, the "valid percent" column provides a count (using base 100) of the number of people who "strongly agreed" to a statement compared with those who were ambivalent.

In most standard statistical computation software, this procedure of counting is called computing the "frequency" of the occurrence of a particular attribute. This computation has several advantages.

Figure 10.1
Typical output from the computation of frequencies

Art Classes (attendance)

		Frequency	Percent	Valid Percent	Cumulative Percent
Valid	Yes	41	9.1	10.8	10.8
	No	339	74.8	89.2	100.0
	Total	380	83.9	100.0	
Missing	9	73	16.1		
	Total	73	16.1		
Total		452	100.0		

First, this procedure can act as an excellent data-cleaning tool. For instance, it is possible that for the question on gender, a data entry person accidentally entered the number 3. Since this is not a valid gender number ("Male, 2" "Female, 1") it needs to be corrected. However, to recognize the problem, it is first necessary to compute frequencies so that such discrepant entries can be identified. This is a key concern in any data processing. Often, due to human error, there are mistakes in data entry. First, there is miscoding. As in the above example, a coder might have entered a 3, which is not a valid response to the question. Descriptive analysis can point out such errors, and once the mistake has been identified, it is possible to find the original questionnaire (based on the identification number) and reenter the correct value in the data set. This is a laborious procedure, and it is better to be careful at the data entry stage to avoid these problems at a later point. A second kind of data entry problem is connected to wrong entries that are within the legitimate limits. In other words, a coder may enter a 2 instead of a 1. If this happens in a systematic manner, the descriptive analysis will provide some pointers. For instance, in the case of gender, if one coder made this mistake in a systematic fashion, it is possible that there are far more 2s in the data set than is logically expected. Such discrepancies should be investigated. However, if this error happens in a random fashion, then the descriptive analysis will not be able to identify them. Thus, it is usually recommended that random checking of the data be done in the course of data entry. For instance, after 100 questionnaires have been entered, it is a good idea to select about 10 at random to see if there are any mistakes. While this is not a perfect method, it can certainly point out problems that might exist in the data entry process.

Second, some counts provide valuable information about the respondents and potential problems that can be corrected. For instance, in a leisure and recreation survey, it is customary to send the survey by first-class mail to residents in the community without attention to gender. It is assumed that due to random selection and assignment, any subject-related bias will disappear. If, however, the results indicate a particularly high female concentration, there would be reason to believe that there was an inadvertent bias in the selection or a bias in the response pattern, calling for post hoc adjustments such as weighting. Very often in leisure and recreation surveys, which use simple random samples, the question of weighting to adjust for special sample design is not addressed. However, there is often a need to weight the data to correct for under- or over-representation of particular groups. The frequency computation provides the data to make the decision.[1]

Thus, the frequency computation provides the beginning for a large range of possible computations. In some cases, the frequency is the only computation that is required. If the scale used is ordinal or nominal, the frequency is often the most important piece of information because the researcher is interested in the number of cases in each category (e.g., race, gen-

---

1. The process of weighting the data involves an adjustment where the overrepresented group is weighted down while the under-represented group is weighted up. However, in order to do so, it is necessary to know the "correct" ratios. Most often, the census data is considered correct. Thus, if a community is made up of 51% women and 49% men according to census, and the leisure and recreation survey shows a ratio of 60% women and 40% men, then it can be argued that the opinions of the women need to be weighted down (adjusted downward by a ratio of 51/60), while the opinions of the men will have to be weighted up (adjusted upward by the ratio of 49/40). After this, further computations can be conducted on the data set. Most computer packages have standard weighting procedures.

der, income, etc.), and later, perhaps, the agency and the researcher may be interested in categorizing other variables by these groups.

The second important descriptive measure is the computation of central tendencies. The notion of central tendency is connected to questions of generalization. While the frequency tells us in detail the way in which characteristics of the community are distributed, the central tendency measure provides information about the average and the most common attributes of the sample and, thus, the population. Based on that measure, further measures can be devised and specific questions can be raised.

The most common measure of central tendency is the mean or the average. This reports the average score on a nondichotomous measure where the scale is set up as an interval scale. For instance, respondents could respond on a scale of 1 to 5, where the two numbers indicate extremes of opinion. It is possible to compute a mean of the measure to indicate the overall average attitude of the respondents. In association with the sampling error of the mean, it is then possible to draw conclusions about the population average. Thus, 4.2 indicates the average attitude, this suggests a positive attitude for the people who participated in the study. Along with that, if the computed sampling error of the mean is 0.12, this suggests that the mean varied between 4.32 and 4.08—still a relatively positive attitude. The mean is computed using the following formula:

mean = sum of (measure*n)/Total n

In the following example, the measures vary between 1 and 5, and the n's associated with each measure are as follows:

	n	n*measure
1	5	5
2	10	20
3	5	15
4	20	80
5	10	50

The sum of the product of the measure and n is 170. The total n is 50, and the computed mean is thus 3.4.

Next, it is possible to compute the measure of distribution and the sampling error. In most cases, the computer does this, but the numbers need to be used in the correct way. It is important to recognize that the mean is most significant in the case of interval scales, and in other scales, other measures of central tendency must be used to make sense of the data. Sometimes multiple measures of central tendency are needed so that the different measures can illuminate the data in different ways.

Another measure of central tendency is the mode. This indicates the category in which most respondents fall. In the above example, the mode is "4," since 20 out of the 50 respondents answered with a "4." What is noticeable here is the fact that the mean is a little lower than the mode, suggesting that while a large number of people responded with a "4," there is still a significant amount who had opinions that fell at a point less than "4" on the scale. This issue becomes even more important in the case of measures such as income. If in the same sample there were 30 people who reported their income to be $35,000 and five people who reported it as $10,000, but there were 10 who reported their income to be $250,000, a little reflection will show that the average income measure would be unreasonably high, since the higher-income respondents would inflate the data. In such cases, both the mean and the mode need to be presented, since they in combination best describe the income category of the population being considered.

A measure similar to the mode is the percentile measure. Sometimes it is not only useful to know the central tendency in terms of the average and most frequent, but it is also important to look at the scores of the top 95% or the 50% break point. This also provides some indication of the central tendency in the data and supplements the understanding obtained from the mean and the mode. In most leisure and recreation surveys, however, such a measure is not usually reported. It is more typically used in the measurement of talent, as in SAT exams and similar test situations where it is important to obtain the data broken down into ranks.

What should be clear from this discussion is the necessity to obtain information that can be organized around centralizing tendencies. While the counts are important, it is also necessary to see how the data congeal around single numbers to help make better sense of the centralizing tendencies of the data.

However, while the frequency provides a preliminary picture of the data, and the mean tends to refine that information, neither measure answers questions about the spread of the data. If, for instance, it is discovered that the average attitude toward golf is 4.5 on a five-point scale, suggesting a positive attitude, the question could arise about how spread out the data is. In other words, did respondents all give values between 4 and 5, or did the responses have greater spread, and is the mean 4.5 because many more people responded with 4s and 5s than with lower numbers? The answer to this question lies in the measure of variance, which estimates the distance of scores from the mean. The variance can take several different forms. As shown in Figure 10.2a, the data could congeal near the mean, whereas in the case of other data, as shown in Figure 10.2b, the spread could be much larger. The spread is an indication of the range over which the respondents expressed their opinions.

Figure 10.2a
Narrow Distribution

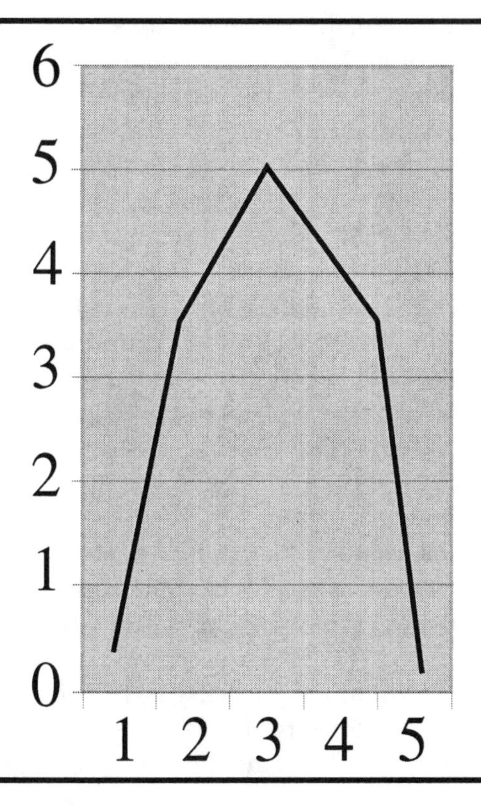

Figure 10.2b
Broad Distribution

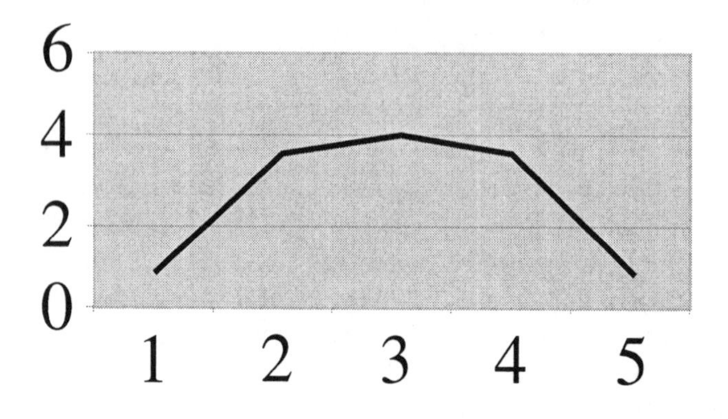

Associated with the variance is the standard deviation, which is the average distance of each score from the mean. Based on the standard deviation, further computations can be done, such as the sampling error and measures of difference.

These computations are based on the fact that there may be a "normal" distribution of data, where the data are equally spread on both sides of the mean. That is, 50% of the scores are less than the mean, and 50% are more than the mean. In the absence of any external effects, this is what would be expected of any distribution. For example, if the entire population of a city had no feelings about an issue related to leisure and everyone answered the issue-related question in a random fashion, the expected distribution would be similar to the normal distribution. However, in reality, people have opinions, and consequently a normal distribution is not expected. However, the extent of the effect of nonrandom elements on opinion can be ascertained by comparing the real distribution to a normal distribution. In this capacity, the standard deviation is an important measure that not only provides a description of the aggregate data but also becomes a stepping stone for further computations.

Once these initial descriptions have been obtained, it is possible to delve further into the data and begin to understand trends based on some of the independent variables.

Analysis of Trends

A common question that parks and recreation administrators raise deals with the way in which different sectors of the community react to their services. This could be an important question in relation to the functional goals of analysis. Board members may be interested in knowing if a particular planning district is in need of a swimming pool or if the elderly feel that there are inadequate recreation opportunities for them. The analysis described up to now does not answer such questions. The descriptive analysis provides the overall aggregate picture without attention to the details of the data. The aggregate picture, however, provides a good starting point to ask questions about the varying interests of different parts of the population. These questions can arise in two different ways.

First, the planners, administrators, and the board could raise these questions. This applies most in the case of development of master plans and long-term planning, where the agency is considering capital investments in the form of new facilities. In such cases, the needs of every constituency must be attended to. Thus, if there is a need for a teen recreation center, then there is a need to know which area would benefit most from such an addition. Similarly, if there are specific deficiencies, for instance, in the area of age-specific programming, then it is important to be able to "break" the data into smaller parts and look at each part to see the way in which differences emerge.

Second, the data itself may indicate differences where none were expected. If the data for a particular measure shows a large spread, or standard deviation, it suggests that there is a large range of opinions about the issue. Such situations raise questions about the way in which the data are spread, who has responded, how, and why. On the other hand, there are conditions where the standard deviation is so low that there is no reason to expect any differences. Thus, for agencies that provide Fourth of July activities in America, there is typically little variance in the interest in such activities. Consequently, doing any trend analysis on such questions is of little value.

The analysis of trends can be done in two different ways. First, it is possible to look at the varying responses in terms of frequencies and see how different groups reacted to a question. This is at the level of count. In Figure 10.3, the response to an attitude question has been broken down into two parts. The first column represents the number of women who responded to the question and how the responses were spread over the possibilities. The second column represents the men. This is called a cross-tabulation by gender. In a similar way, it is possible to cross-tabulate by age, income, or even another attitude question. Thus, it is possible to ask the question: How many people felt strongly positive toward aerobics as well as volleyball? This could be answered by conducting a cross-tabulation of these two variables. Most computer packages offer standard cross-tabulation options. Additionally, the raw counts in each cell can be presented as percentages. Usually, three different percentages are reported. First, it is possible to compute a "column percent," which uses the total of the column as the denominator. Thus, in this example, the column percent would show what percent of the women responded with a "1," how many with a "2" and so forth. Second, it is possible to compute a "row percent," where the raw count in the cell is divided by the row total. This would tell the researcher what percentage of the respondents saying "1" were women and what percentage were men. Finally, it is possible to compute a "total percent" where the raw number in the cell is divided by the total sample size. This would tell what percent of the total population were women saying "1," men saying "2," and so on. It is important to keep in mind that the numerator in all these cases is the raw number in the cell, and the percents are only different ways of representing that same raw count. Cross-tabulation tables thus provide valuable information about the trends in the data and the way in which the data are broken down across the various variables. Usually, the tables are constructed in a way where the independent variable (such as gender) appears as the columns and the dependent variables appear as rows.

A second, similar measure would be an attempt to compare the means of different groups. The procedure involves dividing the raw data into different groups and then computing the mean for each group. In the above example, if the mean for a particular measure is 4.5 and the standard deviation is high, it is possible that there are differences by gender. In such cases, it is possible to compute the mean for each gender and report the two means (the test of difference is a trickier issue and will be dealt with shortly). This provides a more detailed picture than the overall number.

Figure 10.3
Typical Cross-tabulation

ART CLASSES (ATTEND) * gender Crosstabulation

			gender		
			Male	Female	Total
ART CLASSES (ATTEND)	Yes	Count	21	20	41
		% within ART CLASSES (ATTEND)	51.2%	48.8%	100.0%
		% within gender	11.7%	10.5%	11.1%
		% of Total	5.7%	5.4%	11.1%
	No	Count	158	171	329
		% within ART CLASSES (ATTEND)	48.0%	52.0%	100.0%
		% within gender	88.3%	89.5%	88.9%
		% of Total	42.7%	46.2%	88.9%
Total		Count	179	191	370
		% within ART CLASSES (ATTEND)	48.4%	51.6%	100.0%
		% within gender	100.0%	100.0%	100.0%
		% of Total	48.4%	51.6%	100.0%

In these ways, it is possible to describe the ways in which different subgroups react to specific questions in the questionnaire. However, the question that needs to be raised is: Are these differences due to chance or due to a real difference between the groups? For instance, if the mean attitude toward aerobics among men is 2.4 and among women is 4.5, there is certainly a difference, but it cannot be established simply on the basis of the two means whether the difference is due to different opinions between men and women, or merely due to chance. Another question that needs to be raised is: Is the difference found only among the sample of respondents, or would it be seen in the case of the population as well? These questions are connected with the notion of statistical significance. Observing a difference is not usually considered sufficient to make claims about groups. Further tests of the data need to be conducted to establish that these differences are indeed statistically significant within certain acceptable margins of error.

The usual margin of error in the case of leisure and recreation, as well as other opinion and behavior surveys, is 5%. In other words, the researcher needs to be confident that there is only a 5% probability that the observed difference between the groups is due to chance, which means that there is a 95% probability that the difference is indeed due to the different attributes of the groups. This number, 5%, is often called the level of significance. It is expressed not necessarily as a percentage, but as "0.05," and is often also given the abbreviation *p*. Most social science research requires that the *p* value be 0.05 or less for a data to be considered statistically significant. Interestingly, the *p* value is not computed but is held as a standard. Several other measures are computed from the data and compared with standard values, which make the assumption of a normal distribution. If the deviation between the distributions is high enough, then it is possible to claim that the difference is statistically significant, and that the difference observed in the sample could be expected in the population as well.

This notion introduces a fundamental aspect about the enterprise of data analysis. Given the fact that there are flaws inherent in sampling, data collection, and in every other step of the process of conducting a leisure and recreation survey, it is impossible to claim 100% accuracy of results. Most data reports need to have a caveat of probability. In other words, even when policy decisions are made based on the data analysis, it must be understood that there is always a finite chance that the interpretations were wrong. The key is that the margin of error be kept low and acceptable to a larger body of researchers.

In the case of leisure and recreation surveys, that level is 5%; that is, a mistake could result from the 5% possibility that the researcher was wrong. Thus, in the case of aerobics, if the researcher were wrong and the difference in the means were due to chance and not gender, then policy decisions made on the basis of the data, in the form of different aerobics opportunities being offered to men and women, would prove to be ineffective. Yet that is a lesser danger than in the case of medical research, where the significance level is held at 0.01, suggesting that medical doctors need to be 99% certain that the difference is indeed due to the independent variable and not due to chance. That is a much more exacting standard, since life-and-death questions are being settled in that arena. However, even in social science research, if the "p" value is not held to at most 0.10, the data and the research may become suspect.

TESTS OF DIFFERENCE

The critical question in tests of difference is where statistically significant differences exist between groups in the population. It is then possible to make policy decisions about how to deal with the differences. Sometimes the differences are in number, where more people in a particular planning area are interested in a certain development. If it can be established that those in a particular planning area are significantly more interested than those in another planning area, it would suggest that the development occur in the neighborhood of greater need. If there are no significant differences, then it is possible to claim that it would make little difference where the development occurs. Clearly, this is of great consequence. If there is a statistically different need for a facility and the agency does not recognize that, the agency may carry out the construction in an area where it is not needed. Those in the area of greater need would obviously be unhappy, leading to tensions in the community. Indeed, this is not uncommon.

For instance, in one Midwestern city of about 150,000 with a significant "inner city" population, at a public meeting the minority members of the inner city made it clear that the Parks and Recreation department was insensitive to the needs of the community there. While there were "real" needs for facilities in the inner city, the department was continuing to build facilities elsewhere in the service area. While this might appear to be intuitively true or just amount to politically loaded accusations, if the department or the community members had data to back up their respective arguments, this could represent the common ground on which to build a solution. This is precisely where the difference measurement becomes critical.

There are several measures for testing statistical difference. However, in most cases, the measurements can be grouped in the following categories:

- Measurement of the difference in count between two or more groups.
- Measurement of the difference in mean attitude and opinion between two groups.
- Measurement of difference in mean attitude and opinion between three or more groups.

Each of these measurements calls for the computation of different statistics. However, the computations have certain commonalities, and it is important to recognize the common principles that drive the process.

In all the computations, two measures are of great importance. First, based on the data, it is possible to compute a number that represents an indicator of the difference between the groups. The computed number is compared with standard numbers based on the nature of the data. Out of the comparison emerges the level of significance, which indicates, based on the standard measures for that kind of data, what are the chances that the difference between the groups is due to chance. Thus, the decision is dependent on the comparison between the computed measure and the standard measure as well as the nature of the data set. The latter is often described by the degrees of freedom in the data set. This is an indicator of the number of groups and the extent by which the data could vary.

Let's say that there is a question on aerobics, there are 50 members in the sample, and the interest is in comparing the 25 men and 25 women. There could thus be 25 male responses and 25 female responses. Any response has two degrees of freedom in terms of the group—either a male or female response. In a similar fashion, the data could have 50 degrees of freedom in terms of the person who responded. This is an important construct, because the larger the degrees of freedom in terms of groups, the greater the chance of difference; and the greater the degrees of freedom in terms of members in the data set, the better the likelihood of good representation. Based on all the possible degrees of freedom, standard statistical tables report the standard values of the measures of difference. It is thus possible to compute the specific measure and compare that to the corresponding (depending on the correct degrees of freedom) standard value to obtain the level of significance, and then draw conclusions about the statistical significance of the difference between groups.

This procedure holds true for the measures of difference discussed here. In the case where the differences in count between groups are being measured, the appropriate statistic to use is called the chi-squared statistic. The principle behind the chi-squared statistic is simply the assumption that there is an expected frequency or count for any item. Thus, with respect to interest in aerobics between men and women, if gender played no role, the expected number of men interested in aerobics should be the same as the number of women. Thus, for the question "Are you interested in Aerobics?" the corresponding cross-tabulation by gender would produce four cells: men saying "yes," women saying "yes," men saying "no," and women saying "no." The expected frequency for a sample of 100 would be 25 in each cell. However, in reality that would not be the case. The chi-squared statistic measures the difference between the expected and the observed frequencies, and it is then possible to compare that with standard chi-squared tables to see what the significance level is.

Most standard computational packages compute the chi-squared statistic as a part of the cross-tabulation tables, do the comparison between the standard and the computed values, and report the exact level of significance. As shown in Figure 10.4, the cross-tabulation is followed by the computation of the statistics and the reporting of the significance level.

Figure 10.4
Crosstabulation with the Chi-Square statistics

Performing Arts * gender Crosstabulation
Chi-Square Tests

	Value	df	Asymp. Sig. (2-tailed)
Pearson Chi-Square	6.094[a]	2	.048
Likelihood Ratio	6.125	2	.047
Linear-by-Linear Association	.011	1	.915
N of Valid Cases	239		

a. 0 cells (.0%) have expected count less than 5. The minimum expected count is 14.94.

					Total
Performi Arts					82
					100.0%
					34.3%
					34.3%
					127
		Arts			100.0%
		% within gender	45.4%	60.8%	53.1%
		% of Total	22.6%	30.5%	53.1%
	8	Count	16	14	30
		% within Performing Arts	53.3%	46.7%	100.0%
		% within gender	13.4%	11.7%	12.6%
		% of Total	6.7%	5.9%	12.6%
Total		Count	119	120	239
		% within Performing Arts	49.8%	50.2%	100.0%
		% within gender	100.0%	100.0%	100.0%
		% of Total	49.8%	50.2%	100.0%

Very similar to the chi-squared statistic is the way in which the difference between two means can be computed. In the case of the T-test (also called Student's T-test, based on the name of the inventor of the test), the principle is the same except that the comparison is conducted for the mean. Here, too, there is an assumption about the expected average, and the observed mean and appropriate statistics are computed and compared against the standard T-curve. Subsequently, measures of significance are obtained. There are, however, some additional complexities to the T–test.

First, there are sets of assumptions about the variance of the two groups that are being compared. It is assumed in a standard T-test that the variances or standard deviations of the two groups are comparable. In other words, if all the men in the aerobics example gave the exact same responses, while the women gave responses that varied substantially around the mean, then a comparison between the men and women could be flawed. (Which do you think would have a higher standard deviation, the men or the women?) On the other hand, if the variation is comparable between the two groups, then a T-test can be performed. There are ways of getting around this problem by doing higher-level and modified T-tests where the assumption of equality of variance may be violated.

T-tests can also be used for comparing two different time frames for the same group. Consider, for instance, a situation where an agency plans to conduct one needs assessment before building a new multiuse recreation center, and another one after completion of the facility. It may be possible to compare the changes in the attitude of the community by comparing the opinions before and after the building of the facility. Assuming random sampling and comparable variance, a T-test can be performed on the means of the opinions to see if there have been any significant changes in attitude due to the new addition.

While the T-test compares means and makes certain assumptions about the variance, it is possible to do comparisons that take the data analysis to a higher level of abstraction and attempt to compare means as well as variances. The most common of these tests is the one-way analysis of variance, often called simply "one-way" analysis.

In the one-way test, the means of two or more groups are compared along with the variances of the groups. Thus, it is more powerful than the T-test, because it offers the opportunity to compare multiple groups. The one-way is thus the appropriate test to use if the agency is interested in comparing mean attitudes between different income levels or racial groups. Although a T-test can still be used by breaking the multiple groups into pairs), is difficult to identify the exact pair of groups that is statistically significant. This is a critical issue in most tests, since an agency is very interested in knowing if there is a significant difference in planning districts and, if so, which districts are most different.

Consider, for instance, a situation where the service area is divided into five planning areas, where the spatial distance between areas "1" and "2" is far less than between areas "1" and "5." In Figure 10.5, the mean attitude toward building a new multipurpose center is indicated for each area in this hypothetical place. If it can be established that the difference between the means for "1" and "5" is significant, but the difference between "1" and "2" is not, it can be established that area 5 is far more interested in the multipurpose center than "1" and "2" are. This decision is obviously based on the mean attitudes.

Figure 10.5
Examples of differences in means for different planning areas

Area	Mean attitude toward a multipurpose center ("1" Negative, "5" Positive)
1	2.1
2	4.3
3	2.4
4	1.1
5	3.1

In this situation, there is a need to do a more complex comparison, and the one-way analysis is appropriate. In this case a value similar to the T-value and the chi-squared statistic is computed, and then compared to the standard values based on the degrees of freedom and the significance reported. However, it is necessary to do an additional set of computations to determine which particular sets of pairs are indeed significantly different. The most common test used for this is called Scheffe's test, which produces a matrix with the different group means and indicates which are indeed significantly different. The combination of the one-way analysis and the Scheffe's test thus provides a complete picture of where the differences lie, and decisions about specific issues can be made on the basis of these differences.

The one-way test is similar to another test called the analysis of variance (ANOVA), which computes the difference between groups. However, a more complex test is the multiple analysis of variance (MANOVA). The latter test is used in special situations where the effects of multiple groups need to be studied. Again using the example where the attitude toward the construction of a new multi-user recreation center is being analyzed, if it can be argued that the attitude could be controlled by multiple facts, such as the number of children in the household and the income level of the household, then it is important to not only look at the differences based on those criteria of grouping, but also on the combined effect of the groups. MANOVA results would indicate which of the variables—number of children or income level—has the main effect, and what the interaction effects of these variables are. Based on the results, it would be possible to make certain claims about the factors determining attitude. It is important to note that the MANOVA is not often used. It is more of a tool for the experimental researcher geared toward the establishment of cause-effect relationships and testing of hypotheses than for the survey researcher interested in the descriptive task of looking at differences and trends.

In addition to the tasks of looking for trends and differences, it is often necessary to establish relationships between different elements of the data that can shed some light on the possible reasons for a particular behavior. This is the realm of correlation and regression analysis.

ANALYSIS OF RELATIONSHIPS

The descriptive analysis addresses the overall makeup of the data, the trend analysis and cross-tabulations point toward possible areas of difference, and the tests of difference establish the differences to be statistically significant. The question that arises out of the analysis is whether these statistically significant differences show the existence of a relationship that can be statistically established. Furthermore, if the relationship can be established, is there a causal relationship between the variables?

An example illustrates the issue. Most leisure and recreation surveys include a question about the information that the respondents have about agency activities. Consequently, there could be a statement saying, "I am aware of the department's activities," to which a response could range from "strongly agree" to "strongly disagree" on a five-point scale. Such surveys also often have a question about the frequency with which the respondent might attend the department activities. It is thus logical to claim that there could be a relationship between the two. However, that intuitive claim can be measured and a numerical value assigned to the relationship indicating the strength and the direction of the relationship. This value is called the correlation coefficient and is often designated as "rho."

In order to measure the relationship, the first step is to construct a chart that shows the way in which the values are distributed. In Figure 10.5 the chart shows the various values of the attitude question and the corresponding values of the attendance question. Thus, each point in the "scatter" diagram illustrates a response from a single respondent. In the end, a "cloud" of points is formed in the graph. The correlation coefficient first measures the width of the cloud. If the cloud is so dispersed that it looks almost like a circle, as illustrated in Figure 10.5a, then it can be argued that there is little correlation between the variables since no pattern emerges. On the other hand, if the cloud is thin and looks almost like a straight line as in Figure 10.5b, there is a clear relationship between the two variables. If a look at the plot in relation to the axes also illustrates that as attitude increases, the frequency of attendance goes up, this suggests a positive relationship between the variables. However, in some cases, there could be an inverse relationship. If a statement such as "I do not feel safe in the parks" is substituted for the variable on x-axis, it is possible a different distribution be obtained as illustrated in Figure 10.5c, that would constitute a negative relationship.

Figure 10.5a

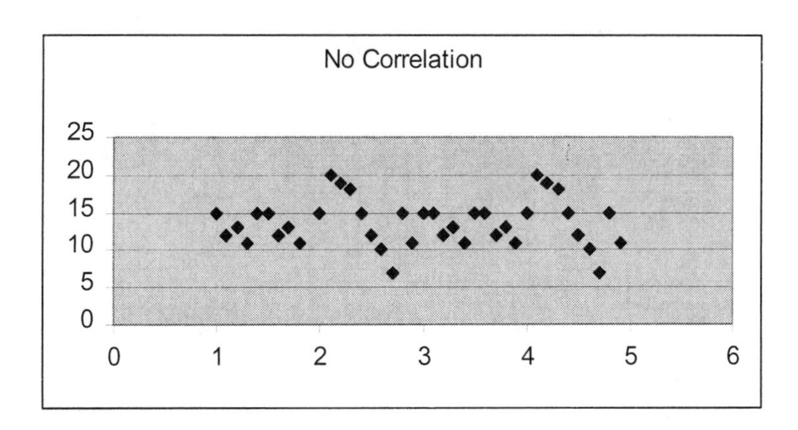

Figure 10.5b

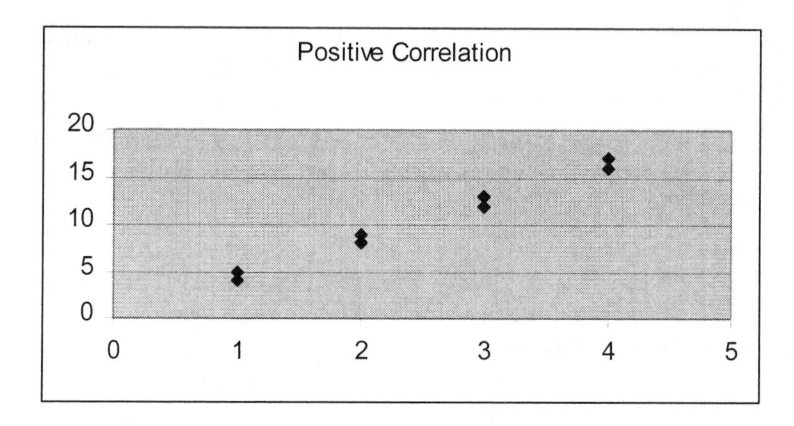

Figure 10.5c

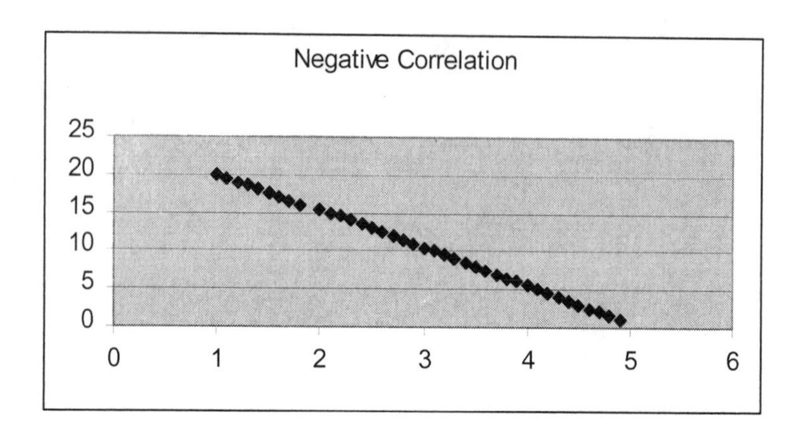

The rho value is thus a measure of two different attributes—the direction of the relationship and the strength of the relationship. The direction is indicated by the sign of the number rho. If it is a positive value, it indicates a positive relationship, and a negative relationship is indicated by a negative value. The strength of the relationship is indicated by the numeric value of rho. In the case of a straight-line relationship, i.e., when the cloud condenses to a straight line, the value of rho is considered to be "1," while in the case of the circular distribution, the value of rho is "0." In other words, rho can vary between +1 and -1, and the computed value can be used to draw some conclusions about the relationship between the variables.

The conclusions about the relationship are primarily based on convention and the needs of the research. In the case of social science research, as with needs assessments and leisure and recreation surveys, a rho value under 0.2 is considered to represent a weak to nonexistent relationship. Values between 0.2 and 0.4 indicate a moderate relationship, those between 0.4 and 0.6 indicate a strong relationship, and values over 0.6 indicate the existence of a very strong relationship. It is not often, however, that rho values of 0.8 or higher are observed. However, in other research—for instance, medical research concerning the use of specific drugs—the relationships need to be defined in a different way due to the rigors involved.

It is important to clarify that correlation measures relationships and their strength, and not causality. Thus, while a high rho value indicates a strong relationship, it is incorrect to conclude that the amount of knowledge about the department activities, for example "causes" particular kinds of behavior in attendance. It is indeed true that there is a relationship, but there is no statistical basis to establish causality (although there may be intuitive or descriptive information to support that). To establish causality, it must be established that the variation in the attendance pattern is explained by the variation in knowledge about activities. This is a fine distinction but a critical one.

The assumption here is that there is a certain degree of variation in the attendance patterns. That is, there is a distribution of respondents who vary between infrequent attendance and frequent attendance. The causality question in such cases is stated as: What causes this variance, and is there a limited number of variables that can explain the majority of the variance in the attendance pattern? This question is answered by the regression analysis, which also provides a mathematical relationship between the variables. Based on this relationship, it is then possible to predict, with a measurable degree of confidence, that if the value of one variable is known, the value of the other variable can be predicted. In the simplest form, the linear regression relationship is expressed as:

$$y = ax + b$$

where "x" and "y" are the variable and "a" and "b" are constants

The previous example of knowledge and attendance will be used to illustrate. Let us assume that the knowledge question is asked on a five-point scale and the attendance question is measured as the number of times the respondent has attended district activities in the past six months. Based on the data, it is possible to establish a statistically significant relationship that is mathematically expressed in a form such as:

attendance = 2*knowledge score + 1

Thus, those who scored a 5 on the knowledge measure are expected to have attended activities about 11 times in the past six months. It is thus possible to ask anyone the knowledge question and, depending on the score, it is then possible to predict, with some degree of accuracy, how many times the person has attended department activities.

The degree of accuracy is measured by the regression analysis as well. The computations not only provide the values of a and b in the equation, but also produce a value called "R-square" which indicates the percent of the variance in y that can be attributed to x. The R-square value is in fact none other than the square of rho. Thus, if the rho value is *1*, it can be argued that there is a perfect relationship, that 100% of the variance in y is explained by x, and there is thus the possibility of establishing a causal relationship. However, if the correlation is lower, even if the rho value is 0.9, the R-square value goes down to 0.81, suggesting now that only 81% of the variance in y is explained by x, and the remaining 19% needs to be explained by a different variable. Thus, it should be clear that predictable, cause-effect relationships are indeed difficult to establish, and there is always an element of unexplained variance in the dependent variable.

This concludes the discussion of the data analysis steps that could be conducted with the survey data. In the next section, further procedures are described that help to verify the reliability and validity of the questionnaire used in the data analysis.

FACTOR ANALYSIS AND RELIABILITY CHECKS

There are sets of assumptions made about the questionnaire that sometimes need to be checked and validated. These assumptions have to do with notions of the internal validity of the research process, which concerns the procedures used in the conduct of the study. Thus, it is important to confirm that the questionnaire is indeed measuring what it is supposed to be measuring, and when conclusions are drawn about such measurements, that they are reliable and valid conclusions. Additionally, the research needs to be externally valid so that the results of the survey can be generalized over a larger population. Many of the concerns over sampling and random selection have to do with the issues of generalizability and external validity.

It is important to be able to establish that items in the questionnaire indeed measure the construct that the researcher is trying to get at. For example, as mentioned earlier, if there is an item in the questionnaire that states, "I feel safe in the parks," there is a possibility that respondents could interpret "safety" in terms of violence to themselves or in terms of the security and maintenance of the park equipment. These are completely different constructs. A recreation department can often do very little to make sure that there are no antisocial elements in the parks, but if safety is related to the maintenance of park equipment, the department is directly responsible for safety. However, the department or the agency has no good way of determining how the community interprets the statement.

In cases like this one, it is possible to do a reliability check on the instrument. This involves comparing the responses of randomly selected members in the community and checking the level of agreement between these members. If there is a large degree of agreement, it can be argued that the community is interpreting the question in the same way, although doubts still linger about the exact interpretation (this is why it is necessary to pay attention to the design and construction of the questionnaire and use focus groups to clarify what the key issues are).

The best way to perform this comparison is to conduct multiple tests. If the same questionnaire is administered to different samples from the same or similar populations then these responses can be compared. However, because these questionnaires are often specifically designed for the needs of a specific community, there might not be a good history of use of the questionnaire to draw upon existing reliability data. Moreover, it is often impractical to administer the questionnaire more than once to different samples just to obtain the reliability data. Consequently, a method called "split-half" is used, where the sample is randomly split into two halves and the responses of the two halves are compared. This provides a good measure of reliability. The common statistic used is called Cronbach's alpha, which can have a value between "1" and "0" where the "1" value represents a highly reliable measure. An alpha value between 0.6 to 0.8 can be considered very reliable.

It is important to note that the reliability measure is done after the data have been collected and cannot affect the data collection procedure. So if unreliable items are discovered in the questionnaire, the department has to be careful about paying much attention to those items, because it is simply unclear how valid those items are and what they are measuring. Needless to say, if the questionnaire is to be used in the future, those items need to be restated or removed. Finally, some of the doubts can be resolved by post hoc focus groups, where members of the population are invited back into group discussions to help interpret some of the data and indicate how the ambiguous items may have been interpreted.

Along with reliability checks, it is also often necessary to conduct analyses to provide information about the way in which the questionnaire measures broad concepts. Very often, particularly with the attitude items in the questionnaire, multiple items attempt to measure the same construct. For example, in one community in the Midwest there was a great deal of concern about nonresidents coming in and using the facilities. The issue was so important that, based on the focus group data, it was deemed necessary to include a set of items in the questionnaire addressing the broad notion of "how to handle the nonresident issue." However, what remains unclear is the extent to which the respondent understands that the items deal with the same issue. Even if the items are grouped together, there could be situations where the responses demonstrate that the items were not interpreted in the way intended.[2]

However, a factor analysis can be used, which computes a set of statistics and then reports different clusters of items. For instance, in a questionnaire with 50 questions, the researcher could have a computer calculate five factors according to which the items can be grouped. At the end of the analysis, the items can be arranged in groups of 10 based on the weight each item had for each factor. If, for example, one item had the weights 0.4, 0.6, 0.2, 0.1, and 0.1 for five factors, it would be assumed that it weights heavily on the second factor and should be grouped on that basis. The researcher can then observe the five

---

2. It is important to keep in mind that it is often a mistake to group such items together because that can lead to the question order effect, where the respondents simply answer the questions without necessarily paying attention to what they are saying. Consequently, similar items are usually distributed across the questionnaire and later tested to see if they indeed measured the same construct.

factors and make the decision as to whether similar items do indeed cluster around the same factor.

Usually there are two outcomes to this analytical approach. First, the researcher might notice that issues unrelated to the "nonresident" problem, continuing the example above, are appearing under the factor that has been labeled the "nonresident" factor. This could call for a finer factor analysis; instead of five factors, it could be necessary to use seven or eight factors and see how the new clusters appear. Second, it is possible that an item that the researcher felt was associated with the nonresident issue does not appear in the cluster. This suggests that the way in which the item was interpreted by the respondents differed from the way it was intended. In such cases, it is instructive to note how the particular item did indeed weight on what factor. Moreover, in such cases it is a danger to include that item in any grouped series. Often, to get a bigger picture, items that load on the same factor can be summed to produce a composite measure that can be used for correlation and other statistical manipulations. In such cases, it is important to be able to determine what are the appropriate scores to group, and the factor analysis becomes critical.

Finally, it is important to recognize that both the reliability checks and the factor analysis help researchers to better understand the questionnaire, but they are not descriptive tools that help to make recommendations for the department. These checks help the researcher to understand how reliable and valid the data are and provide a check on the questionnaire and the data collection process. Often in the final report, this analysis is not reported.

Chapter Eleven

Data Reporting

The final part of the survey process is data reporting, when the results of the data collection and analysis are prepared for presentation to a large audience that includes not only the members of the agency staff but also the general public, since the results of service agency surveys need to be distributed widely.

The process of preparing the report begins with a review of the computer printouts produced. It is the task of the author of the report to take the information and convert it into terms that can be understood by those who might not be versed in the language of statistics and analysis. Additionally, the report will need to contain ample illustrations, graphs, charts and tables to make the information clear and easily accessible. Finally, the report must be written in a fashion that will enable the information to be translated into action, so that the results presented in the report can have some direct impact on the planning process. Various aspects of data presentation in a report are covered in Appendix D.

ORGANIZATION OF THE REPORT

The first part of the report is typically the *executive summary*. The purpose of this section is to provide a clear and concise description of the highlights of the study without focusing on the details of complex methodology and analysis. This section is set apart from the main report, and this is the part that is most commonly read, since it is short and contains the key pieces of information. An example of an executive summary may be found in Appendix B. It is a good idea to write this section without using too much technical language and to include the most significant findings. Usually leisure and recreation surveys contain hundreds of statistics, and the executive summary provides only a few of these so as not to overwhelm the reader with details, but to provide a "snapshot" of the most important elements of the data. Some guidelines for writing the executive summary are:

- Be concise.
- Be selective in terms of what is presented.
- Avoid jargon.
- Explain the key terms.
- Use "action language" to emphasize the connection between the data and planning.
- Be objective.

If these guidelines are followed, the executive summary will be a useful part of the final report that will help both the administrator and planner to identify the most important parts of the data.

The *body* of the report contains more detail. This part is loosely divided into three sections. The first section specifies the goals of the study. It is necessary to clarify that the assessment process was driven by specific objectives related to the overall preparation of the master plan. It needs to be clarified to the reader that there were specific and well–defined ends that were kept in sight in designing the research. This is particularly important since these ends often determine the methodology of the research.

The next section of the body deals with the methodology of the research. This section gives the researcher the opportunity to demonstrate that appropriate methods were used to collect the data. This section contains information about the sampling design used for the study, the process by which the sample size was determined, and arguments supporting the sample selection. After explaining the sampling process, the author needs to describe in clear detail the data collection procedure, including the specific method(s) used and the rationale for the method. Then details of the procedure are presented. For instance, in the case of a mail survey, it is necessary to describe whether the mail was sent first-class, whether return envelopes were included, and whether an incentive was provided. Details of the length of time spent waiting for the responses and attempts at follow-up need to be presented to support the data collection process. Readers may review the methods section looking for flaws in the research process that could invalidate the results, so it is important that every element of the method of data collection be carefully described and defended. If there were mistakes or setbacks, those should be discussed clearly and their implications addressed in depth. This will strengthen the validity of report and allay any fears of deception.

The data collection section should conclude with the reporting of the response rate, since the strength of a methodology often lies in obtaining a high response rate. It should be noted whether the response rate obtained was conventional for the data collection strategy employed. Sometimes problems relating to response rate are beyond the researcher's control. Extraneous factors need to be highlighted in this section of the report so that an outside reader can get a sense of the circumstances of the study.

Finally, the methods section needs to discuss the data analytic tools used in the study in order to inform the reader about the specific methods of analysis and to demonstrate that standardized and conventional methods were used.

The next section reports the broad results of the study. First, this section should discuss the descriptive findings. Often it is best to start with the demographics and provide the reader with a sense of the makeup of the sample and the way the sample compares with known population figures. For instance, if the numbers reveal that there was an over–representation of women in the sample, that needs to be mentioned here and strategies for post hoc adjustment discussed. Appropriate statistics should be reported, including percentages for the demographics, means and standard deviations for the attitude questions, and percentages for other nominal measures (such as activity attendance). This section provides the reader with an overall picture of the community and an indication of the needs, attitudes, and behavior of the community in terms of recreation. This section also addresses questions about the differences in the community.

A second part of the results section deals with trends. Given the fact that numerous cross-tabulations are possible with a large data set, the researcher has to carefully select the trends to include in the report. To include all the trends would be tantamount to writing an epic, which will have very little utility to the agency. Two interrelated criteria can be used in making this decision:

- Are the differences statistically significant?
- Can the trends be translated to "action" on the part of the agency?

A few examples will illustrate the point. One trend that may have been identified is a strong difference in opinion about football between men and women. Even though the difference is statistically significant, it cannot be translated to any action on the part of the agency. There is nothing the agency can or should do about that difference in attitude. On the other hand, if one planning district has a significantly higher need for a swimming pool and there is no aquatic facility in the area, the agency can consider the construction of a pool there. Ultimately the report needs to focus on action and demonstrate to the agency that there are specific things that need to be done based on the data.

The last substantive part of the report is a list of recommendations. An example of a recommendations section may be found in Appendix C. Every recommendation should be phrased in clear, active language so that the reader can translate the statement into an activity or a policy. Second, the statement should be explained and supported by data. The data used to support the recommendation might come directly from earlier sections of the report, but it is also possible that the recommendation is based on data from additional analysis not reported in the results section of the report. In other words, the recommendations are based on in-depth data analysis that the researcher has conducted, even if not all of it was included in the report.

Ultimately, it is this recommendations section of the report that is particularly useful to the agency since it indicates specific directions in which the agency can proceed. Often, writers feel that each recommendation must suggest a new course of action. However, it could be that a new course is not needed and that the status quo is providing a good service to the community. In such cases, it is reasonable to say that the agency should continue to do the good work it is doing in a particular area. Figure 11.1 illustrates how recommendations are data based and often underscore an existing standard of excellence for an agency.

Figure 11.1
Examples of Recommendations

Opinions about PRC, and Water-based Recreation

THE PRC SHOULD CONCENTRATE ON PROVIDING DIFFERENT KINDS OF WATER-BASED RECREATION.

The County residents feel that the role of PRC is to provide a wide variety of water-based recreation in the County. This should be done in cooperation with private enterprise, but that is not to suggest that the PRC should not provide activities that are already provided by the private operators.

THE PRC SHOULD FIND WAYS TO MAKE WATER-BASED RECREATION MORE AFFORDABLE.

In line with the previous recommendation, and since the respondents feel that water-based recreation is too expensive, the PRC needs to provide cheaper opportunities for water-based recreation to the residents of Charleston County.

USING GRAPHICS IN THE REPORT

Graphics is a broad term that includes graphs, tables, and figures used to illustrate, summarize, and strengthen the point being made in the text of the report. It is important to use graphics in a report. First, graphics help to illustrate a point. Figures can show examples of recommendations or past questionnaires to illustrate and provide examples of the various artifacts used in leisure and recreation survey research in order to aid in the understanding of the material. Second, graphics help to summarize information. It is often simpler to condense a large set of similar findings in a summary table that the reader can quickly review instead of having to sift through several pages of text. For instance, most leisure and recreation surveys include a personal opinion section. It is possible to create a table that lists each of the opinion statements and the mean response to the statement. That information is easier to access in the form of a table than as text. Moreover, by rank-ordering the statements from the high to the low mean, the reader can get a notion of the key concerns and opinions of the community. Third, graphics are often used to strengthen a point made in the text by bringing out what is most important in the data. For example, it is certainly possible to claim in the text that there is a significant difference between men and women in interest in aerobics, but showing that in a graph often makes the point clearer and stronger.

Three kinds of graphics are commonly used in reports. Figures and drawings help to demonstrate to the reader a process or a particular idea. For example, the chart in Figure 5.1 was used to establish the connection between attitudes and behavior. Such charts illustrate relationships and make it clearer to the reader how the relationship is established. Reports that are connected with master plans could include drawings that provide a new plan for a construction or a development. Figures could be used to illustrate a process that can be followed to reach a particular goal.

Perhaps the most common form of graphics are tables. It is important that tables include clear labels so that the reader can tell what the various elements of the table are. Additionally, tables should not be crowded with too much information, since the purpose of the table is to summarize and not confuse. A table also needs to be designed so that it can be contained within a single page, so that the reader can glance at it and see the numbers being used to illustrate the point.

Finally, graphs play an important role. While there are many different ways in which numbers can be represented in graphs, The writer should stay within accepted boundaries and limit the use of graphs to bar charts, line diagrams, and pie charts for reasons of consistency. Graphs should not be used to unnecessarily "jazz" up the report but in a meaningful way to make the report stronger. Bar graphs provide a good visual tool for demonstrating differences between groups. If one wishes to illustrate that men and women have different attitudes toward an issue, for example, the bar graph is a good tool. Similarly, bar graphs illustrate the way in which opinion about an issue is distributed by visually presenting the percentage of respondents who fell along the continuum between "strongly agree" and "strongly disagree." Line graphs also help to make this point clear and often provide a better illustration of trends. Finally, pie charts are very useful for the illustration of demographic trends and percentages in the sample. The pie chart brings this information to life by showing how the community is split between different age groups, ethnicities, income groups, and so on.

Graphics need to be used in an appropriate manner and properly selected to fill different needs. It is in the combination of the analysis, writing, and presentation that a compelling report is produced that serves the purpose of planning.

IN CLOSING

This book has attempted to address a series of issues related to the process of research that is a necessary part for the successful functioning of any recreation agency. Planners and administrators of recreation agencies constantly have to make difficult and sensitive decisions about the kinds of services that they need to provide to their constituencies.

These decisions often have long-range impact on the organization as well as the people the organization serves. As students training to be administrators and researchers it is therefore necessary to be able to raise the appropriate questions and arrive at reliable answers. We have offered different ways to arrive at the answers. It is important to note that all methods have their drawbacks, but when the method is correctly chosen and rigorously applied, the answers can be reliable.

The book can be used in many different ways. After reading the book it is possible to develop systems of evaluation and assessment that the reader can use to answer the questions that face him or her. On the other hand, the book provides a set of guidelines to determine the best way to answer the question and evaluate the comparative merit of the different systems of inquiry and analysis. Thus even if the practitioner is unable to do the research, he or she should be able to use the information in the book to evaluate the proposals and work of people who claim to be experts in the analytical work. We have offered many different methods, broadly categorized as experimental and survey methods. However, the reader should recognize that neither method is intrinsically better than the other. Rather it is important to begin with the specific research question and then apply a combination of methods that would help to answer the question best. It is important to remember that recreation is a pragmatic affair, and the answers and decisions have practical implications. Therefore, it is more important to arrive at the methods of leisure research by beginning with the fundamental question, "What's going on?" and then move from there to select the synthesized method that best answers the question. Therein lies the power of recreation research.

References

Adams, G. R., & Schvaneveldt, J. D. (1991). *Understanding research methods.* White Plains, NY: Longman Publishing Group.

Albaum, G., Best, R., & Hawkins, D. (1977, January). The measurement properties of semantic scale data. *Journal of the Marketing Research Society*, 21-26.

Allison, M. T. (1995). The question of relevance: Introductory comments. *Leisure Science, 17*(2), 121-124.

Altheide, D. L. (1987, Spring). Ethnographic content analysis. *Qualitative Sociology, 10*(1), 65-77.

Babbie, E. (1986). *The practice of social research.* Belmont, CA: Wadsworth Publishing.

Babbie, E. (1992). *The practice of social research* (5th ed.). Belmont, CA: Wadsworth Publishing Co.

Backoff, R. W., & Nutt, P. C. (1988). A process for strategic management with specific application to the nonprofit organization. In J. M. Bryson & R. C. Einsweiler (Eds.), *Strategic planning: Threats and opportunities for planners.* Chicago: Planners Press.

Bannon, J. (1985). *Leisure resources: Its comprehensive planning.* Champaign, IL: Management Learning Laboratories.

Bedini, L. A., & Wu, Y. (1994). A methodological research in *Therapeutic Recreation Journal* from 1986 to 1990. *Therapeutic Recreation Journal.* Second quarter, 87-97.

Bialeschki, D. (1994, May). What's happening in our curriculum in recreation, parks resources. *Parks and Recreation*, 27.

Bloch, D. P. (1992). The application of group interviews to the planning and evaluation of career development programs. *Career Development Quarterly, 40*, 340-350.

Bloom, M. (1986). *The experience of research.* New York: Macmillan Publishing Company.

Bodgan, R. C., & Biklen, S. K. (1992). *Qualitative research for education: An introduction to theory and methods.* Boston: Allyn and Bacon.

Bouchard, T. J., Jr., & Hare, M. (1970). Size, performance, and potential in brainstorming groups. *Journal of Applied Psychology, 54*(1), 51-55.

Brewer, J., & Hunter, A. (1989). *Multimethod research: A synthesis of styles.* Newbury Park, CA: Sage Publications.

Britton, R. A. (1979). The image of the Third World in tourism marketing. *Annals of Tourism Research, 6*, 318-329.

Caldwell, L. L., Smith, E. A., & Weissinger, E. (1992). Development of a leisure experience battery for adolescents: Parsimony, stability, and validity. *Journal of Leisure Research. 24*(4), 361.

Cannon, D. (1991). Generation X:The way they do the things they do. *Journal of Career Planning and Employment, 51*(2), 34-38.

Campbell, D.T., & Fisk, D.W. (1959, March). Convergent and discriminant validation by the multitrait-multimethod matrix. *Psychological Bulletin, 56*, 81-105.

Campbell, D.T., & Stanley, J. C. (1966). Experimental and quasi-experimental designs for research. In N. L. Gage (Ed.), *Handbook of Research on Teaching* (pp. 1-76). Chicago: Rand McNally.

Carey, M.A., & Smith, M.W. (1992). Enhancement of validity through qualitative approaches: Incorporating the patient's perspective. *Evaluation and the Health Professions, 15*(1), 107-114.

Chadwick, B. A., Bahr, H. M., & Albrecht, S. C. (1984). *Social science research methods.* Englewood Cliffs, N J: Prentice-Hall.

Churchill, G. A., & Peter, J. P. (1984, November). Research design effects on the reliability of rating scales. *Journal of Marketing Research*, 360-375.

Cooper, H. M. (1989). *Integrating research:A guide for literature reviews.* Newbury Park, CA: Sage Publications.

Cozby, P. C. (1993). *Methods in behavioral research.* Mountain View, CA: Mayfield Publishing.

Creswell, J. W. (1994). *Research design: Qualitative and quantitative approaches.* Thousand Oaks, CA: Sage Publications.

Cronbach, L. J. (1951). Coefficient alpha and the internal structure of tests. *Psychometrika, 16*, 297-334.

Dandekar, H. C. (1988). *The planner's use of information:Techniques for collection, organization and communication.* Chicago: American Planning Association.

Delbecq, A., & Van de Ven, A. (1971). A group process model for problem identification and program planning. *Journal of Applied Behavioral Science*, 7(4), 466-492.

Delbecq, A., Van de Ven, A., & Gustafson, D. H. (1975). *Group techniques for program planning: A guide to nominal groups and delphi processes.* Glenview, IL: Scott, Foresman.

Dennis, M. L., Fetterman, D. M., & Sechrest, L. (1994). Integrating qualitative and quantitative evaluation methods in substance abuse research. *Evaluation and Program Planning, 17*(4), 419-427.

Dillman, D.A. (1978). *Mail and telephone surveys: The total design method.* New York: John Wiley.

Doty, P. (1991). Scientific norm s and the use of electronic research networks. *Proceedings of the ASIS Annual Meeting, 28*, 24-38.

Downs, R. M., & Stea, D. (1977). *Maps in minds: Reflections on cognitive mapping.* New York: Harper & Row.

Edginton, C. R., Hanson, C. J., & Edginton, S. R. (1992). *Leisure programming: Concepts, trends, and professional practice* (2nd ed.). Dubuque, IA: Brown & Benchmark.

Edginton, C. R., Madrigal, R., Lankford, S. V., & Wheeler, D. (1990). Organizational goals: Differences between board members and recreation managers and board or commission members. *Journal of Park and Recreation Administration, 8*(2), 70.

Ellis, G. D., & Williams, D. R. (1987). The impending renaissance in leisure service evaluation. *Journal of Park and Recreation Administration, 5*(1), 17-29.

Ewert, A. (1990). Decision-making techniques for establishing research agendas in park and recreation systems. *Journal of Park and Recreation Administration, 8*(2), 1-13.

Firestone, W. A. (1987). Meaning in method: The rhetoric of quantitative and qualitative research. *Educational Researcher, 16*(7), 16-21.

Fishbein, M. (1975). *Belief, attitude, intention, and behavior: An introduction to theory and research.* Reading, MA: Addison-Wesley.

Fisher, M. A. (1993). Research on a shoestring: A veteran marketer shows data collection needn't be expensive. *Currents, 19*(2), 42-43.

Fridgen, J. D. (1987). Use of cognitive maps to determine perceived tourism regions. *Leisure Science, 9*, 101-117.

Gebremedhin, T. G., & Tweeten, L. G. (1994). *Research methods and communication in the social sciences.* Westport, CT: Praeger Publishers.

Glancy, M., & Little, S. (1995). Studying the social aspects of leisure: Development of the multi-method field investigation model (MMFI). *Journal of Leisure Research, 27*(4), 305-325.

Goldman, A. E., & McDonald, S. S. (1987). *The group depth interview: Principles and practices*. Englewood Cliffs, NJ: Prentice-Hall.

Goodale, T. (1994, December). Leisure science: Impractical? Impenetrable? *Parks & Recreation*, 14.

Goodyear, M. (1982, April). Qualitative research in developing countries. *Journal of the Market Research Society*, 86-96.

Guba, E. G. (1992). *The paradigm dialog*. Newbury Park, CA: Sage Publications.

Guba, E. G., & Lincoln, Y. (1988). Do inquiry paradigms imply inquiry methodologies? In D. Fetterman (Ed.), *Qualitative approaches to evaluation in education* (pp. 89-115). New York: Praeger.

Hammersley, M. (1993). *Social research: Philosophy, politics and practice.* Newbury Park, CA: Sage Publications.

Havitz, M. E., Dimanche, F., & Howard, D. R. (1993). A two sample comparison of the personal involvement inventory (PII) and the involvement profile (IP) scales using selected recreation activities. *Journal of Applied Recreation Research, 17*(4), 331.

Hedges, L. V., & Olkin, I. (1985). *Statistical methods for meta-analysis*. New York: Academic Press.

Hedrick, T. E., Bickman, L., & Rog, D. J. (1993). *Applied research design: A practical guide.* Newbury Park, CA: Sage Publications.

Henderson, K. A. (1991). *Dimensions of choice: A qualitative approach to recreation parks, and leisure research.* State College, PA: Venture Publishing.

Henderson, K. A. (1994, July). Not for researchers only. *Parks and Recreation*, 14-17.

Henderson, K. A., & Bedini, L. A. (1994, January). Emerging cultural paradigms and changes in leisure sciences. *Parks and Recreation*, 24-28.

Henderson, K. A., & Bialeschki, M. D. (1995). *Evaluating leisure services: Making enlightened decisions.* State College, PA: Venture Publishing.

Henderson, K. A., & O'Neill, J. (1995, January). Has research contributed to the advancement of professional practice? *Parks and Recreation*, 17.

Henwood, K., & Pidgeon, N. (1993). Qualitative research and psychological theorizing. In M. Hammersley (Ed.), *Social research: Philosophy, politics and practice* (pp. 14-32). Newbury Park, CA: Sage Publications.

Hines, A. M. (1993). Linking qualitative and quantitative methods in cross-cultural survey research: Techniques from cognitive science. *American Journal of Community Psychology, 21*(6), 729-746.

Howard, D. R., Havitz, M. E., Lankford, S. V., & Dimanche, F. (1992). Panel survey assessment of elapsed time response error in travel spending measurement. *Journal of Hospitality and Leisure Marketing, 1*(1), 39-50.

Howard, D. R., Lankford, S. V., & Havitz, M. E. (1991). A method for authenticating pleasure travel expenditures. *Journal of Travel Research, 29*(4), 19-23.

Huck, S. W., Cormier, W. H., & Bounds, C. H. (1974). *Reading statistics and research.* New York: Harper Collins.

Isaac, S., & Michael, M. B. (1985). *Handbook in research and evaluation.* San Diego, CA: Edits Publishers.

Iso-Aloha, S. E. (1980). *The social psychology of leisure and recreation.* Dubuque, IA: William C. Brown.

Ittelson, W. H. (1973). Environment perception and contemporary perceptual theory. In *Environment and cognition* (pp. 1-19). Proceedings. New York: Seminar Press.

Jaeger, R. M. (1990). *Statistics: A spectator sport* (2nd ed.). Newbury Park, CA: Sage Publications.

Johnson, T., Mitra, A., Newman, R., & Horm, J. (1993, June). Problems of definition in sampling special populations: The case of homeless persons. *Evaluation Practice*, 130.

Kerlinger, F. N. (1986). *Foundations of behavioral research* (3rd ed.) New York: CBS College Publishing, Hold, Rinehardt, Winston.

Knowles-Lankford, J. (1990). *Highway 101–View enhancement study.* Prepared for the State of Oregon Highway Division. Salem, OR: Community Planning Workshop, University of Oregon.

Kramer, G. L. (1993). Using student focus groups to evaluate academic support services. *NACADA Journal, 12*(2), 38-41.

Krathwohl, D. R. (1985). *Social and behavioral science research: A new framework for conceptualizing, implementing, and evaluating research studies.* San Francisco: Jossey-Bass.

Kraus, R., & Allen, L. (1987). *Research and evaluation in recreation, parks, and leisure studies.* Columbus, OH: Publishing Horizons.

Krueger, R. A. (1988). *Focus groups: A practical guide for applied research.* Newbury Park, CA: Sage.

Krugman, D. M., & Johnson, K. F. (1991). Differences in the consumption of traditional broadcast and VCR movie rentals. *Journal of Broadcasting and Electronic Media, 35*, 213-232.

Lankford, S. V. (1988). *Image of place and community economic development: The case of government camp Oregon.* Clackamas County Department of Human Services, Division of Community Development. Eugene, OR: University of Oregon Community Planning Workshop.

Lankford, S. V. (1990). *A study of evaluation competencies of park and recreation personnel in the Pacific Northwest* (Unpublished Monograph). Eugene, OR: University of Oregon, Department of Leisure Studies and Services.

Lankford, S. V. (1994 & 1996). *Na Ala Hele: Island of Oahu biking trails and attitudes survey report.* State of Hawaii Department of Forestry. University of Hawaii: Department of Kinesiology & Leisure Science.

Lankford, S. V. (1995). *Market research strategies and methods.* U.S. Army, Hawaii, MWR Department, Marketing Division. Honolulu, HI: University of Hawaii, Department of Kinesiology & Leisure Science.

Lankford, S. V., & DeGraaf, D. (1992). Strengths, weaknesses, opportunities, and threats in morale, welfare and recreation organizations: Challenges of the 1990s. *Journal of Park and Recreation Administration, 10*(1), 31-45.

Leedy, P. D. (1985). *Practical research: Planning and design.* New York: Macmillan.

Lengua, L. (1992). Using focus groups to guide the development of a parenting program for difficult-to-reach, high-risk families. *Family Relations, 41*, 163-168.

Lincoln, Y. S., & Guba, E. G. (1985). *Naturalistic inquiry.* Beverly Hills, CA: Sage Publications.

Little, J. R., Lankford, S. V., DeGraaf, D., & Tashiro, A. (1995). An exploratory study of issues and trends in therapeutic recreation: A practitioner perspective. *Journal of Applied Recreation Research, 20*(4), 269-282.

Mannel, R. C. (1980). Social psychological techniques and strategies for studying leisure experiences. In S. E. Iso-Ahola (Ed.), *Social psychological perspectives on leisure and recreation* (pp. 62-88). Springfield, IL: Charles C. Thomas.

Majchrzak, A. M. (1984). *Methods for policy research.* Newbury Park, CA: Sage Publications.

McCracken, G. (1988). *The long interview*. Newbury Park, CA: Sage Publications.

McDonald, W. J. (1982, Fall). Approaches to group research with children. *Journal of the Academy of Marketing Science*, 490-499.

McMillan, J. H., & Schumacher, S. (1984). *Research in education: A conceptual introduction*. Boston: Little, Brown.

Merriam, S. B. (1988). *Case study research in education: A qualitative approach*. San Francisco: Jossey-Bass.

Morgan, D. L. (1988). *Focus groups as qualitative research*. Newbury Park, CA: Sage.

Moser, C.A., & Kalton, G. (1972). *Survey methods in social investigation* (2nd ed.). New York: Basic.

Nachmias, D., & Nachmias, C. (1987). *Research methods in the social sciences*. New York: St. Martin's Press.

Naisbitt, J. (1982) *Megatrends: Ten new directions for transforming our lives*. New York: Warner Books.

Nishikawa, N. I. (1988). Survey methods for planners. In Dandekar, H.C. (Ed.), *The planner's use of information: Techniques for collection, organization and communication* (pp. 32-55). Chicago: American Planning Association.

O'Sullivan, E. L. (1991). *Marketing for parks, recreation, and leisure*. State College, PA: Venture.

Patton, M. Q. (1980). *Qualitative research methods*. Beverly Hills, CA: Sage.

Pearce, P. L. (1981) Route maps: A study of travelers' perceptions of a section of countryside. *Journal of Environmental Psychology, 1*, 141, 155.

Phillips, B. (1985). *Sociological research methods: An introduction*. Homewood, IL: Dorsey Press.

Povey, D., Lankford, S. V., & Knowles-Lankford, J. (1989). *Government camp economic development improvement plan*. Clackamas County Division of Community Development. Eugene, OR: University of Oregon Community Planning Workshop.

President's Commision on Americans Outdoors. (1986). *A literature review*. Washington, D.C.: Government Printing Office.

Pryor, C. B. (1992). Schools' defense of children in America at war. *Urban Education, 27*, 7-20.

Quantz, R. A. (1992). On critical ethnography. In M. D. LeCompte, W. L. Millroy, & J. Preissle (Eds.), *The handbook of qualitative research in education* (pp. 447-505). New York: Academic Press.

Robertson, B. J. (1994). Leisure in the lives of male adolescents who engage in delinquent activities for excitement. *Journal of Park and Recreation Administration, 12* (4), 29-34.

Rosenberg, M. (1968). *The logic of survey analysis*. New York: Basic.

Rosenthal, R. (1984). *Meta-analytic procedures for social research*. Newbury Park, CA: Sage Publications.

Rossi, P. H., Freeman, H. E., & Wright, S. R. (1980). *Evaluation: A systematic approach.* Beverly Hills, CA: Sage Publications.

Rossi, P. H., Wright, J. D., & Wright, P. H. (1978). The theory and practice of applied social research. *Evaluation Quarterly, 2,* 171-191.

Rossman, R. J. (1995). *Recreation programming: Designing leisure experiences.* Champaign, IL: Sagamore Publishing.

Ryan, G. J. (1993). Shed a little light: Eight illuminating axioms of market research. *Currents, 19* (2), 40-42, 44-45.

Schatzman, L., & Strauss, A. L. (1973). *Field research: Strategies for a natural sociology.* Englewood Cliffs, NJ: Prentice-Hall.

Schmerl, R. B. (1988). Written communication. In H. C. Dandekar (Ed.), *The planner's use of information: Techniques for collection, organization and communication* (pp. 170-187). Chicago: American Planning Association.

Scholtes, P. R. (1988). *The team handbook: How to use teams to improve quality.* Madison, WI: Joiner Associates.

Short, E. C. (1991). *Forms of curriculum inquiry.* Albany, NY: State University of New York Press.

Slater, D. (1984). *Management of local planning.* Washington, D.C.: International City Management Association.

Smith, J. K. (1983). Quantitative versus qualitative research: An attempt to clarify the issue. *Educational Researcher,* (March), pp. 6-13.

Smith, M. L., & Glass, G. V. (1987). *Research and evaluation in education and the social sciences.* Englewood Cliffs, NJ: Prentice-Hall.

Sommer, R. S., & Sommer, B. B. (1986). *A practical guide to behavioral research: Tools and techniques.* New York: Oxford University Press.

Stewart, D. W., & Kamins, M. A. (1993). *Secondary research: Information sources and methods.* Newbury Park, CA: Sage Publications.

Stoddard, R. H. (1982). *Field techniques and research methods in geography.* Dubuque, IA: Kendall/Hunt Publishing.

Strauss, A., & Corbin, J. (1990). *Basics of qualitative research.* Newbury Park, CA: Sage Publications.

Sudman, S. (1976). *Applied sampling.* New York: Academic Press.

Sylvester, C. (1995). Relevance and rationality in leisure studies: A plea for good reason. *Leisure Sciences, 17*(2), 125-131.

Thomas, J. R., & French, K. E. (1986). The use of meta-analysis in exercise and sport: A tutorial. *Research Quarterly for Exercise and Sport, 57,* 196-204.

Thomas, J. R., & Nelson, J. K. (1990). *Research methods in physical activity.* Champaign, IL: Human Kinetics.

Tillinghast, D. S. (1980, Fall). Direct magnitude estimation scales in public opinion surveys. *Public Opinion Quarterly,* 377-384.

Tuan, Y. (1975). Images and mental maps. *Annals of the Association of American Geographers, 65,* 205-213.

Tuckman, B. W. (1978). *Conducting educational research.* New York: Harcourt Brace Jovanovich.

Tull, D. S., & Hawkins, D. I. (1987). *Marketing research: Measurement and method.* New York: Macmillan Publishing Company.

Twombly, S. B. (1992). Student persectives on general education in a research university: An exploratory study. *Journal of General Education, 41*, 238-272.

Walmsley, D. J., & Jenkins, J. M. (1992). Tourism cognitive mapping of unfamiliar environments. *Annals of Tourism Research, 19*, 268-285.

Wagenaar, T. C. (1981). *Readings for social research*. Belmont, CA: Wadsworth Publishing.

Wesner, B. (1994, February). The value of historical research. *Parks and Recreation*, 30-40.

Williams, A., Lankford, S.V., DeGraaf, D., & Chen, A. (1995). *Pathfinder analysis of motivation knowledge structures: A preliminary investigation* (p. 55) Abstracts of the leisure research symposium. San Antonio, TX: National Recreation and Parks Association.

Williams, A., & Neal, L. L. (1993). Motivational assessment in organizations: An application of the importance-performance analysis. *Journal of Park and Recreation Administration, 11*(2). 60.

Williams, D. D. (1986). *Naturalistic evaluation*. San Francisco: Jossey-Bass.

Williamson, J. B., Karp, D. A., & Dalphin, J. R. (1977). *The research craft: An introduction to social science methods*. Boston: Little, Brown.

Wolcott, H. F. (1994). *Transforming qualitative data: Descriptive, analysis, and interpretation.* Thousand Oaks, CA: Sage Publication.

Yoder, D., McKinney, W., Wicks, B., & Espeseth, R. (1995). The theory and application of triangulation to public park and recreation planning. *Journal of Park and Recreation Administration, 13*(3), 26-40.

Glossary

abstract population: The population about which one ultimately wishes to draw conclusions.

action research: Applied research using the scientific method.

analysis of variance (ANOVA): A procedure for testing hypotheses about relationships among variables under a wide range of conditions for three or more groups.

applied research: Research emphasizing the solution of social and community problems.

attitude scale: A type of questionnaire designed to produce scores indicating the overall degree of favorability of a person's attitude on a topic, such as free time.

attribute: One of the categories specified or implied by a variable.

basic research: Research emphasizing the solution of theoretical problems.

binomial probability distribution: The probabilities associated with every possible outcome of an experiment involving *n* independent trials and a success or failure on each trial.

bivariate analysis: The analysis of relationships among pairs of variables.

census: A complete count of the members of a population; also refers to the count and survey process conducted by the U.S. Census Bureau.

central tendency: The degree to which the quantities of a variable converge.

cluster analysis: An exploratory procedure for combining similar objects into groupings and then using those groupings ("clusters") as a basis for further analysis.

cluster sample: A probability sample in which groupings of elements are selected initially and individual elements are sampled subsequently.

code: A translation from raw data to numbers that can be employed by data entry personnel.

coding: A procedure that assigns data to numbered categories in order to facilitate quantitative and qualitative analysis.

coefficient of determination: A measure of the proportion of the variation in the dependent variable that the independent variable is able to account for.

complete observer: An observational role in which the researcher's behavior is not part of the phenomenon studied and subjects remain unaware of the study and observer.

complete participant: An observational role involving as thorough as possible an entrance into the lives of those being studied.

concept: A linguistic symbol that categorizes phenomena.

concurrent validity: The correlation of results correspond with other results.

construct validity: The degree to which an operational definition categorizes phenomena in the same way as a well-accepted or criterion operational definition. Simply, do items measure hypothetical constructs or concepts?

content analysis: Research procedures for relating symbolic data to their context; systematically describing the form and content of written or spoken material.

content validity: The condition in which the items on the survey measure the content they were intended to measure.

control group: A group not subjected to the experimental treatment, which is used for purposes of comparison. The control group resembles the experimental group in every respect except that it is not exposed to the independent variable(s) in order to control for the effects of extraneous variables on the dependent variable.

controlling on a variable: Cross-tabulating other variables within each of the attributes of the variable, such as female and male, age, etc..

convenience sample: A nonprobability sample drawn primarily on the basis of the ease of obtaining the data.

correlation: A measure of the degree of fit (a coefficient indicating the relationship) between two sets of scores (variables).

corroboration: Confirmation of statements from two or more sources.

cross-tabulation: The distribution of one variable within the categories of another.

cumulative scaling procedures: Techniques for constructing a partially ordered scale that include some testing of that scale's assumptions.

data: Information about the nature of phenomena derived from experience or observation.

degree of relationship between two variables: The closeness of the relationship between the variables, usually measured by a correlation coefficient.

dependent variable: A variable presumed to be influenced by another variable.

discriminant analysis: An exploratory procedure for identifying relationships between nominal-scale dependent variables and more quantitative independent variables, often used to describe group characteristics.

elaboration model: An image of bivariate and multivariate cross-tabulation procedures for making sequential inferences from one-shot data.

ethnomethodology: A theoretical orientation emphasizing people's everyday procedures for solving practical problems in situations through (1) constructing ethnotheories, (2) experiencing phenomena, and (3) constructing common-sense accounts and prophesies.

evaluation research: Applied research using the scientific method to assess the worth or effectiveness of a leisure activity, program, or policy.

ex post facto hypothesizing: Developing hypotheses to fit observed data.

experiment: A method of data collection in which the researcher tests hypotheses by introducing a change in the research situation and observing the results.

experimental group: A group subjected to the experimental treatment.

experimental post test: Observation subsequent to introduction of the experimental treatment.

experimental pretest: Observation prior to introduction of the experimental treatment.

experimental treatment: The change that the experimenter introduces.

exploratory observation: A type of pretest centering on the method of noting and recording ongoing phenomena.

external validity: The degree to which statements about the specific phenomena investigated (the sample) can be generalized to other settings (the population).

face validity: The degree to which an operational definition, on the basis of the researcher's experience and that of other experts, appears to correctly specify the concept it is designed to specify. Specifically, do the items appear to measure what the instrument purports to measure?

factor analysis: An exploratory correction procedure for deriving a relationship among a small number of "factors" or dimensions from a larger set of variables; useful for data reduction, explanation of dimensions, and scaling.

field experiment: An experiment within an ongoing setting.

field observation: The noting and recording of behavior within an ongoing setting.

fixed-alternative question: A question that provides a list of alternative answers with a restrictive scale format (yes/no; strongly agree/strongly disagree).

focused interview: An interview centering on the effects of a given phenomenon experienced by the respondent.

funnel technique: The use of successively more structured and probing questions.

historical method: The process of critically examining the records of the past.

historiography: The imaginative reconstruction of the past by means of the historical method.

hypothesis: A tentative statement of a relationship between two or more variables.

independent variable: A variable presumed to influence or precede another variable (dependent variable).The variable is systematically manipulated by the researcher to determine changes in the dependent variable. Also known as the experimental variable or moderating variable.

internal validity: The degree to which the instrument (statements) or procedure in a study measures what it is supposed to measure.

interval scale: A measurement of a variable which results in the classification of phenomena into a set of attributes with equal distances or intervals separating them (1=Strongly Agree, 2=Agree, 3=Neutral, 4=Agree, 5=Strongly Agree).

intervening variable:A variable that follows the independent variable and precedes the dependent variable, sometimes manipulated to determine effects of the independent variable on the dependent variable through the means of covariation.

investigator effect: The impact of the scientist on the research process.

laboratory experiment: An experiment within a deliberately constructed setting.

laboratory observation:The noting and recording of behavior within a deliberately constructed setting.

Likert-type scales: Measurements employing many of the criteria specified by Likert for summated scaling procedures, usually a three-, five-, or seven-point scale.

measurement:The process of creating a correspondence between a concept and data in specifying that concept.

method of agreement: An experimental method that designates a presumed partial cause of a phenomenon as any factor that occurs together with the phenomenon.

method of concomitant variations: An experimental method that designates as a presumed partial cause of a phenomenon any factor that varies in the same way that the phenomenon varies.

method of difference: An experimental method that designates a presumed partial cause of a phenomenon as any factor that occurs together with the phenomenon and does not occur when the phenomenon does not occur.

method of equal-appearing intervals: A technique for constructing an interval scale based on judges' ratings of a large number of items on the items' degree of "favorableness" to a given variable.

method of paired comparisons: A technique for constructing an interval scale based on judges' choices—for all possible combinations of pairs of items—of items on the basis of their degree of "favorableness" toward a given variable.

multiple correlation: A measure of the degree of fit between actual scores for a dependent variable and the scores predicted by a set of independent variables.

multiple regression: A prediction of the scores of a given dependent variable using the scores of a set of independent variables. Of interest is the relationship between the sets of scores. Can we predict attitude or behaviors based on the influence or presence of a set of variables or conditions (independent measures)?

multivariate analysis: The analysis of relationships among three or more variables at the same time. For example, in a leisure services marketing study, the effects of age, income, and education could be analyzed simultaneously to determine which of the variables would better predict (or explain the largest amount of variation in) nonuse of a program.

nominal scale: A measurement of a variable which results in the classification of phenomena into a set of consistent and non-overlapping attributes (yes, no, male, female, etc.).

nonparametric statistics: Tests of significance that require few assumptions about the population. Use of these statistics should occur when samples are small (fewer than 30 subjects), when subjects were not randomly sampled, or data are not interval level. Chi-square, Spearman rank order coefficient, and Mann-Whitney U are some examples.

nonprobability sampling: A method of selecting a sample from a population that does not yield known probabilities for selecting each sample element. There are three types: quota, purposive, and convenience samples.

null hypothesis: A hypothesis about a population made for the purpose of testing it against sample data; a conservative means of stating the research questions to indicate that the independent variable has no effect on the dependent variable.

objectivity: An unprejudiced or open orientation to information about the nature of phenomena being studied.

observation: The act of noting and recording a phenomenon, often with instruments (cameras, recorders) or note taking.

observer-as-participant: An observational role revealed to others and offering a very limited time for data collection.

open-ended question: A question that does not provide a list of alternative answers, but allows the respondent to express his or her position on a topic.

operational definition: An explicit procedure for defining a variable by the means used to measure it. The personal meaning of leisure can be operationally defined as the responses to a set of involvement profile questions.

ordinal scale: A measurement of a variable that results in the classification of phenomena into a set of ranked or ordered attributes.

parametric statistics: Researchers use these statistics when samples are larger than 30 subjects and are randomly drawn, groups have equal variances, and data are interval. Examples of these statistics are the T-test and analysis of variance.

partial correlation: A procedure for measuring the degree of association between an independent variable and a dependent variable while controlling the influence of one or more other variables.

participant observation: A method of data collection in which the researcher notes and records ongoing social phenomena with the researcher's own behavior constituting part of the phenomena.

participant-as-observer: An observational role involving the relation of that role to others as well as thorough entrance into their lives.

path analysis: A systematic procedure for constructing a casual model of the relationships among a set of variables, assuming linear relationships exist.

Pearson product-moment correlation coefficient (r): a measure of association based on least-squares deviations from a regression line. A widely used statistic for measuring the relationship between two sets of scores that are assumed to be continuously distributed.

population: A set of elements from which a subset may be drawn (a sample). It is the entire group of people, objects, or events in a category.

predictive validity: The condition in which scores predict a criterion measure.

pretest: A trial run of a data collection procedure to determine problem areas or weaknesses in design.

primary source: The testimony of an eyewitness, that is, someone present at the events described.

probability level: An indication of the likelihood that an obtained difference on a statistical test is due to chance alone. A common practice in leisure research, and behavioral and social science research, is to use the .05 probability level (also called the .05 level of significance).

probability sampling: A method of selecting a subset of elements (sample) from a larger set (population) in such a way that each element of the larger set has a known probability of being selected. Two general types are random and stratified samples.

purposive sample: A nonprobability sample chosen when individuals considered most closely related to the issue being studied are selected for inclusion.

quota sample: A nonprobability sample that takes into account the proportion of individuals in different population categories (age, gender, etc.) within the population. This is a nonprobability type of sample method.

randomization: The use of probability sampling to assign subjects to experimental and control groups.

ratio scale: A measurement of a variable that results in the classification of phenomena into a set of attributes. This scale is characterized by an absolute zero point as well as equal distance between attributes.

research triangulation: The use of multiple methods of investigation. The assumption for use of this method is that any bias inherent in the study would be neutralized in conjunction with other data sources and collection procedures. There are two types: within methods and between methods. The within-methods approach utilizes only quantitative (surveys and experiments) or only qualitative (observation and interviews) approaches. The between-methods approach mixes both quantitative and qualitative methods.

regression: A prediction of the scores (or values) of a given dependent variable, based on the scores of one or more independent variables.

reliability: The degree to which an operational definition is stable and consistent under similar circumstances. Reliability amounts to consistency in measurement, the repeatability or replicability of findings. Specifically, reliability applies to measures of item consistency (are item responses consistent across constructs?), test stability (do responses vary when test is given a second time?); and consistency in administration and scoring (were errors caused by carelessness in administration or scoring?).

replication: The repeating of a study to determine if findings can be duplicated. This is important to increase confidence in research results and to establish models.

research ethics: Principles that guide an investigator's choices and procedures. Of concern is maintaining confidentiality of data, preserving anonymity of informants, and using research for the intended (stated) purposes.

sample: A subset of elements selected from a larger set (the population). The sample is used to make generalizations about the population from which it was drawn.

sampling bias: The error introduced by a sampling procedure that favors certain characteristics over others.

sampling error: The degree of inaccuracy of statements about a population due solely to differences between that population and a sample drawn from it; chance variation among samples selected from the same population.

scale: A series of ordered steps at fixed intervals used as a standard of measurement.

scaling: The process of constructing an operational definition with numerical properties. Examples in leisure include scales to determine attitudes toward free time, involvement, barriers, benefits, and tourism impacts. Factor analysis and reliability testing are used for the scaling process.

scattergram: A set of plots for data on two coordinates.

scientific method: A problem-solving process that involves (1) proposing theory, (2) using data to verify theory, and (3) creating more explanations and accurate predictions of the phenomenon.

scientific paradigm: The world view on which a science is based, involving a system of explicit and implicit assumptions.

secondary analysis: The analysis of available data within a framework that differs from that used in the original study..

secondary source: The testimony of anyone who is not an eyewitness.

semantic differential: A questionnaire procedure for measuring the meaning an individual attaches to a phenomenon using opposing adjectives (good to bad; bored to engaged). The scale was developed by Charles Osgood for measuring the meaning of concepts.

semistandardized interview: An interview involving a moderate degree of planned structure established prior to the interview.

simple random sampling: A probability sampling procedure in which each element of the population has an equal probability of being chosen.

spurious relationship: The condition where a third variable precedes, and is seen as a cause of, the independent and the dependent variables.

standard deviation: A measure of variation based on squared deviations from the mean.

standardized interview: An interview involving a high degree of planned structure.

statistical inference: A statement about a population based on procedures for analyzing a probability sample of that population.

stratified probability sample: A probability sample based on selections from different population categories (gender, age, occupation, voter/nonvoter, etc.).

summated scaling procedures: Techniques for developing partially ordered scales by summing scores over a number of items.

survey: A procedure for systematically collecting information from people by obtaining their responses to questions.

systematic sample: A probability sample drawn from a list where every *n*th element is selected, usually after a random starting place in the list.

theory: Explicit ideas about the nature of phenomena. Theory is an interrelated set of constructs (or variables) formed into propositions (or hypotheses) that specify the relationship among the variables.

type I error: The rejection of a correct null hypothesis.

type II error: The acceptance of an incorrect null hypothesis.

univariate analysis: The analysis of single variables as distinct from relationships among variables.

unstandardized interview:An interview involving little or no planned structure. Although the interviewer has a general topic in mind, there is no predetermined order or specified wording to the questions.

validity of measurement: An indication that the measure accurately reflects what it is supposed to measure (see also internal and external validity).

value communication: The researcher's communication of his or her own values.

value neutrality: The avoidance of all pronouncements of an ethical or value-laden character.

variability: The degree to which the quantities of a variable diverge. Variability is the amount of spread or dispersion within a distribution of scores. Common measures of variability are the range and the standard deviation.

variable: A concept specifying or implying more than one category to which phenomena may be assigned. Any characteristic or quality that differs in degree or kind. Variables may be continuous (1, 2,...) or categorical (yes/no, etc.).

Appendix A
Needs Assessment Questionnaires

172 south circle
bloomingdale, il 60108

April ,1997

Dear Bloomingdale Park District Resident:

As part of our commitment to providing quality open spaces, parks and recreational services, the Bloomingdale Park District is preparing a Comprehensive Park and Recreation Plan that will be used to develop short and long-range plans for the delivery of park and recreation services in Bloomingdale.

You can play a very special role in helping us plan these services. You and other members of the Bloomingdale community have been selected by random sample to represent the opinions of our community through the enclosed survey. Please take a few moments to answer the questions in the survey. It is important that you return the questionnaire as soon as possible. When you have completed the survey, please return it in the enclosed postage-paid envelope. **No names are requested and your responses are all strictly confidential!**

We appreciate your time to complete the survey. The information you provide will be very helpful as we plan for Parks and Recreation services into the next millennium.

Thank you.

Sincerely,

Paul L. Becker

Paul L. Becker
President
Board of Commissioners

RECREATION ACTIVITY INTERESTS

Your interest in the following categories of recreation programs is important in determining future programs and services. Please indicate your interest in each of the categories.

Categories	Program Examples	Interested	Not Interested	Not Sure
Visual / Graphic Arts & Crafts	(painting, ceramics, photography, sculpture, etc.)	2	1	8
Performing Arts	(theater, concerts, folk dance, ballet, music, etc.)	2	1	8
Sports, Athletics & Aquatics	(baseball, soccer, wrestling, softball, swimming, etc.)	2	1	8
Environmental	(nature classes, gardening, home landscaping, etc.)	2	1	8
Self-Improvement	(self-defense, teen leadership, home computer, etc.)	2	1	8
Social	(couples dancing, teen club, senior club, bridge, etc.)	2	1	8
Hobbies	(cooking, flower arranging, models, chess, etc.)	2	1	8
Travel & Tourism	(day trips to points of interest within 3-hour drive, etc.)	2	1	8
Special Events	(one- or two-day events, festivals, shows, etc.)	2	1	8

Listed below are many different types of recreational activities that are enjoyed year around. For each activity, please indicate how much interest YOU have in participating in each activity.

	Interested	Not Interested	Not Sure
Children's Art Classes	2	1	8
Painting, Oil, Water, Acrylic	2	1	8
Sewing Classes	2	1	8
Quilt Making	2	1	8
Photography	2	1	8
Ballet	2	1	8
Dancing, Ballroom	2	1	8
Dancing, Jazz	2	1	8
Dancing, Tap	2	1	8
Theater,	2	1	8
Music Lessons	2	1	8
Camping Skills	2	1	8
Home Landscaping Instruction	2	1	8
Tree & Shrub Identification	2	1	8
Gardening	2	1	8
Hanging Flower Baskets	2	1	8
Aerobics/Fitness Classes	2	1	8
Aerobics Low Impact	2	1	8
Aerobics Intermediate	2	1	8
Aerobics Advanced	2	1	8
Aerobics Step	2	1	8
Aerobics Aquatic	2	1	8
Ethnic Cooking	2	1	8
Home Computer, Introduction	2	1	8
H. Computer, Word Processing	2	1	8
H. Computer, Windows 95	2	1	8

	Interested	Not Interested	Not Sure
Basketball	2	1	8
Basketball, Over 40	2	1	8
Floor Hockey	2	1	8
Ice Skating, Indoor Lessons	2	1	8
Golf, Leagues & Tournaments	2	1	8
Gymnastics, Youth	2	1	8
Horseback Riding Lessons	2	1	8
Open Gym	2	1	8
Roller Blade (in-Line)	2	1	8
Roller Hockey	2	1	8
Soccer,	2	1	8
Softball, Men's	2	1	8
Softball, Men's 16-inch slow pitch	2	1	8
Softball, Women's	2	1	8
Softball, Co-Rec	2	1	8
Swim Lessons	2	1	8
Swim Team	2	1	8
Tennis Lessons	2	1	8
Tennis, Leagues	2	1	8
Volleyball, Men's	2	1	8
Volleyball, Women's	2	1	8
Volleyball, Teen	2	1	8
Volleyball, Co-Rec	2	1	8
Water Ballet	2	1	8
Weight Training	2	1	8
Fishing, Clinic or Derby	2	1	8

	Interested	Not Interested	Not Sure
H. Computer, Spreadsheets	2	1	8
H. Computer, Data Base	2	1	8
Martial Arts (Tae Kwan Do, etc.)	2	1	8
Jewelry Making	2	1	8
Bowling	2	1	8
Cards	2	1	8
Concerts in the Park	2	1	8
Day Camps	2	1	8
Before/After School Recreation	2	1	8
Preschool activities	2	1	8
OTHER_____			
Model Making	2	1	8
Hunting Workshop	2	1	8
Baby-sitting Workshop	2	1	8
Teen Activity, Club Events	2	1	8
Entertainment Trips, Live Theater	2	1	8
Ethnic Festivals	2	1	8
Overnight Trips	2	1	8
Ski Trips, Youth and/or Adult	2	1	8
Walking for Exercise Club	2	1	8
Roller Skating Instruction	2	1	8

TIME AND ATTENDANCE

The Bloomingdale Park District wants to schedule recreational programs, as well as special events and activities when it is most convenient for you and your family. Please circle all of the spaces that are generally most convenient for any member of your household to attend. Please mark as many times as you like.

	Monday	Tuesday	Wednesday	Thursday	Friday	Saturday	Sunday
6 a.m. - 8 a.m.	1	2	3	4	5	6	7
8 a.m. - Noon	1	2	3	4	5	6	7
Noon - 4 p.m.	1	2	3	4	5	6	7
4 p.m. - 7 p.m.	1	2	3	4	5	6	7
7 p.m. - 10 p.m.	1	2	3	4	5	6	7

By circling the responses below please indicate how many times, in the past year, you have attended Bloomingdale Park District activities or facilities.

0. Never
1. Once in 12 months
2. Once in 6 months
3. Once in 3 months
4. Once a month
5. More than once a month
6. Once a week
7. More than once a week
8. At least once a day

There are many reasons why people can not, or do not, participate in activities sponsored by the Park District. Please indicate the reasons you have for not participating (circle all that apply).

1. **Getting to the facilities is difficult**
2. **Inconvenient timing of events**
3. **The facilities are crowded**
4. **Lack of information**
5. **Lack of security**
6. **Lack of appropriate staffing**
7. **Better neighboring park districts**
8. **I do not know where they are**
9. **Not interested**
10. **Better private facilities elsewhere**
11. **The user fees are too high**
12. **Poorly-maintained facilities**
13. **I do not have the time**

Please indicate if you or your family have used any of the following Park Districts in the past year (circle the number of all that apply).

1. Medinah	**2. Itasca**	**3. Roselle**	**4. Carol Stream**
5. Wheaton	**6. Glendale Hts.**	**7. Hanover Park**	**8. Other__________**

Please indicate the activity or facility that you have most often used in the neighboring park district(s):
I have used the following activity(s) or facility(s)____________________

SOURCES AND TYPES OF INFORMATION

We are interested in determining the best ways of informing you about the District's activities and facilities. Please circle the appropriate answers below to indicate how effective the following methods are for keeping you informed.

	Very Effective	Effective	Not Effective		Very Effective	Effective	Not Effective
Daily Herald	3	2	1	**Friends, relatives, neighbors**	3	2	1
Chicago Sun Times	3	2	1	**Radio, what station: ________**	3	2	1
Bloomingdale Press	3	2	1	**Cable TV, Channel**	3	2	1
Bloomingdale Village Almanac	3	2	1	**Park District's Program Brochure**	3	2	1
Chicago Tribune	3	2	1	**Flyers sent through schools**	3	2	1
Internet	3	2	1	**Signboard (at the Museum on Bloomingdale Rd)**	3	2	1
Street banners	3	2	1				

PERSONAL OPINIONS

The Bloomingdale Park District (BPD) would like to obtain your personal opinions about a variety of issues. Please circle the number that most closely reflects your attitude.

	Strongly Agree	Agree	Not Sure	Disagree	Strongly Disagree
In general, the facilities I have visited satisfy my needs.	5	4	3	2	1
The BPD should provide a written suggestion/complaint process.	5	4	3	2	1
The BPD's image is good.	5	4	3	2	1
The parks with which I am familiar are well maintained and groomed.	5	4	3	2	1
When I visit the parks I feel safe and secure from physical harm.	5	4	3	2	1
The BPD should conduct periodic user surveys.	5	4	3	2	1
I am proud of the parks and facilities in this community.	5	4	3	2	1
The BPD parks and facilities within the parks compare favorably to those of other park districts within surrounding communities.	5	4	3	2	1
When a development plan for a park or a park facility is being proposed, I would prefer public input before the plans are finalized.	5	4	3	2	1
The amount of park acreage in my neighborhood is adequate	5	4	3	2	1
The amount of park acreage in the BPD seems adequate	5	4	3	2	1
Regarding pets in the park:					
–Do not allow.	5	4	3	2	1
–Allow in restricted areas on leash.	5	4	3	2	1
–Allow in restricted areas off leash.	5	4	3	2	1
The BPD seems responsive to the community recreation needs	5	4	3	2	1
The BPD is an important provider of recreation for me.	5	4	3	2	1
Non-resident use of recreation programs and facilities has not been a problem for me or my family.	5	4	3	2	1
Recreation activities should be provided for:					
–basic instruction and development of skills	5	4	3	2	1
–intermediate instruction	5	4	3	2	1
–advanced instruction	5	4	3	2	1
–competitive (all-star teams, traveling teams, etc.)	5	4	3	2	1
The BPD should increase the collaboration with local businesses to promote and/or sponsor selected activities.	5	4	3	2	1
The BPD should assume an active role in providing child day care.	5	4	3	2	1
The BPD should provide more family activities.	5	4	3	2	1
I am aware of the recreation activities and events the BPD offers.	5	4	3	2	1
The BPD does a good job of advertising its recreation activities and events.	5	4	3	2	1
The BPD needs to increase its promotional material to better inform its residents.	5	4	3	2	1
I receive timely information about the BPD programs and activities.	5	4	3	2	1
The BPD should send its program brochures to local businesses.	5	4	3	2	1
The BPD should use tasteful advertising in selected BPD printed information.	5	4	3	2	1

	Strongly Agree	Agree	Not Sure	Disagree	Strongly Disagree
The nature interpretive trail/wetland at Springfield Park is well advertised.	5	4	3	2	1
The 5% of my real estate tax bill that goes to BPD is just the right amount.	5	4	3	2	1
It is appropriate that the BPD receive revenues from real estate taxes only.	5	4	3	2	1
The BPD seems to spend tax money wisely.	5	4	3	2	1
The BPD should continue to assess each of the community's athletic organizations a surcharge to be used to improve athletic fields and hold down taxes.	5	4	3	2	1
The priorities for expenditure for the BPD should be:					
–Development of New Facilities	5	4	3	2	1
–Land Acquisition	5	4	3	2	1
–Recreation Activities	5	4	3	2	1
–Existing Recreation Facilities	5	4	3	2	1
–Maintenance of Facilities and Parks	5	4	3	2	1
Special interest groups should fund a significant share of projects done at their request.	5	4	3	2	1
The BPD should become more aggressive with user fees.	5	4	3	2	1
I would support a referendum for increased taxes.	5	4	3	2	1
The BPD should attempt to increase its revenue by:					
–Additional property tax costing property owners $5 per year for a $100,000 market value home.	5	4	3	2	1
–Additional property tax costing property owners $10 per year for a $100,000 market value home.	5	4	3	2	1
–Increased user fees.	5	4	3	2	1

EMPHASIS FOR THE FUTURE

BPD has several ideas and projects in mind for improving and increasing recreational services and opportunities. For each of these ideas listed below, please indicate if they should be pursued.

	Yes	Not Sure	No
List parks and amenities in the brochure.	3	2	1
Timely follow-up is needed after questions, concerns, and complaints.	3	2	1
When parks are developed or renovated I would like to see:			
–more passive development (e.g., natural areas, walks, benches, game tables, picnic areas, trees, shrubs, flowers, prairie grasses, etc.)	3	2	1
–more active development (e.g., playgrounds, basketball courts, softball & baseball diamonds, football fields, soccer fields, etc)	3	2	1
–a blend of passive and active development.	3	2	1
Develop a club and activity area for teens.	3	2	1
Develop a teen video arcade.	3	2	1
Develop a Fitness Center for adults.	3	2	1
Develop an indoor ice arena	3	2	1

	Yes	Not Sure	No
Develop a Teen Center	3	2	1
Develop a Senior Center	3	2	1
Develop in-line skating facilities	3	2	1
Develop a Nature Center	3	2	1
Develop a waterpark consisting of water recreation options such as water slides, spray pools, wave pool, lap pool, sand play areas, grassy sunbathing areas, etc.	3	2	1
Increase program activities for adults.	3	2	1
Fine Art show in the parks.	3	2	1
Concerts in parks	3	2	1
Picnic pavilions should be placed in selected parks.	3	2	1
Acquire land for future park development.	3	2	1
Security lighting in selected parks should be considered for:			
–safety and security in playground equipment areas.	3	2	1
–safety and security around high use areas.	3	2	1
Lighting should be used to extend the hours of use for:			
–athletic fields (baseball, softball, soccer, football, etc)	3	2	1
–along sidewalks and paths in parks	3	2	1
Improve the athletic field playing surface conditions.	3	2	1

GOALS OF THE BLOOMINGDALE PARK DISTRICT

The Bloomingdale Park District is in the process of defining its future goals and mission. Some of the possible goals that have been identified have been listed below. Please rank each goal statement between 1 and 5 where 5 represents "very important" and 1 indicates "least important."

	Very Important <—				—>Least Important
Improved maintenance, modernization and operation of existing facilities. (swimming pool, recreation center, museum, etc.)	5	4	3	2	1
Improved maintenance, modernization and operation of existing parks.	5	4	3	2	1
Stay closer to the users by obtaining evaluations of each activity and major facility by way of written evaluations, focus group interviews and periodic community-wide surveying.	5	4	3	2	1
Greater involvement in addressing social issues, (before- and after-school activities, day-care activities, etc.).	5	4	3	2	1
Increase public awareness of the programs offered by the BPD.	5	4	3	2	1
Be the first place a resident will look for close-to-home recreation.	5	4	3	2	1

GENERAL INFORMATION QUESTIONS

The following information is helpful in providing the BPD with the ability to cross-tabulate questions so that better management decisions can be made. Individual answers will be treated with confidence. Please circle the number of the response or fill in the blank.

What is your gender? Male...1 Female...2

What is your age? Under 18...1 19 - 25...2 26 - 33...3 34 - 41....4 42 - 49...5 50 - 54...6 55 - 64...7 Over 65...8

What is your marital status? Single...1 Married...2 Divorced/Separated...3 Widowed...4

What was your household income before taxes in the past year?
Under $11,999...1 $12,000 - $23,999...2 $24,000 - $34,999....3 $35,000 - $47,999...4
$48,000 - $59,999...5 $60,000 - $71,999...6 $72,000 - $83,999...7 Over $84,000...8

How many adults, including yourself, age 19 and above, currently live in your household? ______

How many children in your household are: under age five ______ ages 5 to 10 ______ ages 11 to 14 ______ ages 15 to 18 ______

How many years have you resided in the Bloomingdale Park District? ______

Additional comments: ____

____

This is a map of Bloomingdale Park District. Please locate and circle the number of the area where you live.

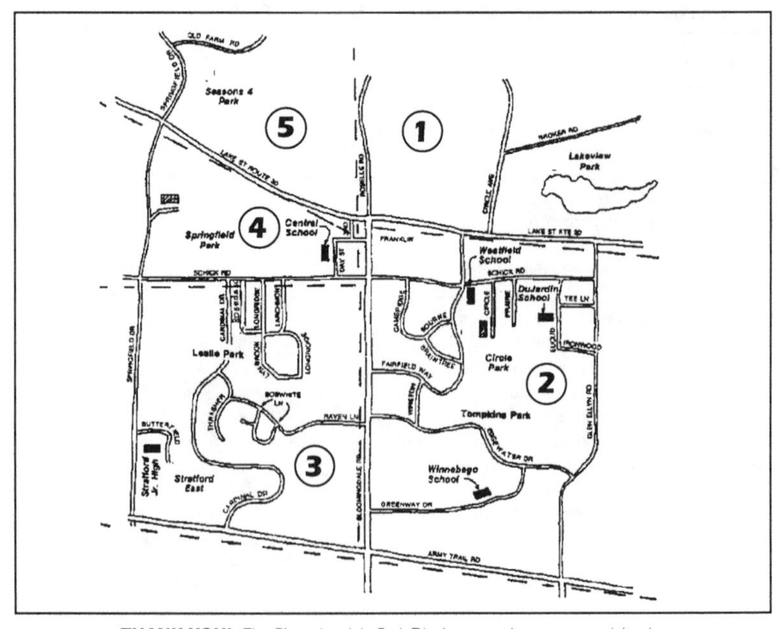

THANK YOU! The Bloomingdale Park District appreciates your participation.
Please use the enclosed postage paid envelope.

Appendix B
Executive Summary

I. EXECUTIVE SUMMARY

The needs assessment study of the Charleston County Park and Recreation Commission (PRC) has been conducted to assist the PRC in the formulation of goals and policies, and for the future development of water-based recreation programs and facilities. The study assesses both the quantity and quality of leisure services and opportunities provided by the Parks and Recreation Commission. This assessment was primarily accomplished through the use of one County-wide survey of residents living in Charleston County. The survey was specifically designed for these evaluative and planning purposes, and it also incorporates information about the geographic, economic, and social characteristics of the population. Responses to the survey items provide helpful input into the future planning decisions, both long and short term, of the Parks and Recreation Commission.

The basic purposes of the survey were as follows:

(a) to gather information that the Charleston County Parks and Recreation Commission may utilize to gain a better understanding of its constituency;

(b) to evaluate current and ongoing water-based recreation opportunities in terms of individuals' desires to participate;

(c) to explore the most effective methods of disseminating information to the public about programs, facilities, and opportunities concerning water-based recreation;

(d) to ascertain the attitudes and opinions of the residents of Charleston County about Charleston County Park and Recreation Commission programs, facilities, policies, and services as they relate to water-based recreation; and,

(e) to afford County residents the opportunity to offer suggestions, comments, and concerns about the leisure opportunities provided for them by the Charleston County Parks and Recreation Commission.

A. *Method*

A survey was designed to achieve the objectives of the study. The drafting of the survey instrument entailed preliminary meetings with the Parks and Recreation Commission staff, as well as discussions with the residents of Charleston County. These group discussions were conducted as focus group meetings. Representatives from nearly seventy County organizations met with the consulting team. These members were able to candidly share their concerns about the role of the PRC in the County. The participants included representatives of special interest groups focusing on specific water-based recreation, local government agencies, and private providers of recreation and citizens of the County. The mailing to a randomly selected sample of 3,000 resulted in 402 usable surveys, which corresponds to an overall response rate of 15.2% (this response rate incorporates the 350 non-deliverable surveys), and a sampling error of less than 3.0%. Statistical procedures were used for the detailed breakdown of the information into demographic categories.

B. *General Findings*

The first part of the questionnaire was designed to determine the types of water-based recreation programs citizens would enjoy. A rather extensive list, including a wide variety of water-based leisure activities, was shown to residents, and they were asked how interested they were in participating in those activities.

In general, what emerges is a pattern of general interest in passive activities such as walking and relaxing by the water, in which the majority of the County is highly interested and participate frequently. Next, there are a set of special interest activities, such as boating and fishing, in which fewer people are interested and fewer participate. Finally, there are some activities such as jetskiing that seem to have selective participation and interest. In most case, the general interest activities are provided by public agencies, whereas the special interest activities have private providers.

Residents were also asked specifically about future improvements to the Parks and Recreation Commission programs and facilities. The results reflected the interest areas expressed in the earlier section of the questionnaire. There is also considerable interest in instructional programs that teach specific skills that can help in the enjoyment of water-based recreation. More than 70% of the respondents also indicated that it was necessary that PRC develop programs for people with disabilities as well as youth at-risk. Among specific activities, swimming was listed as one of the more popular activities. The PRC should thus consider expanding their offerings in the area of swimming.

The respondents were also asked how they get information about PRC and the reasons for not attending water-based recreation. In general, the County was well informed about PRC and the facilities operated by the agency. For instance, more than 90% of the respondents recognized that the facilities at James Island were operated by PRC. On the other hand, the primary reasons for non-participation were cost and access. The respondents indicated that it was too expensive to do water-based recreation, and often it was too difficult to access the facilities. There was also some concern about the fact that there was sometimes lack of information about water-based recreation in the County.

Finally, there was a section to elicit the personal opinions of the respondents. Overall, the respondents gave a positive opinion about water-based recreation in Charleston County. The residents obviously enjoy activities around the water. There is clearly some concern for cost, and a large proportion of the residents feel water-based recreation is too expensive.

These findings have been used to make a set of recommendations to the PRC. All the recommendations are presented in this executive summary along with brief references to data to justify the recommendation. The recommendations are divided into sections corresponding with the different parts of the survey. It is, however, *necessary* to read the entire report carefully before attempting to judge the recommendations. While each recommendation is followed by a brief reference to the data, more detailed information is contained in the body of the report. Further data are also available in the CompuRec database.

Appendix C
Report Recommendations

Demographics and Market Segments

THE PRC SHOULD ATTEMPT TO MEET THE NEEDS OF THE POWER BOAT OWNERS IN THE COUNTY.

The respondents indicate that 28% own power boats. The PRC should explore their specific needs and attempt to meet those needs since this represents a significant portion of their clientele.

THE PRC NEEDS TO CONSIDER THE INCREASING NUMBER OF OLDER PEOPLE IN THE COUNTY, AND ADDRESS THEIR SPECIFIC WATER-BASED RECREATION NEEDS.

The results indicate that there is a growing number of older (55 and above) people in the County. Their water-based recreation needs could be different from the younger population. However, given the changing demographics, the needs of the older people need to be addressed.

Current Water-Based Activities Offered by PRC

THE PRC SHOULD PROVIDE OPPORTUNITIES FOR WALKING BY THE WATER.

A large percentage of respondents indicated that there was a high level of interest in this activity. Moreover, nearly 66% of the respondents indicate that they participate in this activity frequently (more than 6 time a year) and 21% of the respondents do this activity in spaces provided by public water-based recreation agencies. The PRC should *increase* the opportunities for walking by the water.

THE PRC NEEDS TO PROVIDE OPTIONS FOR RELAXING NEAR THE WATER BY GIVING OPPORTUNITIES TO GO TO THE BEACH, WATCH THE HARBOR, AND GO TO WATERFRONT PARKS.

More than 60% of the respondents indicated high levels of interest in activities such as relaxing by the water, going to the beach, watching the water and going to waterfront parks. More than half of the respondents indicated that they do these activities more than 6 times a year. Further, the majority of the respondents indicated that they do these activities on their own in public spaces. The PRC thus needs to continue to provide these opportunities and encourage these activities.

THE PRC NEEDS TO PROVIDE OPTIONS FOR RELAXING NEAR THE WATER BY GIVING OPPORTUNITIES TO GO TO THE BEACH, WATCH THE HARBOR, AND GO TO WATERFRONT PARKS.

More than 60% of the respondents are very interested in waterfront dining, and about 60% of the respondents are going to private dining establishments. The PRC should consider collaborating with the private providers to open dining establishments.

THE PRC SHOULD FOCUS ON OFFERING PASSIVE WATER-BASED RECREATION OPPORTUNITIES.

In general, the most popular water-based activities involved the passive use of waterfront parks, beaches and the harbor as well as picnicking by the water and camping by the water. The PRC should concentrate its efforts on making these activities more attractive and convenient.

THE PRC NEEDS TO PROVIDE SWIMMING POOLS FOR THE RESIDENTS OF CHARLESTON COUNTY.

Nearly half the respondents indicated a high level of interest and frequent participation in swimming at pools. However, 32% of the respondents also indicated that they go to private providers for this activity. The PRC needs to consider the construction of public swimming pools to attract residents of the County to public facilities.

THE PRC SHOULD STEER AWAY FROM PROVIDING SPECIAL INTEREST ACTIVITIES SINCE THOSE NEEDS ARE BEING MET BY THE PRIVATE PROVIDERS.

There are a set of activities such as deep sea fishing, and jet-skiing in which *relatively* few people are interested. However, those who are interested in these activities are having their needs met by the private providers, and the PRC does not need to involve itself with such activities.

THE PRC NEEDS TO GENERATE INTEREST IN ACTIVITIES THAT ARE ALREADY POPULAR.

Nearly 44% of the respondents indicated a high level of interest in special events such as boat races as well as activities like camping by the water. The PRC needs to provide more opportunities to meet this County-wide need.

Informing the Public

THE PRC SHOULD MAKE EFFORTS TO INFORM THE PUBLIC THAT THEY OPERATE THE COOPER RIVER MARINA.

Only 22% of the respondents realize that the Cooper River Marina is operated by the PRC. The agency should make efforts to make this fact known to increase its visibility in the County.

THE PRC NEEDS TO MAKE ITS QUARTERLY PROGRAM CALENDAR A MORE EFFECTIVE MEANS OF INFORMING THE PUBLIC.

Even though 85% of the respondents indicated that the quarterly calendar of events was an effective way of informing the public, it was ranked lowest among the seven methods listed in the questionnaire. Since this calendar provides significant amount of information, the PRC should make attempts to make it more effective.

Increasing Participation

THE PRC NEEDS TO BEGIN A CONCERTED ATTEMPT TO INCREASE ITS VISIBILITY IN THE COUNTY.

Nearly 38% of the respondents indicate that they do not participate in PRC activities because they are unaware of the programs and facilities. Even though this means that 62% claim that they know about the PRC activities, those who are unaware are a significant part of the County. The PRC needs to address this issue and make itself more visible in the County.

THE PRC NEEDS TO MAKE ITS WATER-BASED PROGRAMS AND FACILITIES MORE AFFORDABLE.

The PRC needs to address the issue that 23% of the respondents felt that the water-based recreation programs are too expensive. The agency can consider collaborating with the local businesses to seek sponsorship and find other means of making the programs and activities more equitably available to the residents of the County.

THE PRC NEEDS TO CONSIDER WAYS OF TRANSPORTING PEOPLE TO ITS FACILITIES AND MAKING THE FACILITIES MORE EASILY ACCESSIBLE.

Nearly 15% of the respondents indicated that the PRC facilities are too far away, while 16% of the respondents claim that water-based recreation in general is too far away. For such respondents, PRC needs to provide ways of transportation and access, perhaps by providing bus services to residents who do not have easy access and transportation to water-based

Future Improvements to Water-Based Recreation

THE PRC SHOULD CONSIDER OFFERING INSTRUCTIONAL PROGRAMS PARTICULARLY IN THE AREA OF BOATER SAFETY AND SAILING.

There is considerable interest in instructional programs that teach specific skills which can help in the enjoyment of water-based recreation. Nearly 80% of the respondents felt that boater safety instruction is necessary, and 77% are willing to pay for it with user fees, just as 60% of the respondents felt that sailing instruction is necessary. Further, 82% are willing to pay for sailing instruction with user fees. The agency should consider offering these programs and expanding any of its current offerings in this area.

THE PRC NEEDS TO ADDRESS THE NEEDS OF SPECIAL POPULATIONS SUCH AS PEOPLE WITH PHYSICAL DISABILITIES.

More than 70% of the respondents indicated that it was necessary that PRC develop programs for people with disabilities as well as youth at-risk. These two sectors of the population need different kinds of attention, but it is the feeling of the Charleston County residents that PRC has to play a significant role in providing water-based recreation to these groups. For people with disabilities, the PRC can consider providing expanded opportunities for water-based recreation, and easier access to water-related facilities.

THE PRC NEEDS TO PROVIDE ADDITIONAL RESTROOMS, PICNIC AREAS BY THE WATER, AND BOAT RAMPS.

A significant number (nearly 70%) of the respondents indicate that these are necessary future improvements and the PRC should try to make these additions. It is likely that such modifications would increase the number of users of PRC programs and facilities.

THE PRC SHOULD CONSIDER EXPANDING BOTH INDOOR AND OUTDOOR SWIMMING OPPORTUNITIES.

Swimming was listed as one of the more popular activities. Moreover, 54% of the respondents feel that an outdoor swimming pool is a necessity, while 48% feel that same way about the indoor swimming pool. While these might rank relatively lower in the range of general improvements, the proportion of people interested in these two facilities is quite significant. The PRC should thus consider expanding their offerings in the area of swimming.

THE PRC SHOULD CONSIDER EXPANDING ITS WATER-RELATED RECREATION SUCH AS WATERPARKS AND FACILITIES WITH WATER SLIDES.

Nearly half the respondents indicate that there is a need for Waterparks and facilities with water slides. Given that the James Island Waterpark is extremely popular, it might be wise for PRC to consider expanding these offerings.

THE PRC SHOULD CONSIDER MAKING SOME SPECIFIC IMPROVEMENTS. THESE SHOULD INCLUDE:

1. MORRIS ISLAND LIGHTHOUSE PRESERVATION,
2. BUILDING A WALKWAY ALONG CHARLESTON HARBOR,
3. BUILDING A FAMILY WATER PARK IN NORTH CHARLESTON, AND
4. BARRIER ISLAND PURCHASE.

More than 60% of the respondents indicated that all of the above specific improvements and additions were necessary. The PRC should consider ways in which it can fulfill the above needs. According to the respondents, taxes should be used for the first two options, and user fees should be the way of financing the last two options.

<u>Opinions about PRC, and Water-Based Recreation</u>

THE PRC SHOULD CONCENTRATE ON PROVIDING DIFFERENT KINDS OF WATER-BASED RECREATION.

The County residents feel that the role of PRC is to provide a wide variety of water-based recreation in the County. This should be done in cooperation with private enterprise, but that is not to suggest that the PRC should not provide activities that are already provided by the private operators.

THE PRC SHOULD PROVIDE CHEAPER ACCESS TO WATER-BASED RECREATION THAN WHAT IS PROVIDED BY THE PRIVATE OPERATORS.

The residents of the County overwhelmingly support the fact that the PRC is expected to provide water-based recreation at a lower cost than the private operators because the PRC already has tax support. The fact that this could ruin some private operators does not appear to be very important to the respondents.

THE PRC SHOULD CONSIDER A 25% HIGHER USER FEE FOR ITS NON-RESIDENT USERS.

There is enough support to suggest that the PRC should charge its non-resident users a 25% higher fee. About 72% of the respondents indicated that the PRC should charge non-resident users a higher fee. There is thus significant County-wide support for this.

Appendix D
Data Presentation

One of the issues that often poses a problem to researchers and practitioners is the best way of presenting information that has been produced out of statistical analysis. While to the researcher involved with the analysis, the information might appear to be quite self-explanatory, when that information has to be disseminated to a large audience it is important to keep certain parameters in sight. This appendix would provide a series of guidelines or "tips" that can be used when presenting data.

Tip # 1: Analyze your audience

As in the case of all public communication it is extremely important that the audience characteristics be considered carefully. Different kinds of audiences have different levels of expertise and different expectations.

If the data has to be presented to the general public, it is incorrect to assume that everyone would be very conversant with statistical language. In such cases, it is important to provide a simple and concise presentation that captures the essential elements of the data without confusing the findings with unnecessary statistical detail. In such cases tables need to be clearly marked and all the information should be presented in an easily understandable format. The information should be unambiguous and not cluttered with unnecessary details.

On the other hand, if the audience is made up recreation professionals, they are not only interested in the findings, but also the way in which the findings translate to policy and action. In such cases, the data has to be supplemented with statements that contextualize the findings with specific actions that follow from the findings. In many cases, such statements become recommendations that the audience can use to modify their activities. It is important to note, however, that recommendations and conclusions have to relate to the audience and be supported by the data.

Finally, researchers could also find themselves writing for an audience who is more interested in the theoretical and global implications of the findings of the research. This audience is often less interested in the specific policy-related recommendations specific to a recreation provider, but are more interested in knowing how the research speaks to the broader and more fundamental aspects of leisure and recreation. In such cases, the author often has to provide great amounts of detail about the data and clarify all the different statistical implications of the data. Often, that requires the presentation to contain detailed statistical information.

Thus depending on the audience, the presentation can take on three different forms: simple factual presentation, detailed presentations with policy implications, and detailed presentations with theoretical implications.

Tip #2: Be Consistent

The strategies of data presentation in social sciences has increasingly been conventionalized. In most cases, organizations such as the American Psychological Association (APA) have produced standardized ways of presenting data. While these handbooks provide in-depth and detailed information about data presentation, here are some fundamental guidelines for the presentation of charts and tables.

- Always use a simple and easily understood title for all tables and charts.
- All columns in tables and all parts of a chart should have labels.
- Indicate the unit of measurement in tables and charts; e.g., if presenting percentages then clearly label them as such.
- In the case of factorial tables and in presenting results of cross-tabulation, present the independent variable in the columns and the dependant variables in the rows.
- When presenting percentages it is a good practice to indicate the total "N" so that the reader can easily compute the number in each category or "cell."
- When presenting means it is a good practice to indicate the standard deviation along with the mean.
- When presenting advanced statistics, such as the results of a T-test, ANOVA, or correlation, it is important to include all the relevant and related statistics such as the degrees of freedom (df), level of significance (p), and specific ratios such as the "F" statistics.
- Clearly number charts and tables and make references in the body of the report to these numbers so that the reader can easily find the tables and charts when reading the report.
- Use different-sized typefaces to distinguish between different parts of a table or chart.
- Use formatting strategies such as shading, italics, and underlining to distinguish between different parts of a table or chart.

Tip #3: Clarity

It is always important to be able to provide the information in a clear and well labeled format. In the case of creating tables it is important to note the following guidelines:

- The tables in a report or manuscript should be consistent in format.
- The table should be brief and explanatory.
- The table should have a brief but clear title.
- Every column should have a column heading.
- The table should be referenced in the text.

The next illustration shows a sample table.

Illustration 1: Sample Table

Table 2: Activities with High (OVER 50%) Interest (N=300)

Activity	Interested	Not Interested	Not Sure
Concerts in the Park	71%	21%	8%
Gardening	58%	25%	17%
Home Landscaping Instruction	55%	34%	11%
Entertainment Trips, Live Theater	54%	37%	9%
Aerobics/Fitness Classes	52%	36%	12%
Aerobics Low Impact	51%	38%	11%

In the case of charts (sometimes referred to as "figures") it is important to consider the following issues related to clarity:

- Verify that the figure augments the text rather than duplicates it.
- Verify that the figure conveys only the essential facts.
- The figure should not have visually distracting details.
- The purpose of the figure should be obvious.
- The figure should be easy to read.
- Different parts of the figure must be easy to distinguish; for example, bars in a bar graph should be clearly shaded to differentiate between them.

- In most cases, the horizontal axis of a bar graph should contain the independent variable.
- In the case of bar graphs with two independent variables, the horizontal axis represents first independent variables and each bar in a cluster represents the second independent variable.

The next illustration shows a clustered bar graph with all its essential elements.

Illustration 2: Sample Cluster Bar Graph

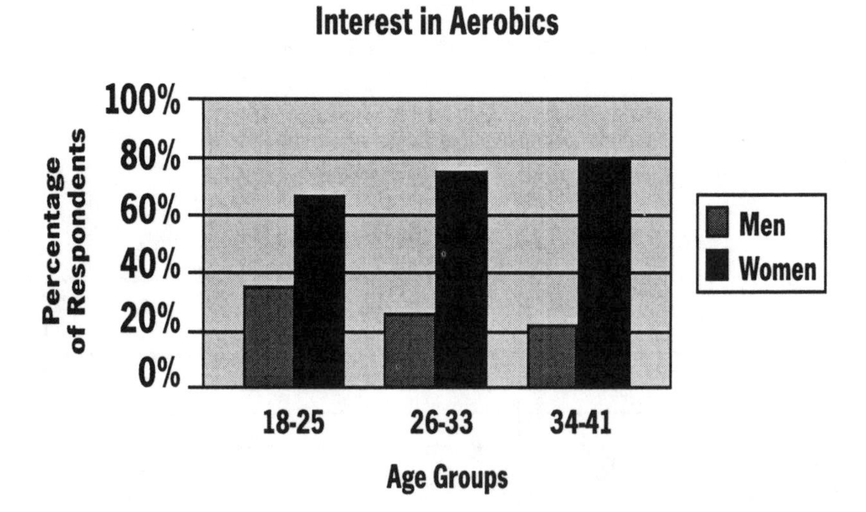

Authors' Page

Dr. Ananda Mitra is an assistant professor in the Department of Communication at Wake Forest University, Winston-Salem, NC. Prior to taking his current position, he served as the head of the sampling section of the Survey Research Laboratory of the University of Illinois. He now lives in Winston-Salem with his wife and son and continues to do research in the areas of leisure and recreation, evaluation, and needs assessment.

Dr. Sam Lankford is an associate professor and director of the Recreation & Leisure Science Degree program within the Department of Kinesiology and Leisure Science at the University of Hawaii-Manoa. He also serves on the graduate faculty of the School of Travel Industry Management at the University of Hawaii–Manoa. His professional experience, research interests, and publications are in community development and change, citizen involvement programs, and how planners can facilitate planning and development processes to encourage a wide range of opinions and values. He has a particular interest in how these issues are related to parks, open space, tourism, and ultimately, the development of communities.

Other Titles from Sagamore Publishing

The Wilderness Within: Reflections on Leisure and Life, Second Edition
Daniel L. Dustin

The Wilderness Within is a collection of eighteen essays that explore the meaning of recreation, parks, and leisure in Dustin's own life. Many of the essays are about adventure-based outdoor recreation experiences and are set in the contexts of mountains, forests, deserts, and tundra. More recent essays are based on the realization that much of what makes life interesting flows out of everyday pastimes: visiting with friends, playing games, enjoying good food, listening to music, appreciating the landscape, connecting with family, and self-reflection.

6x9 Softcover • ISBN 1-57167-253-2 • $19.95

. . . .

The Management of Clubs, Recreation, and Sport: Concepts and Applications
Thomas H. Sawyer and Owen R. Smith

The Management of Clubs, Recreation, and Sport: Concepts and Applications is a comprehensive compilation of concepts and practical subject matter published for the sport management student, professional, and practitioner. The book focuses on those activities that a club manager, recreational sports manager, or competitive sports manager faces everyday on the job. The content of the book focuses on those activities that are the most important for either a club manager, recreation sports manager, or competitive sports manager. Each chapter provides explanations of various management concepts important for the reader to understand and how-to information that applies to the concepts in realistic situations.

7x10 Hardcover • ISBN 1-57167-027-0 • $44.95

. . . .

Leisure Resources: Its Comprehensive Planning, Second Edition
Daniel D. McLean, Joseph J. Bannon, and Howard R. Gray

Leisure Resources provides detailed information about strategic planning and master planning and about support systems related to these two types of planning. Included in the book as support information is how to create organizational alignment, establishing a program evaluation system, working with surveys, and defining other methods of information gathering. The book is written to be used. It provides examples of strategic plans and master plans. The use of examples and guides allows the reader to develop a comfort level with the processes of planning. This book will find a ready place on any practitioner's reference shelf and be an excellent asset in the park and recreation planning class.

7x10 Hardcover • ISBN 1-57167-025-4 • $44.95

For more information on these titles call 1-800-327-5557 or visit us at **www.sagamorepub.com**

Index

D

E

J

K

L

M

N

O

P

Q

T

U

V

W

Y